STORIES OF MÉTIS WOMEN

TALES MY KOOKUM TOLD ME

COMPANION DOCUMENTARY

AVAILABLE ON VIMEO

Stories of Métis Women

Directed and Edited by Matt LeMay, 2021

Password: durvile2021

Video *(55 min.)* – https://vimeo.com/559638135

STORIES OF MÉTIS WOMEN

TALES MY KOOKUM TOLD ME

Bailey Oster & Marilyn Lizee

DURVILE & UpRoute Books

Calgary, Alberta, Canada

DURVILE &
UpRoute Books

UpRoute Imprint of Durvile Publications Ltd.
Calgary, Alberta, Canada
www.durvile.com

Library and Archives Cataloguing in Publications Data

STORIES OF MÉTIS WOMEN
Tales My Kookum Told Me

Oster, Bailey; Author and Editor
Lizee, Marilyn; Afterword and Editor
Audrey Poitras; Foreword

Northern Michif translation; Morin, Mary SkyBlue

1. Métis People | 2. Aboriginal | 3. Indigenous | 4. Canada | 5. Reconciliation

The UpRoute "Spirit of Nature" Series
Series Editors, Raymond Yakeleya and Lorene Shyba

Issued in print and electronic formats
ISBN: 978-1-988824-21-5 (pbk); 978-1-988824-68-0 (e-pub)
9781988824697 (audiobook)

Front and back cover image of original beadwork, Krista Leddy.
Book design, Lorene Shyba. Typeset in Utopia.

Durvile Publication Ltd. Is committed to reducing the consumption of
nonrenewable resources in the production of our books.
We make every effort to use materials that support a sustainable future.

We acknowledge the traditional land of the Treaty 7 Peoples of Southern Alberta: the
Siksika, Piikani, and Kainai of the Niisitapi (Blackfoot) Confederacy; the Dene Tsuut'ina;
and the Chiniki, Bearspaw, and Wesley Stoney Nakoda First Nations.

We also acknowledge the Homeland of the
Otipemisiwak Métis Government of the Métis Nation within Alberta..

Durvile Publications would like to thank
The Government of Canada through Canadian Heritage Canada Book Fund
and The Government of Alberta, Alberta Media Fund
for their financial support.

New Dawn Society would like to acknowledge the financial support of
Aboriginal Affairs and Northern Development Canada.

Printed and bound in Canada. Eighth Printing. 2024.

Dedication

We dedicate this book to all Métis women and girls across the Homeland; you are the backbone of our People. Throughout history, the voices of Métis women and girls have so often been forgotten, yet, you continue to do the hard work — the work that has built this nation. We are publishing this book with the hope that we can give voice to the amazing strength that Métis women have always had.

It is also dedicated to all the missing and murdered Indigenous women, girls, and 2SLGBTQ+ individuals who have been taken from us far too soon. We pray that your spirits will find their way home, and that those who you had to leave behind can take comfort knowing that you will never be forgotten.

Author and editor proceeds will go to
New Dawn Society Métis Women MMIWG Fund.

Contents

Cover Artist Note

AS A MÉTIS ARTIST, every beaded piece I make carries the stories and encouragement of my Kokums, Aunties, and every person who has guided me in my journey. This piece contains the beauty, medicine, and life of the women who have walked before me, with me, and the women who will walk this path in the future.

I took the traditional teachings of our floral beadwork and combined them with contemporary expressions to represent that our stories will live on so that these stories will be told to our great-great grandchildren. That like our infinity, we as Métis women, and as a People, will walk this land forever.

— *Krista Leddy*

Note on the Translation

All the women's stories within this book, told by the women themselves, have been translated into Northern Michif. Michif is the language of the Métis People. It is a mixed language which, at its very basic elements, combines Cree verbs with nouns from French and occasionally from English.

Various dialects of Michif are spoken across the Homeland, each of which may incorporate more Cree, French, or English words, and even have elements of other Indigenous languages within them. All dialects of Michif are currently classified as endangered, with only a few hundred or thousand people who currently speak the language. Most, if not all these speakers are older, which leaves the language in a very vulnerable position for future generations.

Some early Métis have also been known to speak a language called Bungee. This language is a variety of English intermixed with some Cree and Ojibwe. The Métis who spoke this language were mainly the children of Orkney or Gaelic men, and Cree or Ojibwe mothers. However, only a handful of speakers are still known to exist.

The stories in this book are translated into Michif Cree with a Cree "y" dialect as it is the language of our translator, and contributor to the book, SkyBlue Morin.

We recognize the importance of preserving our language so that it is not lost, and so future generations are able to connect with this text through Michif.

Foreword

Audrey Poitras

As PRESIDENT OF THE MÉTIS NATION OF ALBERTA, it gives me great pleasure to endorse the book *Stories of Métis Women: Tales My Kookum Told Me.* We fully support initiatives like this, initiatives that not only celebrate the lives of women, but tell their stories of hardship, tragedy, and triumph.

At the Métis Nation of Alberta, we truly believe that women are the keepers of our culture; they are our nurturers, they are the keepers of our children and they are the backbone of our communities. They are the teachers who pass along their traditional knowledge and teachings to our children so they can grow into proud individuals — proud of who they are and proud of where they came from, and to truly know where they want to go.

I would like to quote our Métis Region 6 Elder:

> [Our goal is] to respect women as givers of life, to teach self-respect to young girls and women, and recognize children as gifts. These teachings need to be shared.
>
> — *Angie Crerar*

Identity is very important to me, to the Métis Nation, and to our citizens. Gender equality is just as important. We all have a role to play and, as such, we should all be recognized equally. That does not always happen, but there is hope. This book is a great opportunity to promote and support women, to acknowledge them and uplift their spirits and show the world they can do whatever they set their minds to. If we do not write our stories down or pass them on to our children in other ways, we risk losing precious memories, precious wisdom, our culture, and our traditions. I would like to encourage you all to talk to your Kookums, grandmothers, aunts, and moms. Listen to their stories and write them down, for there is nothing more precious than a beautiful lesson learned from your Kookum.

I truly believe we need to support each other, not just as women supporting women, but all of us supporting each other. Then and only then will we reach true gender equality. In these days of ever-changing times, gender equality and gender identity are discussed and acknowledged much more than before. We all have a role to play, and for all of us to feel supported and to feel valued, we need more publications recognizing the contributions made by not just Métis women but all women.

I want to thank New Dawn Métis Women's Society for the dream and vision of completing this book. I want to thank all the strong beautiful Métis women, who willingly shared their stories. I want to also thank Lorene Shyba of Durvile Publications for believing in New Dawn's dream. This book only tells a fraction of the stories of our strong, beautiful Métis women within the Métis Nation — women who work in the background to ensure that other women can get the support and encouragement they need to succeed in life; women who sacrifice a piece of themselves so others can prosper, and women who work tirelessly behind the scenes to move our Nation forward. I hope that this is only the beginning and that New Dawn

Métis Women's Society will be able to capture more stories in the future.

So often our stories go untold, our voices go unheard, our songs are never sung, and our dreams get left by the wayside. But the strength of women, even after all these trials and tribulations, continues to drive us forward, to continue our journey, not just for ourselves but so our children and communities can prosper. That is where our wisdom guides us. We are the keepers, the healers, and the givers of life.

With that I am going to leave you with a few words to think about. There is a saying by Gloria Steinem, well-known journalist and feminist, that goes,

> Women grow radical with age. One day an army of gray-haired women may quietly take over the Earth.

Enjoy this beautiful publication.

—Audrey Poitras, 2021

Audrey Poitras

President, Métis Nation of Alberta

Introduction

my grandmother stories follow me,
spill out of their bulging suitcases
get left under beds,
hung on doorknobs

— Marilyn Dumont, *A Really Good Brown Girl*

KOOKUM, which there are many different spellings of across the Homeland, is the Cree term for grandmother. *Stories of Métis Women: Tales My Kookum Told Me* is a book created from the need to share the stories of Métis People, specifically, Métis women. At our core, the Métis People are natural storytellers. We love to visit, to laugh, to share our joy, and our sorrow with each other and the world. Our families are inextricably linked through shared histories, and through those histories we can connect with each other on a deeper level of understanding. We connect through storytelling and its innate power to create and strengthen kinship ties.

The idea for this book came from a presentation given by my mom, Colette Poitras, at the New Dawn Métis Women's Society AGA in 2018. It was a presentation surrounding the importance of preserving Indigenous stories, and the different ways we can go about doing this. As a librarian, she works tirelessly to promote and preserve the knowledge and power that books can hold for their readers. However, books cannot be created without the stories of the people within their pages. Following her presentation, we began to hear the women in attendance share their stories with us, and with each other. The value of these stories was quickly apparent, and we began to brainstorm ways to preserve them, and through those conversations the idea for the book was born.

New Dawn Métis Women's Society is the voice for Métis women within Alberta. It is our job as a society to protect and promote the voices of our mothers, sisters, daughters, aunties, cousins, friends, and every other Métis woman and 2SLGBTQ+ person throughout the Homeland. Our culture was built by the strong women who came before us, and we carry weight of these histories with us, every step we take throughout our lives.

Within the pages of this book, we share the stories of Métis women, in their own words. The women within this book each have a unique and interesting story to tell. While I know that there is no way we can tell the stories of all Métis women, we hope the experiences of these select few will help give insight into the vital role Métis women play within our culture and our society.

We begin this book by delving into a brief history of the Métis People, our ethnogenesis as a Nation, and the role of the Buffalo Hunt as an early form of governance for the Métis, for we must understand how our Nation was built in order to understand where we are headed. Throughout this section about nation building, I hope readers will understand that Métis women have never been silent bystanders to history; their strength, creativity, and perseverance have pushed our Nation forward, and continues to do so.

The next section on culture is dedicated to sharing the distinct traditions of Métis People. The Métis are, and have always been, a joyous people who love to share their unique talents and passions with the world. We want to showcase this part of Métis culture, as it is truly what brings us together as a community above all else.

Undoubtedly, the Métis have faced many hard times in the past two hundred years. There is no escaping the darkness of this history, and the adversity that Métis women have faced. We need to hear these truths, we need to believe them, and we need to continue the path of reconciliation. While much of this book is dedicated to celebrating the strength of the women who are here today to tell their stories, there are many women who are not. In the section Dark Times, we honour and acknowledge the lives of the women who were taken from us too soon, who were not given the opportunity to tell their truth. As I am writing this introduction, the news is breaking about the remains of 215 children who have been found at a former Kamloops Residential School site. This news is not a surprise to me, rather a stark and gut-wrenching reminder of the people we have lost to colonial violence. We want to celebrate our culture and our history, but we cannot lose sight of those who were stolen from us, and the needless suffering Indigenous Peoples have experienced.

The women whose biographies follow tell their stories throughout the pages of this book. Each of them has a unique and varied experience, which symbolizes the collective knowledge of the Métis as a people. Threatened with assimilation, many Métis families and communities practiced endogamy to maintain Métis culture and identity. Others hid in "plain sight" as a coping mechanism to keep their family and their community safe from continued persecution. Each of these stories is valid and part of the Métis experience.

Our stories are important, and we hope this book can be a small piece of our Nation's story. By nature, storytelling is a powerful gift. It is more than just a symbol or a tale from the past. It is a resource for generations of Métis from which to build strength and to navigate challenges that they otherwise may not have felt prepared to take. Storytelling develops intergenerational connections that can carry us through our lives. Stories of the people who came before us are vital to our survival as a Nation. Throughout history,

Métis People have fought many battles. Some fought for our rights as a People, while others simply fought to survive in a world that, at times, seemed like it did not want them.

Within this book, we explore these stories to better understand the truth of what it means to be *Otipemisiwak*, the People who own themselves.

— *Bailey Oster, 2021*
Vice President,
New Dawn Métis Women's Society

The Women

Norma Spicer. Born and raised in Manitoba, Norma Spicer is the current Knowledge Keeper for the Métis Nation of Alberta Provincial Head Office. She has worked with the MNA for many years, both as Knowledge Holder and as President Audrey Poitras' Executive Assistant. Norma is passionate about Métis history and culture and is a strong representative for Métis women across the Homeland.

Angie Crerar. Angie grew up in Fort Resolution, NWT. Her fondest memories are those of family, and of living off the land — canning, hunting, gardening, and fishing. Through her parents, she was taught many great values and life skills. She knows what it means to have a wonderful life, to be Métis. However, this did not come without hardship. In 1947, her way of life changed. She was taken from her home, her family, and her community and placed in the Fort Resolution Residential School. For years Angie struggled and endured adversity at this school. Angie persisted, and stood up for what she believed in; she was determined to not let her spirit be broken and has spent her life standing up for those who cannot stand up for themselves. Angie is a survivor. She is a role model for Métis People everywhere, and we are proud to share her story within these pages.

Murial Stanley-Venne. Muriel has dedicated her entire life to helping Indigenous women. She aims to help them find their pride, to keep them safe, and ultimately to find their place in life. Muriel has many accomplishments under her belt, all of which are very well deserved. Throughout her life, Muriel has faced adversity time and time again, and has always persevered. She leaves a legacy of hope, determination, pride, and most of all, strength. Muriel has made a name for herself as a champion of human rights in the Province of Alberta. Muriel was presented with the Alberta Human Rights Award on the 25th Anniversary of the Alberta Human Rights Commission. She founded the Institute for the Advancement of Aboriginal Women, an organization that strives to promote opportunities for women. Today, Muriel continues the fight for Métis women alongside her daughter, Rochelle.

Doreen Bergum. Doreen has served as the Métis Nation of Alberta Region 3 Elder since 2011. She is a talented artisan, and a champion jigger who has won competitions across the Métis Homeland. From an early age Doreen was taught the importance of her Métis history and culture, even when they had to practice it in secret. Today, she proudly practices her culture and traditions, sharing her knowledge and skills with Métis and non-Métis people across the Homeland. She won an Esquao award in 2019 for her amazing work within the Métis community, and has spent much time working within communities and schools to promote Métis history and culture.

Bertha Clark Jones. Bertha joined the Royal Canadian Air Force at the age of 18 in 1940. She devoted her life to supporting Indigenous veterans and fighting for the equality of Indigenous women within Canada and became one of the country's first outspoken voices on the movement. In the late-60s she co-founded the Voice of Alberta Native Women's society to represent Indigenous women in Canada in the fight for equal rights. The organization eventually became the Native Women's Association of Canada (NWAC), where she served as its first President in 1974. NWAC is to this day a powerful voice for Indigenous women and children in Canada, and that is due in part to Bertha's strong leadership and hard work. Bertha passed away in 2014 but is remembered by her community as a strong and compassionate advocate for Indigenous women. Within these pages, her daughter, Gail Gallupe, tells Bertha's story through her recollections of her mother.

Pearl Calahasen. Born and raised in Grouard, Alberta, Pearl Calahasen represented the electoral district of Lesser Slave Lake in the Legislative Assembly of Alberta from 1989 to 2015. She was the Minister of Aboriginal Affairs and Northern Development, and the first Métis woman to be elected as an MLA in Alberta. Pearl has dedicated her life to advocating for Indigenous People across Alberta and working hard to improve the lives of people within her northern Alberta community.

Delia Gray. Delia Gray became the first Provincial Elder of the Métis Nation of Alberta in 1996 following the election of MNA President, Audrey Poitras. She was born at Wabasca Lake, Alberta in 1917 and devoted her life to preserving the language and culture of the Métis People. She cared deeply about her Métis community, and to honour her memory, the Métis Nation of Alberta named their then-recently-purchased head office building, The Delia Gray Building. Although Delia passed away in 1999, her story is remembered through the lives of her daughters, granddaughters and great-granddaughters who remember their Kookum through their stories of her life, and the time they got to spend with her. The members of Delia's family who have contributed to this book are her daughters, Roberta Marie (Bobbi), Anne, and Elizabeth (Betty); granddaughters, Cynthia Marie and Krista; and great-granddaughters, Josephine Marie and Sullivan.

Lisa Wolfe. Lisa is a retired officer of the Edmonton Police Service, and an ex-member of the Royal Canadian Air Force. She is a strong Métis woman, a wife of 30 years, a mother of four and a grandmother of two. Lisa has a deep cultural knowledge and understanding of Métis culture that has been passed down from her mother, Yvonne Glaubitz (Cardinal). She enjoys beadwork, making moccasins, sewing, and learning about her cultural identity. Lisa spends time with her parents learning about the old ways of growing up in the North. As a result, she enjoys camping off-grid and teaching her children and grandchildren about their Métis heritage and traditions.

Dianne Ludwig. Dianne is the Métis Nation of Alberta Region 1 Elder. She grew up in the small Saskatchewan community of Buffalo Narrows where she spent hours on the trapline with her parents and grandparents. Currently, Dianne lives in Lac La Biche, Alberta where she passionately works at the Aurora Middle School as the Elder in Residence. Students at the school call her "Kokum." Dianne is passionate about working with Indigenous students and cares deeply about connecting them to their culture.

Beatrice Demetrius. Beatrice was born in Big Prairie, Alberta to Helen Chalifoux and Joseph Jobin. She grew up with an older sister, and five brothers, and the family moved to High Prairie, Alberta when she was eleven. Beatrice is passionate about Métis history, and worked as the Head Genealogist for the Métis Nation of Alberta for many years until she retired in 2018. She led the charge in developing the MNA Genealogy and Research Center into what it is today. Beatrice is an amazing storyteller who is passionate about educating people about Métis history and the importance of knowing our past.

Juanita Marois. Juanita Marois is the Executive Director for MNA affiliate, Métis Crossing. As a child Juanita's Métis culture was not passed down to her from her parents and grandparents. However, as she grew older and began to put the pieces of her family history together, she began the journey of reconnecting with her culture and community. Today, she runs Canada's first major Métis cultural gathering center and is a strong advocate for Métis tourism across Canada.

Doreen Poitras. Doreen was born in Elk Point, Alberta in the early 1940s to Pierre Poitras and Margaret Garneau. She grew up on a farm by Elk Point with her parents and five brothers. Since retiring in 2000, Doreen has spent most of her time volunteering with the Edmonton Indigenous Seniors Center, painting, golfing, reading, and berry picking. However, her biggest joy comes from spending time visiting with her friends and family. Doreen is passionate about her Métis community and has been an active member of the Métis Nation of Alberta (MNA) for many years.

Caroline Charlebois. Born in 1892, Caroline Charlebois (Poitras) was a Métis woman whose family was one of the first to settle in St. Paul des Métis during the development, and eventual disbandment of the Settlement. Before her death, she spoke on tape with Gordon and Audrey Poitras about her memories of growing up on the ill-fated Settlement. We have a transcription of part of this interview within this book.

Mary SkyBlue Morin

Mary "SkyBlue" Morin is a Michif cultural knowledge keeper and a speaker of the Michif Cree and Ile-a-la-Crosse Michif language. She learnt the language as a child and has continued to speak it to this day. She has been working as a Michif Cree writer, translator, and teacher since 2010.

Jobin Family Gathering
Photo: Beatrice Demetrius

Upper: Métis Camp with Red River Carts
Photo: Saskatchewan Provincial Archives R-A3955
Lower: Métis camp and women baking, Pembina area, MB
Illustration: Glenbow Archives NA-1406-27

Chapter 1

Nation Building

The Métis Nation's ancestors sought freedom, and with that freedom they chose to become a separate People. It was a grand imagining, and the Nation has spent two hundred years fighting for the freedom to continue that dream. In the course of that long battle, they have had to convince others of their existence as a collective. The Métis Nation has been forged in this battle for freedom, recognition, land, resources and rights.

—Jean Teillet from "The North-West is our Mother: The Story of Louis Riel's People, the Métis Nation."

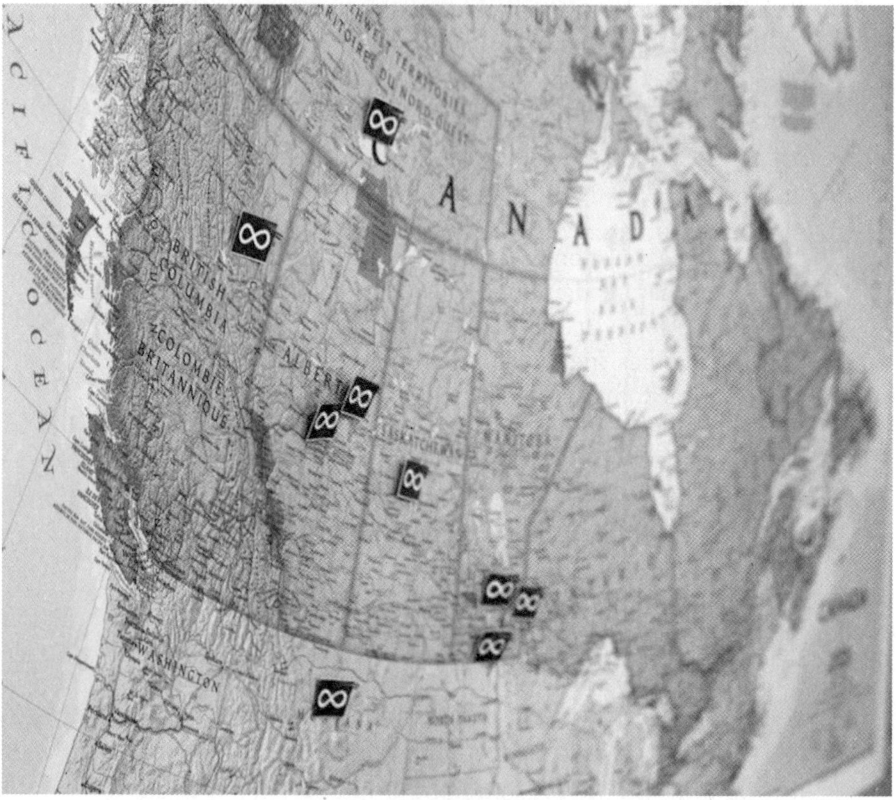

Map of the Métis Homeland
Source: Métis Nation of Alberta

OTIPEMISIWAK PEOPLE

THE MÉTIS have been known by many names: *Otipemisiwak* (the People who own themselves), *Bois Brules* (Burnt Wood), *Apihtawikosisan* and *Apeetogosan* (half-breed) are just a few. We have also been known as rebels and traitors to Canada. Few know our story, for we are also known as the "Forgotten People." When people speak of Canada's Indigenous Peoples, they often equate that to the First Nations Peoples, leaving the Métis out of the narrative altogether. Many think that Métis simply means "mixed" — it does not. We are a People with a unique and proud history and nationhood. Only now in this era of reconciliation has there been an influx of titles that explain the *Otipemisiwak* People's story, the Métis Nation, from our perspective.

Since 1982, the Métis have been recognized as one of the three distinct Aboriginal Peoples of Canada. From a historical perspective, the Métis are a culture whose ethnogenesis originated from the union of European fur traders and First Nations women in the 18th century. We are a post-contact Indigenous Nation whose descendants of these country marriages would go on to form a distinct culture, collective consciousness, and nationhood in the Northwest. The Métis developed distinct communities throughout the Métis Homeland and governed ourselves by the laws of the Buffalo Hunt. We developed unique cultural, linguistic, and political traditions which remain strong to this day. By 1869, the Red River Settlement was the largest Métis community in the Homeland and one of the largest settlements in North America, with over 10,000 Métis living there.

Throughout history, the Métis have fought many battles for our rights as a People. We first came together as a nation under Cuthbert Grant at the Victory of Frog Plain (also known as the Battle of Seven Oaks) in 1816. Later we

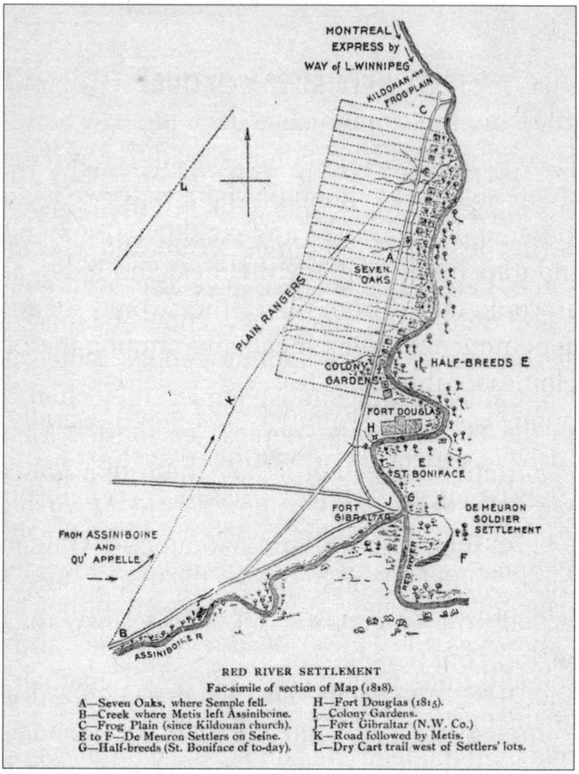

Red River Settlement 1818 [1910] by Manitoba Historical Maps
Licensed under CC by 2.0

fought the Sioux in the Battle of the Grand Coteau (1851), the Red River Resistance (1869–70), and of course, the Battle of Batoche (1885). At Batoche, the Métis would again fight for our land, and stand up for our rights as a Nation against the Government of Canada. Louis Riel, the leader of the Métis, was executed shortly thereafter, and many Métis fled persecution once again. Of course, this history is, for the most part, very well documented. While Métis culture and history are not well known to many, almost every Canadian has heard about Louis Riel. Some may view him as a hero or a martyr, others a traitor, but they have undoubtedly heard of him.

Since the Métis Nation's ethnogenesis, we have always stood up and fought for our rights as a People. However, as is so common when observing the historical record, this history has so often been told by men. The men may have led the battles, but the women have been the backbone of our culture, communities, and families. Within Métis communities, both men and women played a vital role in sustaining economic development and stability. The men would hunt and trap, bringing home the meat and hides, and the women would take it from there. They would spend hours making pemmican, drying meat, and tanning the hides to make clothes for their families.

In many cases, the women were often the family's economic drivers, especially when times were tough. The pemmican they would make out of dried meat (usually buffalo), melted fat and berries was a valuable trading resource for Métis People. Métis women were also well known for their prolific beadwork designs — so much so that they became widely known as the "Flower Beadwork People" and would often sell and trade their work across the Canadian plains and into the northern United States.

While men did lead the battles, the women were by no means silent bystanders either; there are many historical accounts of Métis women taking an active role in the fight. They nursed the wounded, cared for the vulnerable, provided supplies, and in some cases aided the men in developing a battle strategy.

In her book, *The Free People - Li gens Libres,* Métis historian Diane Payment recounts the following stories of Métis women's roles during the Battle of Batoche in 1885.

> Marguerite Caron (née Dumas) persuaded Riel to send reinforcements to *la couli des Tourond* (now Fish Creek), and her sister Christine Pilon (née Dumas) was one of the leaders at *la loge des femmes* (the women's camp) along the riverbank, rounding up the cattle, cooking, and caring for the sick. Marie Letendre Champagne protested vainly when the government soldiers started rounding up her horses and cattle but managed to hide sacks of flour and some meat from them. It was the women who made bullets out of melted lead during the battle and picked

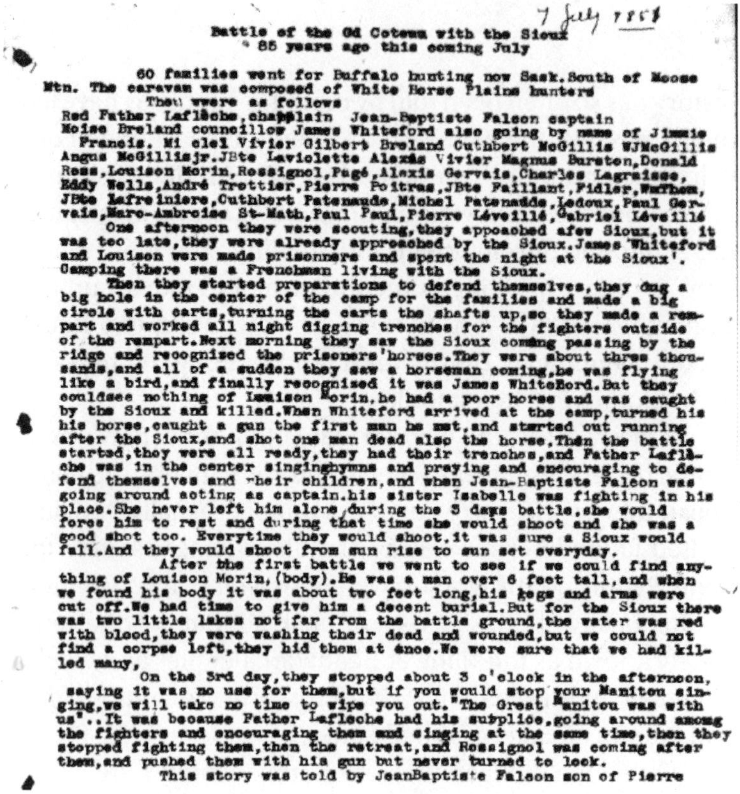

7 July 1951

Battle of the Gd Coteau with the Sioux
85 years ago this coming July

60 families went for Buffalo hunting now Sask. South of Moose Mtn. The caravan was composed of White Horse Plains hunters

They were as follows

Red Father Laflèche, chaplain Jean-Baptiste Falcon captain Moise Breland councillor James Whiteford also going by name of Jimmie Francis. Michel Vivier Gilbert Breland Cuthbert McGillis WJMcGillis Angus McGillisjr. JBte Laviolette Alexis Vivier Magnus Burston, Donald Ross, Louison Morin, Rossignol, Pagé, Alexis Gervais, Charles Lagraisse, Eddy Wells, André Trottier, Pierre Poitras, JBte Faillant, Fidler, Wuthem, JBte Lafreiniere, Cuthbert Patenaude, Michel Patenadde, Ledoux, Paul Gervais, Marc-Ambroise St-Math, Paul Paul, Pierre Léveillé, Gabriel Léveillé

One afternoon they were scouting, they appoached afew Sioux, but it was too late, they were already approached by the Sioux. James Whiteford and Louison were made prisonners and spent the night at the Sioux'. Camping there was a Frenchman living with the Sioux.

Then they started preparations to defend themselves, they dug a big hole in the center of the camp for the families and made a big circle with carts, turning the carts the shafts up, so they made a rampart and worked all night digging trenches for the fighters outside of the rampart. Next morning they saw the Sioux coming passing by the ridge and recognised the prisoners' horses. They were about three thousands, and all of a sudden they saw a horseman coming, he was flying like a bird, and finally recognised it was James WhiteBord. But they couldsee nothing of Louison Morin, he had a poor horse and was caught by the Sioux and killed. When Whiteford arrived at the camp, turned his his horse, caught a gun the first man he met, and started out running after the Sioux, and shot one man dead also the horse. Then the battle started, they were all ready, they had their trenches, and Father Laflèche was in the center singinghymns and praying and encouraging to defend themselves and their children, and when Jean-Baptiste Falcon was going around acting as captain. his sister Isabelle was fighting in his place. She never left him alone during the 3 days battle, she would force him to rest and during that time she would shoot and she was a good shot too. Everytime they would shoot, it was sure a Sioux would fall. And they would shoot from sun rise to sun set everyday.

After the first battle we went to see if we could find anything of Louison Morin, (body). He was a man over 6 feet tall, and when we found his body it was about two feet long, his legs and arms were cut off. We had time to give him a decent burial. But for the Sioux there was two little lakes not far from the battle ground, the water was red with blood, they were washing their dead and wounded, but we could not find a corpse left, they hid them at once. We were sure that we had killed many,

On the 3rd day, they stopped about 3 o'clock in the afternoon, saying it was no use for them, but if you would stop your Manitou singing, we will take no time to wipe you out. "The Great Manitou was with us".. It was because Father Lafleche had his surplice, going around among the fighters and encouraging them and singing at the same time, then they stopped fighting them, then the retreat, and Rossignol was coming after them, and pushed them with his gun but never turned to look.

This story was told by JeanBaptiste Falcon son of Pierre

Battle of the Grand Coteau with the Sioux
Source: Archives of Manitoba microfilm

up the dead afterwards. Many of them were left alone to raise large families and rebuild the community as many of the men were sent to prison, were forced into exile, or left in search of work in the years following the armed resistance.[1]

Clearly, by this account, the women were very much present during the resistance. They may not have seen the battlefield itself, but they were fighting a war of their own.

In another account from the Battle of the Grand Coteau, Jean Baptiste Falcon, Captain of the Hunt and son of Métis fur trader and composer Pierre Falcon details his sister, Isabelle Trottier's actions through the three nights of fighting. The Battle

1. D. P. Payment, (2009). *The Free People = Li gens libres: A history of the Métis community of Batoche, Saskatchewan.* University of Calgary Press.

of the Grand Coteau was fought in 1851 between the Red River Métis buffalo hunters and the North Dakota Sioux. This was the last battle fought between the two groups, and the Métis were victorious. From the Battle of the Grand Coteau microfilm, seen on the opposite page,

> My sister Isabelle was fighting in the place of her husband, Andre Trottier. She never left me alone during those three days of battle. She would force me to rest, and during that time, she would shoot, and she was a good shot too. Every time she would shoot, it was sure a Sioux would fall. And we would all shoot from sunrise to sun fall every day.

Historically, Métis women have always been deeply entrenched in the social and political spheres of their communities. More recently, many women have gained political and social power, and recognition within the Métis Nation and the Canadian state. They are paving the way and enabling us to follow in their footsteps.

Buffalo Hunt Red River
Illustration: Glenbow Archives NA-1406-7

MÉTIS BUFFALO HUNTERS AND MÉTIS MATRIARCHS

as told by **Métis Knowledge Holder, Norma Spicer**

> This comes from family history and from both oral and written history that I've researched. — *Norma Spicer*

INTO THE EARLY 19TH CENTURY, buffalo herds roamed the prairies of North America. I've heard they would move from north to south in the fall and return for the fresh grasslands after the spring rains. I've also heard it wasn't unusual to see herds of ten thousand of these animals migrating in search of fresh grassy plains.

Prized for their hides, meat, sinew and bones, these animals would not only feed Métis communities but were also essential to the fur trade. Forts and posts along the Red, Assiniboine and North Saskatchewan rivers purchased the products of these hunts.

I've read that the Métis buffalo hunts across the Homeland began in the late 1700s with the last hunt recorded by Oblates in 1881.

Summer hunts lasted from June to early August. It was an ideal time to make dried meat (pemmican) and for the buffalo tongue so prized by the Hudson Bay Company and traders who came on the hunt. The autumn hunt lasted from September to late October or early November.

Métis would keep about half of their pemmican and dried meat and bring back fresh meat preserved by the cold fall temperatures. The rest of their hunt would be sold to the traders for the forts and trading posts.

In the early spring there was a hub of activity in Métis communities. I've heard that men sowed their fields and readied their Red River Carts, livestock, guns, ammunition, lumber (for the drying racks) and tools. Women planted their gardens, gathering their clothing, bedding, wash tubs, pots, pans, and provisions needed to sustain the family over

A Métis family at their camp in Manitoba, with Red River Cart
Photo: Rice Studio. Library and Archives

the next few months. They would also bring their lye soap they'd made with fat and wood ashes and the quilts they had fashioned from used pieces of cloth. Children would load lots of firewood into the carts. It was also a time for packing the beaded and embroidered clothing, moccasins and things crafted over the long winter months. I've heard they would all look forward to see families and friends who were joining in the hunt from other Métis Communities.

These journeys would sometime be over hundreds of miles, travelling ten to twelve miles a day. The noisy Red River carts were brightly decorated, and horses were proudly adorned with intricate beadwork decorations.

The women would make fires, boil water for tea, fry up some bannock and set out food for their families. Once watered and fed they all would set out again on the trail. The last stop of the day was a hub of activity. Fires were lit and

Métis camp and women baking. Pembina area, Manitoba
Photo: Glenbow Archives NA-1406-27

the major meal of the day was prepared, families fed, dishes were cleaned, tents were set up and little ones were bedded. Weather permitting, it was also a time to talk with the others and maybe listen to a tune or two. A strong sense of community and friendship made it a good place to be.

Métis hunting brigades were created to lead the buffalo hunts. Métis families followed matriarchal lines and it was through these ties that the brigades were formed. Women played an important role in the creation, formation, leadership, and maintenance of the brigades. When you think of a Métis hunting brigade, you often think of the men's role in the hunt. However, women played a pivotal role in the connection and kinship ties that was the foundation of the brigades.

I have heard as the hunters, traders, and their families arrived, the camp was set up. Their tents were lined in multiple rows at one end of the camp, their horses, and other animals at the other end. In the evening, the buffalo ponies were always kept in a circular enclosure of Red River Carts and heavily guarded. These horses were prized by the Métis and coveted by horse thieves.

The Métis buffalo camps and hunts were organized and carried out with military precision. There were "Laws of the Hunt," Métis hunters had established and followed throughout their homeland. This is important because it shows that the Métis had their own unique ethnic identity and a structure of laws in place long before Canada was country.

The Captain of the hunt coordinated the men, women, and children as well as the carts and horses. They were responsible to plan every detail to make the hunt as efficient and as safe as possible. The Captains also appointed their own guides whose duty was to enforce the laws of the hunt.

Here are the specific laws that were developed by the Métis in 1840 Laws of the Hunt:

1. No buffalo to be run on the Sabbath-Day.
2. No party to fork off, lag behind, or go before, without permission.
3. No person or party to run buffalo before the general order.
4. Every Captain with his men, in turn, to patrol the camp, and keep guard.
5. For the first trespass against these laws, the offender to have his saddle and bridle cut up.
6. For the second offence, the coat to taken off the offender's back, and be cut up.
7. For the third offense, the offender was flogged.
8. Any person convicted of theft, even to the value of a sinew, to be brought to the middle of the camp, and the crier to call out his or her name three times, adding the word "thief" at each time.

The Buffalo Hunt Laws have become the basis for Métis self-government today.

Following the hunt, the hard work began. Women and older children brought their Red River Carts and butchered the buffalo. The carts were then loaded with the meat and furs and brought back to camp.

They would spend several days processing the meat. The meat would be cut into strips and hung for three days to dry in the summer sun. On dull or rainy days, the meat was dried inside their tents or cabins.

Métis families would also be busy picking saskatoons and chokecherries to make pemmican. When the buffalo meat would dry, they would place it on the buffalo hides and pulverize it. The bison fat was then added to the mixture with berries for flavouring. The ingredients were then mixed with a shovel and left to congeal. The women would put the pemmican into large rawhide sacks and sew them closed with sinew. I've heard that the women would also use the rawhide sacks to store dried berries for use later on. These berries would last a very long time and were a nutritious food for their families.

Another job of the women would be to scrape the buffalo hides. They would use these hides for many things such as tent covers, sleeping robes, clothing, and moccasins. The Métis could use nearly every part of the buffalo; the horns were used as drinking vessels and containers for gun powder, bones could be fashioned into tools, the ribs could be made into sled runners, bladders into water bags, just to name a few.

Other daily activities at the buffalo hunting camp started early; fires were lit, and women cooked the food needed to sustain everyone during the heavy workday ahead. This demonstrates the strength and importance of Métis women as leaders within Métis communities and families.

The Métis brigades would always bring a priest along on the hunt. They would always lead the camp with a prayer for the success of the hunt and bless the daily bread.

Sunday would be the day of rest from the hunt and the harvest. The priest would always start Sundays with a mass. Sometimes, the Métis would hold baptisms and weddings. Weddings were known to last up to two days, or longer. The Métis have always loved to celebrate whenever they could; to this day, the Métis are renowned for their fiddle music and dance skills. They always take time to gather, share food, play music, sing, dance, laugh and tell stories.

In the spring, the Métis would often trade their pemmican and hides. The women would also sell the many items they had crafted over the winter months. They were famous for their floral beadwork designs and embroidery that they would add to jackets, bags, leggings, gloves, vests, and pouches. These items can be found all over the world today.

When the fall came and the weather got colder, the Métis would hold boisterous parties to celebrate the success of the hunt. Lively dancing, fiddle music, card playing, storytelling and feasting were all part of the festivities. Warm embraces were shared, and tears overflowed as families and friends parted.

The families slowly travelled the long journey home; their carts laden with pemmican, hides and the things they had bought from the traders. They would reminisce on the days of the hunt and the joyous times they'd had with family and friends. The work had been hard, but the memories of the good times were plenty. As the carts squeaked and brought them ever closer to home, they would take in the beauty that the fall colors brought to the prairies. They looked forward to seeing those they had left behind to tend the stock and the gardens.

That is the story of the Métis buffalo hunts. These hunts could not have been possible without the hard work of the Métis men, women and children who all played an important role.

INTRODUCTION TO THE WOMEN

Olive, Ken, and Beatrice Jobin
Photo: Beatrice Demetrius

BEATRICE DEMETRIUS (JOBIN)

I was born at a farm in Big Prairie, Alberta to Helen Chalifoux born 1912, and Joseph Jobin, born 1902. I had an older sister, Olive, and five brothers. We were a typical Métis family of fair, medium, and darker skinned. My parents were Métis, my father's family was from Manitoba and mothers were from Lac La Biche.

Ni kê pimâtisiyân ânta uskênân ântê Big Prairie, Alberta ochi Helen Chalifoux kê pimâtisit 1912, mêna Joseph Jobin kê pimâtisit 1902. Ni k'âyâwâk omisimaw, Olive, mêna nêyânan nistesak. Nêyanân ôma mwechi la Métis famille ochi wapasow musakiy, âhpétaw kuskétiwâw musakiy mêna kuskétiwâw musakiy. Ni nékéhikowak wêyâwâw Métis, ni papa son famille wêyâwâw ochi Manitoba mêna ni mama sa famille ochi Lac La Biche.

My brother Fred and I found all the newspapers at the archives; the obituary stated that Louis Jobin was a Lieutenant and joined Louis Riel, along with his brothers in 1885 at Batoche, Saskatchewan.

Ni stes Fred mêna nêyâ kê miskâmân âchimow'usinahikuna ântê tânta kâ kunawêyih'tamihk kâyâs ispayiwina; ânta âkatuskêwin kê itustêk Louis Jobin kê Lieutenant mêna kê wêchêwat Louis Riel, usichi o'sitêsa ispê 1885 ântê Bâtoche, Saskatchewan.

The Jobin family lived at Manitoba, my great-grandfather Ambroise senior married Marguerite Mandeville and they had five boys and five girls.

La famille Jobin kê wêkichik ântê Manitoba, ni châpân-moshomimâw Ambroise Sr. kê wêkimat Marguerite Mandeville mêna wêyawâw kê âyâchik nêyânan napêsisak mêna nêyânan iskwesisak.

Ambroise worked for the Hudson Bay Company and was sent to Sawridge and to Fort Chipewyan. He returned to Manitoba where he retired.

Ambroise âtoskêt kichi Hudson Bay Company mêna êtsâhiht ântê Sawridge mêna ântê Fort Chipewyan. Wêya pê kêwew ântê Manitoba ikotê pooni'atoskew.

Ambroise Jr. was born 1851 and was a council member of Louis Riel's Provisional Government. In 1885, he took Métis to Fish Creek where a battle broke out. He was wounded in the leg, on the last day of the battle at Batoche he was shot in the same leg and was arrested. His leg ended up being amputated and he died.

Ambroise Jr. kê pimâtisit 1851 mêna nêkân pêstamâkew ochi Louis Riel Provisional Government. Ispê 1885, k'itohtahât li Métis ântê Fish Creek ikotê notintowin kâ mâchipâyêk. Miswâw miskat, iskoyânihk kêsikâw notintowin ântê Bâtoche, kê pâskisohk pêyakwun miskat mêna otiht-inâw. Wêyâ miskat wanuskoch kêskikatêskwâw mêna kê nipit.

I was eight years old when my father drowned. That summer he bought me a little wringer washing machine, big enough to wash doll clothes. I carried that precious little toy for years, until my little stepsisters played with it and lost parts. That same year Olive and I made our first communion, we wore our communion dresses to father's funeral.

Helen Jobin (Beatrice's mother), Helen's half-brother Joseph, and Magdelaine Johnson (Beatrice's maternal grandmother)
Photo: Beatrice Demetrius

Nêyâ ôma âyinânew kê si piponyân tânispê ni papa kâ nistâpâwêt. Êkospê nêpin k'âtâwestâmowit âpsâsik sêniki'wâskwâhikun kisêpê'kinikun, êkohk kê misâw tâ sêpêkinâmân âwâsêhkân âyiwenisa. Ni k'itâhkonâ'mân êkwâ'nimâ âyiwâki teyihtâkwun mêtâ'wânâkun iskô uskêwina, iskô âpsêsichik nimisâk êhkâwinâ kê mêtâwâkechik mênâ kê wânetâchik pâhkina. Ânimâ pêyakwun uskêwin Olive mêna nêya k'osetâyâhk nêyanân nêkân suskumowin, kê potskâmâk nêyanân suskumowin usâkiya êkotê yisi ni papanân nâhinokêwin.

We moved to High Prairie when I was about eleven, where we went to a Catholic school.

K'âchipichiyâhk ântê High Prairie nântâw nêyâ pêyakosâp, tântê êtohtêyâhk ânta Catholic kiskinohumâ'kewin.

When I was about sixteen, I started asking my mother how grandfather died; I had heard from one cousin that someone shot him. Is it true he was with Louis Riel at Batoche? She would hush me up; she did not like to talk about the deceased.

Tânispê nântâw ikotosik'osâp, ni mâchi kwêchimâw ni mama tânisi ni moshom kê nipit; kê pêhtaman ochi pêyak ânâ ni wâhkomâkun âwiyak kê niskusinêt wêya. Tâpwe chê êkê wêchiwât Louis Riel ântê Bâtoche? Wêya nohtê êti kiyâmapihit, nâmoya kê mêyotâhk tâ pêkiskwâtomâk ânihi onipowak.

Sometime later she would tell me little bits of our family history, it was frustrating for me, and she said I was too nosy.

Mwesteses wêyâ kê wêhtâmowit âpsis pâhki ânihi nêyanân famille histoire, êwuko pekwiyitâk ochi nêyâ, mêna wêyâ êtwew nêyâ ôma sâm mistâhi kâtâch kâhkiyâw wi kiskêyih'tumân.

DOREEN POITRAS

Francois Poitras and his second wife, Madeleine Boudreau (Maggie's sister) Photo: Poitras Family

I was one of six children of Pierre Poitras and Margaret Garneau.

Nêya ôma pêyak ochi nikotosik âwâsisâk ochi Pierre Poitras mêna Margaret Garneau.

The Poitras and Garneau's were proud Métis families of the Red River Settlement, loyal supporters of Louis Riel, who fought in the Battle of the Grand Couteau. Pierre Poitras, my father's great grandfather (also named Pierre), was the grandson of Cuthbert

Left: Lawrence and Eleanor Garneau
Right: Pierre Poitras and Margaret Garneau
Photo: Poitras Family

Grant Sr. He served on the Riel Provisional Government of Manitoba. Many of my ancestors are buried at Batoche.

Li Poitras mêna Li Garneau wêyawâw kistêyimowâhk Li Métis familles ochi Red River Settlement, tâpwêwêwin'iwiw pumihew ochi Lois Riel, kâ notinkêchik ânta Battle of Grand Couteau. Pierre Poitras, ni papa ochâpâna (wêstâ ê-sekâsot Pierre), wêya châpân'ikosis ochi Cuthbert Grant Sr. Wêya âtoskâtâhk ânta Riel Provisional Government de Manitoba. Mistâhi âniki ni wâhkomâkunâk ê-nâyinewchik ântê Bâtoche.

My mother, Margaret Garneau, was a grandchild of Lawrence Garneau and Eleanor Thomas. Much has been written on the history of Lawrence Garneau, who on leaving Edmonton, settled in St. Paul des Métis. The Garneau district in Edmonton is located on his river lot.

Ni mama, Margaret Garneau, kê chapânâsis ochi Lawrence Garneau mêna Eleanor Thomas. Mistâhi kê mâsinahikêwin ânima l'histoire ochi Lawrence Garneau, âwêna kâ nâkâtâhk Edmonton, okistapit ântê St. Paul des Métis. Li Garneau district ântê Edmonton ê-chêpatâstek ânta son rivyer tipâskânis.

My paternal grandparents were Francois Poitras and Maggie Boudreau. Francois loved classical music (on the radio), which we kids thought was strange and we didn't like it one bit. He was a kind and gentle old man. She (Maggie) is buried in Fishing Lake Métis Settlement where the Poitras lived after leaving St. Paul. The early (Métis) settlers at St. Paul des Métis resettled mainly in Fishing Lake or Elizabeth (Métis Settlement).

N'ohtâwênakisi châpânâk Francois Poitras mêna Maggie Boudreau. Francois sâkihitâht mooniyâw kitochikêwin (ânta pehtumowâkun), tâna neyanân âwâsisâk kê têhtumahk mâhmâtâwun mêna moya kê mêyotâmâhk sôskwach. Wêya kê mêyotaht mêna kê kisêwatsit kêhtaya nâpew. Wêya (Maggie) kê nâyinewiht ântê Fishing Lake Métis Settlement tânita Li Poitras kê wêkichik êyikohk kâ sepwêtêchik Saint Paul. Kâyâs Li Métis okistâpiwak ântê Saint Paul des Métis kê okistâpichik âsumêna ântê Fishing Lake âhpo Elizabeth (Li Métis Settlement).

DOREEN BERGUM (DUMONT)

My name is Doreen Bergum, born in Olds, Alberta and raised in Sundre, Alberta. My mother was Mary Vaness, my father was Ambroise Dumont. I have been blessed with a rich Métis ancestry and culture — number six in a family of five boys and five girls. My parents taught us how to survive with the values of honesty, respect, love, sharing, caring, courage, kindness, spirituality, and the meaning of kinship, caring for your own. They also taught us how to work.

Ni wêhowin ôma Doreen Bergum, kê pimâtisiyan ântê Olds, Alberta mêna kê opikiyan ântê Sundre, Alberta. Ni mama wêya Mary Vaness, ni papa wêya Ambroise Dumont. Nêya kê sawêyih'tâkosiyân âschi wêyôtisew Métis wâhkomitowin mêna nistum pimâchihowin. Âkêhtâsoyan nikotosik ânima la famille ochi nêyânan napêsisak mêna nêyânan iskwesisak. Ni nêkehikowak kê kiskino'humâkew'iyâhk tânisi tesi pimâtisiyahk âsichi itâhkitewina ochi kwayeswâtisiwin, kistêyihitowin, sâkihitowin, pâhkwênumâwiwin,

Upper: Doreen Bergum's family. Lower: Doreen Bergum and parents
Photo: Bergum Family

kânâwêyihtâmowin, kourage, kisewâtisiwin, mânitowâtisiwin, mêna itwêmukahk wâhkotowin, tâ kânâw'êyihtâm'âsoyin. Wêyawâw mêna kê kiskino'humâkew'iyahk tânisi tesi âtoskêyâhk.

I was raised as a southern Alberta Métis. My father was a faller of trees. My mother worked alongside him in the same logging camp as a cook, that was 30 to 40 miles outside of Sundre. Our parents taught us how to survive, and how to be parents when they left on Sunday night and returned the following weekend.

Ni kê ohpikihewiyân tâskoch li Métis sâwânohk ochi. Ni papa kê kâwâwhêt mêtosa. Ni mama kê âtoskêt kê wêchiwât ânta pêyakwân mistik âtoskew'êniw okupesi'win kê pinawâsot, êkwa'nima nistomtanâw âhpo nêyomtanâw mistika tipahikuna kêchi tipiskan kâ kisipustêk ochi Sundre. Ni kêhikowak kê kiskino'humâkew'iyahk tâ pimâtsiyâhk mêna tânisi tâ kêhikowak ispê kâ sêpwêtêchik ispê Âyimihaw kêsikâw tipskâhki mêna kê kêwêchik pimâtisihikew kisipipayiw kêsikâw.

JUANITA MAROIS

I don't have memories of being on the land with my Kookum or anything like that. I guess that's part of the story. I guess I didn't start to identify until I was a young adult.

Nâmoya nitâ'yân kiskisiwina ochi kê pimâtisiyahk ânta uskê n'ohkom âschi âhpo kêkwîy ikosi. Ni miskwêyitumân êkwâa'nima pâhki ânima âchimowin... Ni miskwêyitumân êkâ kê mâchitâyân istâwêyih tâkosiwin iskô kê oskîya âyisêniw.

So, my name is Juanita Marois and I grew up just outside of Edmonton on the boundary of the Enoch Indian Reserve. My heritage comes from the Cunningham line, so my family has scrip from the river lots in what is now St. Albert. It's interesting though. I remember a conversation as a very, very little person of my grandparents sitting at the table with my parents talking about being Métis. My grandmother said to my mother who is Norwegian Irish and very blonde, and to my father who is French Métis. My grandmother said [to them], "Your kids don't look it, you don't need to deal with it."

Ikosi, ni wêhowin ôma Juanita Marois mêna kê ohkpikiyân kêchi tipâskân kâ kisipustêk Edmonton mêna Enoch nêhiyaw uskê. Ni ânisko'kumâkewin ochi Cunningham, ikosi musinahêkêwin kâ kiskêtâmân ma famille kâ'yachik ânikê li rivyer tipâskânsa êkote ôma êkwa St. Albert. Êkwa ânima pisiskâpumâw mâka. Ni kiskisin pêkiskwê'totâtowin kâ mitoni, mitoni âpisâs'iyân âyisêniw. Mêna ni châpânahk kê âpitchik ânta la table âschi ni kêhikowak. Mêna n'ohkom kê wehtâmwat ni mama wêya Norwegian Irish. Mitoni osawâw mêschakâsa mêna ni papa wêya French Métis mêna n'ohkom. Ikosi, n'ohkom êtwew, "Ki'tawâsimisâk êka êsinâkosichik, moya kâtâch kêkwîy tâ totâmêk êkwâ'nima."

BERTHA CLARK-JONES (HOULE)
as told by her daughter, Gail Gallupe

Bertha Clark Jones
Photo: Gail Gallupe.

Hello. I am Gail Gallupe. Tansi. I am the president at this moment with McMurray Métis local 1935. I am here to talk about my mother, the late Bertha Clark-Jones. Her maiden name was Houle. My mother was born in Clear Hills, Alberta on November 9th, 1922. Mom always joked with us and would never tell us her age because she was sensitive about it, but we found out eventually. She did live to the ripe old age of 92 only just passing, in 2014 on October the 21st.

Tânsi. Nêya ôma Gail Gallupe. Tânsi. Nêya ôma nêkânew mêkwâch âsichi McMurray Métis Local 1935. Ota âyâyân tâ pêkiskwâtâmân ni mama, kâkê pimâtisit Bertha Clark-Jones. Wêya kâ pê pimâtisit wêhowin ânima Houle. Ni mama kê pimâtisit ântê Clear Hills,

Alberta November 9th, 1922. NI mama kâkikê wuwêyut'wêwin usichi nêyanân mêna nâmoya kê wehtâmi'kawiyahk tânima'koh êsi piponêt âya ochi wutakumisiw êkwa'nima ochi, mâkâ nêyanân êti kiskêyihtâmahk. Wêya kê pimâtisit iskô 92 wêya puko kê pônipimâtisit 2014 on October 21st.

Just to give you that little bit of information. While my mom was here, she was an amazing woman. She was of course a role model to me as I got older and could appreciate her work. and her work of course, was with the Indigenous population and the women and families, especially in Fort McMurray in around the 1960s.

Mwechi tâ mêyitâwâw âpsis puko âchimostâtowin. Mêkwâch ni mama ota k'âyât, wêya kê mitoni kêchi iskwew. Wêya tâpwê ânima okiskinowâpâtih nêya kichi kâ êti kihtayoyan mêna mêyeyihtam wêya âtoskêwin, mêna wêya âtoskêwin kê âniki âyinewak yâhkêmowin mêna iskwêwâk mêna li familles wâwes êkwa ântê Fort McMurray mêna wâsakâmê ânihi 1960s.

Mom became very much involved with the Métis population of Fort McMurray where we lived after having moved from Hawk Hills, Alberta, which is close to High Level, Alberta. My mom is the fifth of fourteen children born to Emilie St. Arnaud and Louis Houle.

Ni mama mitoni kê âtoskâta usichi li Métis âyisêniwâk ochi Fort McMurray tântê kê wêkiyahk êyikohk âchipichêyâhk ochi Hawk Hills Alberta tâna chêki ântê High Level, Alberta. Ni mama wêya nêyânan ochi neyosap âwâsisâk kê pimâtsichik ochi Emille St. Arnaud mêna Louis Houle.

She grew up as a farm girl and so of course when she got older, she had some amazing athletic skills from working out in the farm, because they only had the three boys, and the rest were girls. She eventually, in her teens, made a move to Grand Prairie to get out of the homestead with her sister and her brother-in-law while their mom enrolled in the air force.

Wêya kê opikihit tâskoch kistikwêkan iskwesis mêna tânispe wêya k'êti kehte'hên'iw, wêya k'âyât mitoni kêchi sâsâwinêkêwin kuskihowin ochi âtoskêyân ânta kistikân, âyis wêyawâw puko âyâchik nisto nâpêsisâk. mêna kotukik iskwesisak. Wêya, kâ oskîyit kê osêtaht âchipichêwin ântê Grand Prairie tâ sipwêtêchik kâ otinâskehk usichi osêma mêna ostesa in-law mêkwâch omamawa êti musinahikêt simâkunseh kâwinihk.

WW1 had begun. She was 18 and it was 1939 or 40. She enlisted and became a member of the Royal Canadian Air Force. She remained with the army until the war ended. Then she moved to Calgary where she met my dad, George Clark.

WW1 êti-mâchi payêk. Wêya kê êyinanew-osâp mêna ikospê ânmâ 1939 âhpo 1940. Wêya kê musinahikêt simâkunseh kâwinihk mêna mâchi owêchihew ânihi Royal Canadian Air Force. Wêya ikota âyâw usichi simâkunsiw'êniwak iskô notinitowin kâ pônipayêk. Êkospê wêya âchipichew êkote'yisi Calgary tânitê kâ nâkiskâwât ni papa, George Clark.

LISA WOLFE

My name is Lisa Wolfe. I was born in Edmonton. I'm a Métis woman of the Edmonton area. I have Métis heritage on both sides of my family.

Ni wêhowin ânima Lisa Wolfe. Ni kê pimâtisiyan ota Edmonton. Nêya ôma Métis ochi Edmonton. Ni'tayân Métis ânisko'kumakêwin nêswayi ochi nêya ma famille.

On my father's side, as well as on my mother's side my family heritage goes up back up through Lac La Biche region and the Métis mission. It was a major route way back in the early 1800s so that's kind of where it starts.

Ni papa anima wâhkomâkunâ, âyâ mêna ni mama anima wâhkomâkunâ nêya oma famille ânisko'kumakêwin êsipayêk sapotew Lac La Biche region mêna la Métis âyimihew'kamik. Êkwa'nima kêchi pimotêskunâw kayâs ochi ispê 1800s ikosi êkote kâh mâchi'payêk.

My mother's side is a Cardinal, but also MacDonald. So, that's up from Fort McMurray. My great-grandfather was a Cardinal that lived up in the Lac La Biche, Fort Chipewyan region. So when I moved back to Lac La Biche, that's where we kind of more self identified as being Métis and started meeting different relatives and family members.

Ni mama wâhkomâkunâ ânihi Cardinal, mâka wêstâwâw MacDonald. Ikosi ochi êkwâ'nima ochi Fort McMurray. Ni châpân'moshom wêsta Cardinal kâhwêkit antê Lac La Biche, Fort Chipewyan kituskênâw. Ikosi k'âpichewiyân kâwi antê Lac La Biche, êkote ânima nâwâch istâwey-ih'tâkosiwin nêyanân ôma Métis mênâ kê mâchi nâkiskâwâchik pêtos nêchi'sânak mêna la famille owêchihêwak.

PEARL CALAHASEN

My name is Pearl Calahasen. I was born and raised in Grouard, Alberta, from a proud, Métis and proud First Nation family. [Grouard) probably was the smallest little community, but once upon a time would have been the largest community where there are a lot of Métis and First Nations People [who] lived there and influenced what happened in that middle community.

Ni wêhowin ôma Pearl Calahasen. Nêya kê pimâtisiyân mêna kê opi-kiyân ântê Grouard Alberta, ochi ânâ kiste'yimow'ichik Métis mêna kiste'yimow'ichik First Nation la famille. [Grouard) êtikwê ânima mitoni âpisâsik mâmâwi'e'âyâhk, mâkâ pêyakwâw nâwâch kê misâw mâmâwi'e'âyâhk tânitê mêchêt Métis mêna First Nations âyisêniwak kâkê wêkichik êkotê mêna wêyâwê'nâkohtâw kêkwîy kâ ispayêk êkota ânima tustâ'wayi mâmâwi'e'âyâhk.

I was born on a very cold day in December and my mother woke up my dad and said, "It's time, the baby's coming and I need you to go get the midwife."

Ni kê pimâtisiyân mitoni êtâhkâyâk kêsikâw ispê December mêna ni mama kê kwâskwayihat ni papawa mêna êtwêt, "Ikosi ôma êkwâm, âwâsis wi pêtohtew mêna nitâwê'tên kêya tâ nâtaht muskêkê'iskwew."

The midwife was a lady from Grouard, and she was one of the older ladies who actually was probably the only midwife in that little community. My father had to saddle up the horses and go and get the midwife to come and help my mom. And when I was born, I was only less than two pounds. They thought I would never make it as an individual or a person who would survive.

Ânâ muskêkê'iskwew ânâ iskwew ochi Grouard, mêna wêya ânâ pêyak ochi âniki kêhtaya iskwêwak âwêna êtikwe wêya puko êkota ânima âpsis mâmâwi'e'âyâhk. Ni papa puko êstat uspupowina ânihi têhta pêwâtimok mêna tâ nâtât ânihi muskêkê'iskwew tâ pêhtotêt mêna tâ wêchihat ni mama. Mêna kâkê pimâtisiyân, nêya puko kêkâch niso kosikwuna. Wêyâwâw kê têhtâchik namoya nêya tâ kâskêtayân tâ pimâtisiyân.

And so, the midwife laid out some actions for my mom to do, to deal with. With that came the fact that I grew up from a less than two pounder to over 200 pounds. So, I think that says that if you do what the women of our world, whether it's Métis or First Nations, that they have lessons to tell us, they give us gifts that we can move on with.

Mêna ikosi, ânâ muskêkê'iskwew âstâw âtêht tohtumihk ni mama kichi tâ tohtahk. Usichi êkwa kâ pesipayek tâpwêwin ânima nêya opikiyan ochi puko kêkâch niso kosikwuna iskô paschi niso mitâtaht'omitanâw kosikwuna. Ikosi, ni têhtên ânima êtâstêhk ânima kêspin kêya t'itotâmin kêkwîy iskwêwak ochi kêyânâw misiwe'uskê, mutwânchê ikonânki Métis âhpo First Nations, ânima âyâchik kiskinohumâ'kêwina tâ wêhtâmâkoyakik, wêyawâw kê mêkiyâhk mêkiwina kêyanâw.

And that midwife gave my family and myself the gift to survive. That gift to survive was to be able to make sure that I could challenge things as I went on and grew up in the world. And that began with the fact that I left home early to go ensure that I would get my Grade 12. With that came the fact that it was very lonely, very, very lonely, but it was my mom and my grandma and my aunts, because I come from a matrilineal and matriarchal society that I was able to rely upon that.

Mêna ânâ muskêkê 'iskwew kê mêkoyahk ma famille mêna nêya ânima mêkiwin tâ pimâtisiyahk. Êkwa ânima mêkiwin tâ pimâtisiyahk tâ kêchi'nâhowiyahk ânima nêya mâwinwêhiwin kêkwîy kâ êti opikêyân mêna êti êsipwetêyân misiwê'uskê. Mêna êkwa ânima kê mâchipayik usichi tâpwêwin ânima kê sêpwêhtêyân ni wêkinân tâ kêchi'nâhowiyân tâ kâhtinâmân ânima Grade 12. Usichi êkwa ânima p'ispayin tâpwêwin êwuko mitoni pêkis'kâtum, mitoni, mitoni pêkis'kâtum, mâka êwuko ânima ni mama mêna n'ohkom mêna ni mitosisak, âyis nêya ochi ânima okimâkan'iskwewak mêna okimâkan'iskwew society ânima nêya kê kâskêtâyân t'uspê'yimoway kêw'ânima.

MURIEL STANLEY-VENNE
as told by herself and her daughter, Rachelle Venne

Buildings, Pakan, Alberta
Photo: Glenbow Archives ND-3-468a

My name is Rachelle. I am the daughter, youngest, and only daughter of Muriel Stanley Venne. I just wanted to talk a little bit about her and her stories that she's shared.

Ni wêhowin ôma Rachelle, nêya ôma otânisa... âwâsisa, mêna puko otânisa ochi Muriel Stanley Venne. Nêya mwechi kê nohtê pêkiskwâtâmân âpsis nântâw wêya... wêya âchimona kâkê pâhkwênumawêt.

My mom was raised [in] Pakan or they referred to it as Pakan, which is pretty close to where Métis Crossing is.

Ni mama kê pê opikihiht... êsêkâtêk Pakan âhpo wêyâw itsâwew ânima Pakan, tânima chêki ânima tânitê Métis Crossing kâ âstêk.

Her dad was American, he came from North Dakota and Illinois. Both the families came here for land and her mother was from Prince Albert, Saskatchewan originally. They settled in the area around Métis Crossing. She (Muriel's mother) was a fantastic lady. Her name was Jessie Whitford and she did apparently drive a Red River cart and after being widowed quite young, she spent most of her time alone. My mother had a very close relationship with her grandmother and that's [where] she learned a lot of her Métis history.

Ôpapawa âna êyinew North American ochi, ochi North Dakota mêna Illinois. Nêswayi li familles kê pê tohtêchik ochi uskê mêna ômamawa ochi Prince Albert, Saskatchewan nistum ochi. Wêyawâw kê kistapêchikântâ uskê wâsakâmê Métis Crossing. Wêya (Muriel o'mamawa) kê mitoni mêyo'wâtisiw . Wêya wêhowin Jessie Whitford mêna wêya êsa kê puminat ânâ rivyer rooze karte mêna mwestes kâ pê moosiskwêwit mitoni kê oskîyit, wêya mêstinam tânito tipâhikun kê yâkwâpit. Ni mama êki âyat mêyo wâhkotowin usichi ochâpânâ mêna êkote ânima kâ kiskêyitahk mistâhi ânima Métis kâyas âta'yohkun.

My mom had very fond memories of growing up in Alberta. She said she was a product of Canada, and so she really enjoyed the opportunity to share her experiences.

Ni mama k'âyât sakihitaw kiskisi'wina ochi kâ pê pimâtisit ântê Alberta. Wêya k'itwew wêya k'osêhtahk ochi Canada, mêna ikosi wêya mitoni mêyohtum kâ nâhipayik tâkê pâhkwê'numawêt wêya kiskêyih'tumowin.

She was the oldest of well, I guess there was ten children in the family. The oldest one went to live with an aunt and my uncle who is my mom's twin. He ran away at thirteen. So, my mother was kind of the oldest in the home. She had seven younger siblings at home so she was the mom when her mother wasn't there and so [she] took a lot of pleasure in raising the young ones.

Wêya nâwach kê kêhtê'hiyit ochi, ni mêskwe'yitaman mitataht âwâsisâk ânta la famille. Ânâ nâwach kê kêhtê'hiyit isipwêtew tâ wêkit âsichi ânâ mitosis mêna mon oncle âwêna ni mama nêsotew, kê tâpasêt kâ mitâtâht nisto. Ikosi, ni mama tâpiskoch wêya kêhtê'hiyit ânâ wêkih. Wêya kê âwât têpâkoph âwâsisâk osêmisa ântâ wêkih ikosi wêya ni mamanaw ispê wêya ômamawa êk'âyachik ikota mêna ikosi (wêya) otinâm mistâhi mêyo'wâtomowin ê opikihat âniki âwâsisâk osêmisa.

ANGIE CRERAR
(also featured in Memories of Residential Schools)

I'm here to tell my story — I'm starting to feel the pain already — because it's something that I had buried for so many years. As a child I was raised in a Métis community with my three sisters and four brothers. We had a happy life, my mother did a lot of gardening, and she did a lot of herbal medicine. My dad worked at the Hudson's Bay Company and also as an interpreter. We had a very happy childhood and my dad instilled in us the value and the pride of being Métis. I lived a very happy life and was a happy child. We all were. My mother did a lot of sewing and we always had new parkas, new mittens and mukluks, and so on. We always had adequate food as my mother was a very good cook. She could cook from scratch and that's something she taught me which I brought down to my own children.

Nêya ôma otah ê pêkiskwâtamân n'âta'yohkun. – Ni mâchi moositân wêsukê'yihtumowin sâsiy – âyis kêkwîy ânima kâkê nâyinewyân kâyâs ochi. K'âwâsisoyân ni kê ohpikin ântâ Métis mâmâwi'ê'âyâhk âsichi nisto nisêmisak mêna neyo nistesak. Nêyanân n'âtâyân mêyo pimâtisiwin, ma mére mistâhi êtotâhk kistikânisa, mêna wêya êtohtaht mistâhi muskêkêya kâ moona'humihk. Mon pére âtoskêk ânta Hudson's Bay Company mêna âsichi twesta'makew. Nêyanân k'âyâyâhk mitoni mêyowe'yihtâm k'âwâsisi'wiyahk mêna mon pére âchi'puko ânima itaki'tew mêna ânima kiste'yimowin ochi li Métis. Ni kê pimâtisiyan mitoni mêyo'wiyihtam pimatisiwin – k'âyâyân mêyowe'yihtam k'âwâsisi'wiyân – kâhkiyâw nêyanân. Ma mére itohta mistâhi kuskwâs'oyon mêna nêyanân âyâyâk oskîyi kêso'wusa'kiya, oskîyi ustisak mêna pâhpêkin'weskisina, mêna kotuk kêkwîy. Nêyanân kâkikê âyâyâhk êkoyikohk mêchowin âyis ma mére wêya mitoni mêyo opinawusot. Wêya kâskitâw t'opinâwusot from scratch mêna êkwâ'nima kêkwîy wêya kiskino'humâkit nêya tânâ ki pêhtatâyân yisi n'otâwâsimisak.

DIANNE LUDWIG

My name is Dianne McKay, my married name is Dianne Ludwig and that's what I go by. I was born in a northern community in northern Saskatchewan — it was Buffalo Narrows, and I lived there until I was seventeen and then I moved to Fort McMurray. Then we lived in Fort McMurray for thirteen years and then we moved to Lac La Biche.

Ni wêhowin ôma Dianne McKay, ni wêkêhtôwin wêhôwin ôma Dianne Ludwig mêna kêkwîy êkwa'nima ni sêhkasôn. Nêyâ kê pimâtisiyân ântâ kêwêtinohk mâmâwi'e'âyâk ântê kêwêtinohk Saskatchewan - êkwâ'nima Buffalo Narrows, mêna nêyâ kê wêkiyân êkotê iskô têpa'kôhp'osâp mêna êkospê ni âchipichin yisi Fort McMurray. Êkôspe nêyanân kê wêkiyâhk Fort McMurray iskô nistô'sap uskêwina mêna êkospê nêyanân kê âchipichiyâhk yisi Lac la Biche.

MARY SKYBLUE MORIN

I was born in 1951 in Ile-a-la Crosse, Saskatchewan, but my home community is Green Lake, Saskatchewan. The hospital was in Ile-a-la-Crosse, so my mother went to visit her sister and I was born there. I was one of two children of Suzanne Morin. In the 1960s, I met my brother Tony (Antoine) who had been living on a farm as a foster child. He was 21 years old, the legal age to leave foster care in the 1960s. n'ohkom Mary "Lâpis" Morin (nee Aubichon) lived in Green Lake taking care of my cousin Josephine. At times, my mother and I would stay with n'ohkom Lâpis. Her house stood on a hill at the east end of main street.

Ni kê pimâtisiyân 1951 ântê Île-à-la-Crosse SK mâka nêki mâmâwi'e'âyâhk ânima Green Lake SK. Ahkosew'kâmik ânima kê âstêk ântê Île-à-la-Crosse. Ni mama kê itohtêt tâ kêwikâ'wât osêmisâ mêna ni pimâtisin êkotê. Nêya ôma pêyak ochi nêso âwâsisâk ochi Suzanne. Ni nâkiskâwâw nistes Tony (Antoine) âwena kâke wêkit ânta uskê'tipâskânis tâskoch foster child. Wêya âna nêstânâw'pêyak'osâp piponiya e'âyât, kêchi ispehti'sêwin tâ sepwetêt ochi foster care êkospê 1960s. n'ohkom Mary "Lâpis" Morin (nee Aubichon) kê wêkit ânte Green Lake ê kunâwêmat ânihi ni wâhkomâkan Josephine. Âskaw mâna, ni mama mêna nêya ê kê âyâyâk usichi n'ohkom Lâpis. Wêya wâskihikun kê chêpatâstek tâhkoch ispasinâsiw ânta sâkâstenohk ânima kêchi mêskunas.

A few years of researching my grandmother's Aubichon family and the five generations of grandfather's Morin family geneology learning facts about my ancestry. I learned that my great-grandfather Louis Morin Sr. and seven of his fourteen adult children had been granted Métis Scrip in the 1870s. Louis Morin Sr.'s father, Antoine Morin worked for the North West Company (1820) and then the Hudson's Bay Company (1821-1957) as a voyageur and an interpreter. He worked in Great Slave Lake, Fort Chip, Norway House and Ile-a-la-Crosse. The Aubichon family was through Jean Baptiste Aubichon Jr. (1871-1921) and Sr. (1840-1912). My fifth generation grandfather Pierre Aubichon (1797- 1857) worked for the Hudson's Bay Company as a voyageur (1826-1848). Later, he worked for the Red River (1852 - 1854). I thought maybe I would go to my grave without proving my heritage. At fifty-five years, I got my Métis I.D. card from the Saskatoon Métis local.

Âtêht uskêwina tâ nutoni'kewiyân nêyânan ânisko'tâpâna ochi n'ohkom Aubichon li famile mêna ni moshom Morin li famille wâhkom'itowin mâchi kiskêyih'tâmân tâpwê'wina ochi ni wâhko'towin. K'itikiskêtâmân ânima ni châpân Louis Morin Sr. mêna tepa'kohp ochi ânihi neyo'sap âwâsisâk kâ opikichik ê kê mêkâwichik Métis Scrip ispê 1870s. Louis Morin Sr.'s ôpapawa, Antoine Morin kê âtoskêkatahk ochi NorthWest Company (1820) mêna tânispê ânima Hudson Bay Company (1821-1957) tâskoch voyageur mêna tâskoch twestâ'mâkew. Wêya âtoskêt ântê Great Slave Lake, Fort Chip, Norway House mêna Ile-a-la-Crosse. Âna Aubichon li famille ânima ochi Jean Baptiste Aubichon Jr. (1871 - 1921) mêna Sr. (1840 - 1912). Ni niyânan ânisko'tâpân moshomnan âna Pierre Aubichon (1797

-1857) kê âtosket ânta Hudson Bay Co (1826 – 1848) tâskoch voyageur. Mwestes kê âstokew ânte Red River (1852 – 1854). N'itehtên âhpwetikwê tâ nipêyân pâmyêse tâ kêchi'nâhoyân wâhkom'itowin. Kâ isipipon'iyan niyânan'omtinaw niyân'osâp, ni kâchitinên Li Métis ID kêchi musina'hikun ochi Saskatoon Li Métis Local.

DELIA MARIE GRAY (CUNNINGHAM), *as told by* her daughters, granddaughters, and great granddaughters

These are some of the teachings of Delia Gray, as told by her daughters, her granddaughters, and her great granddaughters.

Ohi âtêht kiskino'humakêwina ochi Delia Gray, kê wêhtâmkâwiyak ohpime'yisi otânisa, wêya nosisim otânisa mêna wêya ânsko nosisim otânisa.

Delia was a matriarch of such womanly strength that we did not know there was any other way to be. When Bob, her husband was alive, he was a force to be reckoned with. Like Delia, his first language was Cree. He was a veteran of the air force. He was a social worker. He was known to be a snappy dresser. Probably most importantly for Delia, he was a musician, she loved music. Music could make her dance and sing but she loved it most when music made her cry. With her strong and accomplished husband, she shared the role of the head of the family.

Delia kê okimâkan'iskwew êkoh iskwew kê muskâwisêt ânima nêyanân nâmoya kê kiskêtâmâhk kotuk kêkwîy t'âyâyâhk. Ispê Bob, onâpêma kâkê pimâtisit, wêya totu'mohâw t'îteyih'tumwit. Tâskoch Delia, wêya nêkan pêkiskwêwin kê Nêhiyâwewin. Wêya âna kêhtê'yisêniw onôti'nikewa ochi air force. Wêya ânâ social worker. Wêya êpêkiskêmhit wâwêsew âyiwinsa kâ potskak. Âhpo êtikwe nâwach kêchiyi'wun kichi Delia, wêya âna kitoh'chikew'eniw, wêya kê sâkitam kitoh'chikêwin. Kitoh'chikêwin kê puminikot tâ nêmêhitot mêna tâ nakamot mâka wêya mêchet nâwach mêyotum ânima tânispe kitoh'chikêwin mutwê mâtow. Usichi wêya kâ muskawisêyêt mêna kâ pehkotah'masot onâpêma, wêya kê pâhkwê'numawew âyâw totumowin âna okimakân la famille.

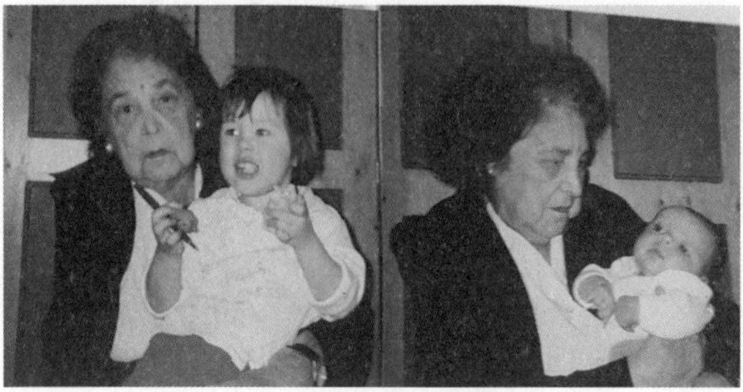

Delia Gray with her granddaughter
Photo: Delia Gray's family

Bobbi (Roberta Marie) (Delia's daughter)

Bobbi is the eldest daughter, a very special place in Métis families. There is recognition but there is also so much responsibility. It is to Bobbi that all of us children and grandchildren are grateful that she preserved the teachings Delia gave her.

Bobbi wêya nistum osân otânisa, mitoni kêchi tânitêkê âhiht ânita li Métis familles. Êkota nistâwi'nâtowin mâka êkota mitoni nâkute'yichikêwin. Wêya ânâ Bobbi âniki kâhkiyâw nêyanân âwâsisâk mêna châpân'âwâsisak kâ nânâskomochik ânâ wêya kê kuniwêyihtâk ânihi kiskino'humâkêwina Delia kâkê mêyat.

Before I get into explaining some things that I learnt from my mom, it is important to her memory that I give some information in regard to her family background, as she used to say, "Know who your relatives are."

Pâmweyês nêya tâ pêkiskwâtâmân âtêht kêkwîy kâ kiskêyihtâmân ochi ni mama, kêchiyiwun êwuko kiskisiwin ânima ê mêkiyân âtêht âchimostâtowin âyâ ochi sa famille wâhkotowin, âyis wêya kê itwêt mânâ, "tâ kiskêmâchik âwina ki wâhkomâkunak."

Both my mom and my dad have given us a rich Indigenous and Scottish bloodline. My mom always used to mention the fact that

Delia's husband Bob
Photo: Delia Gray's family

she was born in Wabasca on March 17, 1917, she was quite proud of this. How this came to be is that her dad worked in Wabasca for Revillon Frères, a fur trading company that rivaled the Hudson's Bay fur trading company.

Nêswayi ni mama mêna ni papa kê mêkoyâkihk oyotsowin Indigenous mêna Scottish bloodline. Ni mama mânâ kê itwew tâpwêwin ânima kê pimâtisit ânte Wabasca March 17, 1917, wêya mitoni kiste'yimow ôma. Tânisi ôma kâ p'âyispayek ânima opapa âtoskêt ântê Wabasca kichi Revillon Freres, ânima âhtiy mêskotoni'kêwin mâmâwêtowâk ânima mâwinê'hitowin âna Hudson's Bay âhtiy mêskotoni'kêwin mâmâwêtowâk.

One of the things that was important to my mom was who her parents and grandparents were; her dad was Henry Cunningham (1869–1955) and her mom was Mary Rowland (1874–1948).

Pêyak âniki kêkwîy nâwach kêchiyi'wun ochi ni mama kê wêya nikêwêhikowak mêna ohêkê'omâwa âyâchik; ôpapawa âna Henry Cunningham (1869–1955) mêna ômamawa Mary Rowland (1874 –1955).

Métis Child and Family Jiggers at Métis Crossing
Photo: Métis Nation of Alberta

Beaded Gauntlets
Photo: Métis Nation of Alberta

Upper and Lower: Matt Hiltermann finger weaving a Métis sash at Métis Crossing
Photos: Métis Nation of Alberta

Chapter 2

Métis Culture and Identity

Métis New Year's Day celebrations at Lac La Biche, Alberta, 1895
Illustration: Glenbow Archives NA-1185-5

New Year's Day celebrants, Elizabeth Métis Settlement
Illustration: Glenbow Archives NA-5127-7

MÉTIS CULTURE AND IDENTITY

Métis Child and Family Dancers at Métis Crossing.
Photo: Métis Nation of Alberta

MÉTIS CULTURE AND TRADITIONS are vast and varied. The Métis People are generally known to be very social people who have, for as long as we've been around, maintained a practice of respect, reciprocity, and relationality. The Métis have always valued our kinship relations and have connected to each other for centuries through our shared language, unique artistry, storytelling practices, humour, and our music and dance.

Celebrations & Social Life

The Métis have always been a celebratory People. Often, stories are told about old-time kitchen parties, where friends, family, and neighbours would come from miles around to gather in an old farmhouse. They would push the furniture out of the way, sometimes out of the house altogether and a fiddle player would play all the old-time Métis tunes such as the Duck dance, The Reel of Four, and Drops of Brandy, but none was more favoured than the Red River Jig. The Red River Jig is the most popular

Brianna Lizotte playing the fiddle

Photo: Métis Nation of Alberta

Old Metis Keep Alive Custom of 200 Years

1940

(Special Despatch)

LEBRET, Sask., Jan 3. — Old Metis buffalo hunters and their friends, gathered for the annual celebration of le jour de l'an, New Years day, and kept alive a custom among their ancestors of more than 200 years. The time honored menu of pemmican, la potine, les boulets and les bugnes croches, was featured, by the remnant of these fast disappearing pioneers, who roamed the prairies during the days when countless buffalo made it their habitat.

Since the demise of Cuthbert St. Denis, 96, Zacharie Blondeau, 81, and Mrs. Joseph Racette, 103, the grim reaper has not visited the old valley colony.

Grew First Wheat

The grand old lady, Mrs. Thomas Kavanaugh, 96 years old, who helped her husband grow the first wheat in the Qu'Appelle valley in 1875, took the place of honor at the head of the table. Next to her was Johnny Blondeau, 92, who in a vivid manner told of passing the winter at Wood Mountain in 1879 and seeing there, Sitting Bull. He also remembers seeing the Marquis of Lorne passing through Lebret 58

regret's services were also much in demand in those days as a horse doctor. Professional vets were practically unknown. Other guests were Mrs. Clem Peltier, 82, a granddaughter of Cuthbert Grant, governor of the North West Fur Company, who out-generalled the Hudson's Bay Company's army in the battle of Seven Oaks in 1816. Stanislaus Desjarlais, 74, whose brother, Michael Desjarlais, fought under Gabriel Dumont and was killed at the battle of Fish Creek in 1885. Others who attended were: Mrs. Joseph Delorme, 89; Pierre Pelletier, 86; Joseph Ouillette, 85, son of Moise Ouillette, councillor to Louis Riel in 1885; Mrs. J. B. Parisien, 86; Nelson Henry, 87; Mrs. Chrysostome Robillard, 87; Pierre Desjarlais, 82, Pierre Blondeau, 74, and Francois Demarais, 76.

Tanned Hides

Mrs. Kavanaugh recounted in detail how she tanned buffalo hides and provided her Irish better half with a pair of buffalo robes which was necessary in those days for a complete winter driving turnout. She also told how 60 years ago the buffalo inhabited the western plains of Canada and the United States in countless thousands, and how the

SIR W

Mul

Ind

Era

TOR

Muloc

era of

200-Year-Old custom newspaper clipping

Photo: Beatrice Demetrius

Métis dance. It is a structured competition dance between two partners that involves hardly any movement of the body above the knees as all the work is done with the feet. Dancers at these parties would dance in pairs, showing off their best jigging steps for the whole party to see.

Still to this day, Métis People will take any opportunity we can to gather with friends and family to visit, listen to music, and dance the night away. There are even stories of some weddings and holiday parties lasting for over two days. However, of all the holidays, New Year's Day is historically one of the most important and celebrated for Métis People. While Christmas was a religious holiday for the Métis, New Year's Day was often one of the Métis' largest social celebrations of the year. Often many families, or even entire communities would come together to eat, drink, dance, and visit for hours, or even days.

Some Métis even took to calling New Year's Day "Kissing Day," or "ochetookeskaw," because people would visit house to house and shake hands and kiss. An old newspaper from Lebret, Saskatchewan reports the 200-year-old tradition of the Métis New Year's festivities, and recounts their traditional food, religious practices, and celebrations.

Beatrice Demetrius: The Beaudrys were a Métis family who lived up the hill; they played fiddles and guitars, and sang — they were very talented. There was a young shy girl named Yvonne, everyone would ask her to jig, someone gave her a quarter, she would finally get up and dance the Red River Jig.

Li Beaudry wêyâwâw la famille Métis kâ wêkichik ispimihk wâchiy; wêyâwâw kê mêtâwêchik li viôlôn mêna kitochike'wina, mêna kê nâkâmochik, wêyâwâw âyâwin mitoni kuskêtâmowin. Êkota kê oskîyit iskwêsis Yvonne êsêkasot, kâhkiyaw ê'kwêchimachik tâ nêsosimowit, âwiyahk ê'mêyât pêyak soniyâs, wêya pêyês ê'pâsikot mêna ê'nêmihitot la Rivyer Roozh Nêsosimowin.

After harvest there would be a dance at the schoolhouse, and everyone came. Mothers would place their babies in the cloak room on all the coats on the floor, they made coffee and baloney sandwiches, there would be cakes and cookies.

Mwestus kâ mâwiso'konamihk kistikana ikota k'âyâchik nêmihitowin ântê kâkiskino'humkamihk, mêna kâhkêyâwiyahk ê'pêtohtêchik. Ni mamawahk âhâchik otâwâsimsahk ântâ miskitâkiy piskikipâhikun ântâ kâhkêyâw miskitâkiya âstêki li plâncher, wêyâwâw ê'ositâchik pêhkâte'wapoy mêna pâhpêtos wiyâs nêsonikuna, êkota âyâchik wêhkikusina.

I remember going to Midnight Mass on Christmas Eve; my father would take us by sleigh, the church was about two miles away.

Ni kiskisin ê'tohtêyahk Midnight Mass ântâ Christmas Eve, ni papa kê tohtâhikoyahk pipon tâpânâsk, ânimâ âyamihew'kamik nânto niso mistika wâhiyâwes.

After Midnight Mass, we hung our stockings up. There would be an apple, orange, and some hard Christmas candy. We were thrilled; we got one present, usually a doll with a porcelain face and rag body, or a set of little dishes.

Mwestes ânima Midnight Mass, k'âkohtiyâhkik usikunuk. Êkotâ âyâkik li pomme, l'orange, mêna muskâwpayiw sêwachikânsa. Ni tukâhke'yihtumnân; nâyanân pêyak mêkêwin, mânâ awasêhkan usichi mêkisiwoyakun mêhkwakun mêna âyânis mêyaw, âhpo âpsâsiki wêyâkunâ.

Christmas was a religious time for the families, the next day we would go by sleigh to our relative's farm to see the tracks Santa made on a little hill near their place.

Christmas ânimâ âyimihâwe wâtisiw kêsikâw ochi li famille, kotuk kêsikâw nêyanân ê'tohtêyahk usichi pipon tâpânâsk ântê ni wâhkomâkunahk wêkêwin uskêhk tâ wâpâhtâmahk kê pimohtew êsâ Santa kâ ositâht ântâ âpisâsik âyâputinâw chêki wêyâwâw uskêhk.

New Year's Eve was a big celebration, where the families would gather at someone's house, there would be music and dancing.

Oskîyi Pêyak Uskê Otakosiki ânima mistâhi mêyo kêkwîy êwêyospayik, ispê li famille kâ mâmâwâpichik âwlyâk owâskâhikâni, êkotê êyâchik kitochikêwin mêna nêmihitowin.

Doreen Bergum: At the end of the week, it was time to relax. Keeping in Métis tradition, they would throw out the furniture, and the families would haul in food (bannock and harvested meat, and cakes) fiddles, guitars and even the spoons — to dance, sing and laugh to enjoy their Métis culture.

Kâ ponipayêk pêyak âyimehâw kêsikâw, nuhêyi'kok âyâ tâ wêpiwin. Tâ kânâwêyihitâmahk ântâ Métis ânisko'totumowin, kê wayi'wepinakihk kêsâpowina, mêna li famille âwâtâki mêchowina (pâhkwesikun mêna kâ mâwiso'konâmihk wiyâs, mêna wêhkêh'kusikuna) li viôlôns, kitôchikuna mêna li couilleurs. Tâ nêmihitoyahk, nâkâmoyahk mêna pâhpêyahk tâ mêyo wâhtumâchik wêyâwâw Métis nistum pimâchihowin.

As a young girl of five, I remember sleeping under the table at these events listening to the fiddle and the fun. That's how I learned to do the Red River Jig. In fact, I learned from the best — my mother was a champion jigger.

Kâ iskinê'k'iskwêwiyân nêyânan ochi, ni kiskisin kê nipâyân sepâ la tâble chêki ohi kêkwîy êw'ispayik ê-nitohtâmahk la viôlôn mêna kâ mochikehtayahk. Ikosi ânima kiskêyihtumân tâ itotâmân li Rivyer Roozh Nêsosimowin. Tâpwêwin, ikosi ânima kiskêyihtumân ochi mâmweyes kê mêyosik – ni mama kê otâhowew kâ nêsosimot.

The gathering would last until the sun came up. I watched feet flashing around the floor to the Red River Jig, Drops of Brandy, Heel and Toe Polka, Reel of Eight, Broom Dance and the Sash Dance. Our Métis spirit was alive!

Ânima mâmâwupowin k'ispayêk iskôpêsim kâ pê tâpun. N'âsâ wêyihtumân misita wâskotêpayiki wâsa'kâmisi la plânche ânima Red River Jig, Drops of Brandy, Heel and Toe Polka, Reel of Eight, Broom Dance mêna ânima Sash Dance. Nêyanân Métis âchâhk ochi kumisew pimâtâkun.

My parents and my community taught us how to work with our hands, head, and heart.

Ni nêkêhikowak mêna mâmâwi'e'âyâhk kê kiskino'huma'kâwiyahk t'âtoskêyahk âschi michêchêyâ, mistikwan mêna mitê.

Doreen Poitras: We entertained ourselves in those days. Our dad played the fiddle and any other musical instruments too, it seemed. So, our house was the gathering place for the community. We danced often — all the traditional Métis dances: the Red River Jig, Drops of Brandy, the Duck Dance, the Rabbit Dance, all the old reels and square dances with my Uncle Lloyd calling.

Nêyânân mêyo wâtumohewiyahk ikospê. Ni papanân kê mêtâwêt li viôlôn mêna nikotwâw kotuk kêkwîy kihtochêkunahk itêyihtâkwun. Ikosi nêkinân ôma kê mâmâwupihk nâkiskato-kamik ochi mâmâwi'e'ayahk. Ni nêmêh'tonan mêchêtwaw – kâhkiyâw kâyâs ochi kâkê p'itotumihk li Métis nêmêh'tona: ânima Red River Jig, Drops of Brandy, ânima Sesep Nêmeh'towin, ânima Wapoos Nêmeh'towin, kâhkiyâw kwâskwêpichikun nêmêh'towina mêna âyineyo kâ nêmêh'tochik âyâ âschi mon oncle Lloyd kâ tâhtêpwêt.

Bertha Clark-Jones (as told by Gail Gallupe): We used to get together for holidays and reunions. We still do every three years. My grandpa played the fine fiddle. He played his fiddle at my wedding and, they played guitar and they sang. There was music and dancing. That was something my mother loved, and she did that whenever she had the opportunity. She just loved dancing, as did her family.

Kê mâmâwapiyâhk âyiwêpew'kêsikâw pêyak oskân kêw'kâtowâka. Kêyapich ni tohtênân âna nisto pêyak uskêwina. Ni moshom kê mêtâwêt mêyosit la viôlôn. Kê matêwêt wêya la viôlôn ânta nêya kâ wêkihtoyân mêna, wêyawâw kê mêtawêchik kitochikun mêna wêyawâw kê nâkâmochik. Êkota mistâhi kitochikêwin mêna nêmêh'towin. Êkwâ'nima kêkwîy ni mâmâ kê sâkihitâk, mêna wêya k'itohtâhk pukwêspê kâ nâhi'payik. Wêya mwechi kê sâkihitâk nêmihitown, tâskoch sa famille.

SkyBlue Morin: Although we were poor, my mother and her common-law husband knew how to have fun. Sometimes, people came to visit and make music. Someone would make music with a fiddle and another would play the spoons. He would hold the spoons together in one hand, do a fancy tap to the spoons with his other hand and fingers to make different sounds. They sounded great! Another person would start to jig fancy steps joined by another in competition. I would get a quarter each time I did the jig. I made money, lots of quarters. I became quite a good jigger and was very proud of that. When I fought with kids, I told myself they couldn't do the jig as fast or as long as me as it was a test of endurance.

Âtâwe'yâ nêyanân kê kitimakisiyahk, ni mama mêna wêya common law napêma kisikêtâmawak tânisi tâ mâchikêtachik. Âskâw, âyisêniwak kê pê kihokêchik mêna kitochikêwahk. Âwêyak tâ mêtâwew la viôlôn, mêna kotuk tâ mêtawew li cuilleres. Wêya kê michiminat li cuilleres usichi pêyak michêchê, tâ mêyo wêwêhtitâw li cuilleres usichi kotuk michêchê mêna michêchêsâ tâ osêtâht pêtos itêhtâ'kwuna. Mitoni mêyo itêhtâ'kwuna! Kotuk âyisêniw tâ mâchi kunâhkite'simow mêna êti nêsosimochik. Nêya ni kê mêkâwin pêyak'sooniyas tâhto ispê kâ nêsosimoyân. Ni sooniyahkân, mêchet pêyak'sooniyâsak. N'êti mitoni mêyo nêsosimowin mêna ni mêchimon ochi êkwâ'nima. Tânispe kâ notinkeyân usichi âwâsisak, ni wêhtamason nâmoya kâskêtâwak tâ nêsosimochik tesi kwêyâhochik âhpo kinwês tâskoch nêya âyis êkwa'nima sêpêhtamowin.

Sometimes, they would sing, *Kêspin Ki Sakihin,* a song they sang for their girlfriend. When they sang, they told a story, to prove that they were better at doing things or better at story telling. They sang about going to a city like Edmonton or going up north. They sang about hunting ducks and rabbits. I thought those were great stories and I would sing along: "Kê-spin, ki sa-ki-hin, sê-mak pê o-chê-min (If you love me, right away kiss me). Métis are proud and the song could be a long story.

Âskâw, wêyawâw kê nikamowâhk "Kêspin Ki Sakihin", nikomowin kê nikamochik âyâkichi nitohtêm'iskwew. Kâ nikamochik, kê âchimochik, tâ kêchi'nâhochik ânima wêyawâw nâwach kê mêyo tohtâkik kêkwîy âhpo nâwach kê mêyo âchimochik. Wêyawâw kê nikamochik kê tohtechik otênaw tâskoch Edmonton âhpo kê tohtêchik kêwêtinohk. Wêyawâw kê nikamochik ochi kâ mâchêchik sêsêpak mêna wapoosha. N'itêyitên êkonânihi mitoni mêyosikik âchimona mêna nêsta ni nikâmon: "Kê-spin, ki sâ-ki-hin, sê-mak pe-o-chê-min." Li Métis kiste'yimow'ichik mêna ânima nikamowin kâkê ispayen kinwês âchimowin.

Storytelling

Telling stories has always been an essential part of who the Métis are as a People. It is a way in which we can share life lessons, pass down our history and learn from each other. Storytelling is often intergenerational; grandparents will pass their story on to their grandchildren, who will then pass those stories along to their own children and grandchildren. It is how we come to understand our family history and it is how we keep our culture alive. Some of these stories are educational, some delve into folklore, others are touching. However, many are joyful, and hilarious. Any Métis function is full of storytellers, cracking jokes and sharing their merriment with anyone who will listen.

> Within each person lies a story that has the power to change their lives and, if shared, the potential to transform the world of others. As life reveals, some stories call out to us, some stories lay hidden in the recesses, and still others overtake all else — it is this living quality of stories that make them such a potent tool of transformation, and of domination. As the Métis People of Canada, we have only to think about how our history has been taught in schools to affirm this reality.
>
> — Yvonne Poitras Pratt from *Digital Storytelling in Indigenous Education: A Decolonizing Journey for a Métis Community,* UK Taylor & Francis.

Dianne Ludwig: My grandmother often tells stories; she tells a lot of stories. We used to get really scared especially at nighttime when we wanted to go home, and she wanted to tell stories.

N'ohkom mêchet'wâw wêhtâmakit âchimona; wêya wêhtâmakit mêchet âchimona. Nêyanân kê koskwêtayâhk wâwes êkwa kâ tipskâk tânispê kâ nohtê kêwêyâhk, mêna wêya nohtê wêhtâmâkit âchimona.

"No, you guys have to all sleep here," she would say. So, she used to put her grandchildren there and then she'd tell us stories, but I don't think it wasn't for nothing that she told us those stories.

"Nâmoya, kêyawâw puko kâhkiyâw tâ nipâyêk ota." wêya nohtê itwew. Ikosi, wêya mâna âstêhat osisima êkotê mêna êkospê wêya wêhtâmâkoya âchimona, mâkâ nâmoya ni'tihitên mâkêkwîy kichi wêya kâ wêhtâmâkoya ikonânhi âchimona.

She used to tell us that all the time. Stopping us from going there. So, one day we asked our grandmother, "Where do babies come from?"

Wêya kê wêhtâmâkoya tâhki tipahikun. Nakinikâwiyahk ochi t'itohtêyâhk êkote. Ikosi, pêyak kêsikâw nêyanân kê kwêchimâyâhk n'ohkomnân, "Tânte âwâsisâk pêtohtêchik ochi?"

So, we asked her. Our grandmother said, "Oh my dear grandchildren!"

Ikosi, nêyanân kwêchimâyâkik. N'ohkomnân itwew, "Oh, n'âmê noosisimak!"

So, we said, "You got to tell us now, Grandma."

Ikosi, nêyanân itwêyâhk, "Kêya puko tâ wêhtamoyâhk n'ohkom."

"Well, you know how your grandfather makes a garden, and those seeds that we put in the cabbage patch?"

"Well, kiskeyihtên tânisi ki moshomnâw ê osêtaht âna kistikânis, mêna ikonânhi kistikewi'mênis ânihi kê âstayahk ânta otêhi'pukwa kistikânis?"

"Yes," she says, "in the cabbage that's where babies come from," she used to say. And that's the way we were told things.

"Tâpwe," wêya itwew, "ânta otêhi'pukwa êkotê ânima âwâsisâk ochi kâ pêtohtêchik," wêya kîtwêt. Mêna ikosi ânima kâkê wêhtamâ'kâwiyak kêkwîy.

So, for a while longer we didn't know where babies came from. So we just were told stories that's all. Grandmother used to tell us a lot of things.

Ikosi, âcheyaw kinwesês nêyanân nâmoya kiskêyihtênân tânte âwâsisâk pêtohtêchik ochi. Ikosi, nêyanân mwechi wêhtama'kâwiyak âchimona ânima ikosi. N'ohkomnân kê wêhtama'kâwiyak mistâhi kêkwîy.

And then me too, I've told my children. I told them. I used to tell stories to my children. They used to laugh a lot.

Mêna ânima nêya nêsta, ni kê wêhtam'wâwak n'otawasimisak. Ni kê wêhtam'wâwak. Nêya kê wêhtam'wâwak âchimona ochi n'otawasimisak. Âchimona wêstawâw mêna.... wêyawâw kê pâhpichik mistâhi.

"No, it can't be that way," they say.

"Nâmoya, ikosi tâ k'ispayen." wêyawâw itwêwak.

I said to them "Yes it was like that," and they would say "Yeah right!"

Ni kê wêhtam'wâwak "Tâpwe ikosi ânima," mêna wêyawâw kê twêwak "Tâpwe ânima!"

But everything that my grandmas and grandfathers told me ... teaching lessons that they used to tell me.

Mâka kâhkiyâw kêkwîy ânima n'ohkomak mêna ni moshomak kâ wêhtamochik... Kiskino'humakâwîyak kâkê wêhtamochik.

My mother used to tell us stories, like don't ever look in the mirror when there's a lightning storm. Cover up all the mirrors you know, that's how she was. And then they would say "Mom, how come Kookum covers us up and puts us to bed when there's a lighting storm?" but she used to do that! "Don't cover up all the mirrors," she used to tell my daughters when there was a lightning storm. Yeah, she was a beautiful woman.

Wêya (Dianne omâmâwa) kê wêhtamachik wêyawâw (Dianne otânisa) âchimona. Tâpiskoch kâya wâhpâtâ pêchîy wâpamon tânispe mêkwâch kâ wâskote'payik mâyi kêsikâw... tâ kwunahâmâhk kâhkîyaw âniki wâpamona, kiskêyihitên, ikosi ânima wêya. Mêna êkospe k'itwêwâk "Mom... tanêhki k'ohkomnaw kê kwunahoyahk mêna kâwsimo'nahêwiyâhk tânispe kâ wâskote'payik mâyi kêsikâw?" mâka wêya kê tohtak ânima! "Kâya kwunâha kâhkiyâw wâpamona," wêya kê wêhtâmowât ni tânisa tânispe kê wâskote'payik mâyi kêsikâw. Tâpwe... wêya kê mêyona'kohew iskwew.

Doreen Poitras: Another memorable occurrence from about the time of the Lac Ste. Anne Pilgrimage, was at the Treaty Day. Again, we had a [concession] booth put up not far from the old school. On this day there was a big lineup of people — all ages going into the school, so I lined up too. Inside, two women were sitting at a table who asked my name and said, "Do you belong to this reserve?" I said yes, thinking... well I'm here with my family so I must belong. Anyway, I waited my turn and was called up to get a chest x-ray.

Kotuk kiskise'itohte'payêk ispayêwin ochi pêyakwun tipahikun (tâskoch ânimâ Lac Ste. Anne Pilgrimage), mâka ôma tipahikun ântê okimâw usotumâkêwin. Âsumêna ê'chimatâwyâhk mêchowin mâmâwupi'wina moya wâhiyo ochi kâyâsiyâhk kiskino'humato'kamik. Êkôma kêsikâw êyistêk mitonih êkinohk kiposkâtowin êyinêwuk

Métis beaded gloves
Photo: Métis Nation of Alberta

Métis beaded bag
Photo: Métis Nation of Alberta

– tântâhto ê-piponêchik êtohtêchik pêhchiyek kiskino'humato-kamik, itam ni kiposkâton nêsta. Pêchîyi, nêso iskwewuk ê-âpichik chêki li table âwêna kâ kwêchimchik ni wêhowin mêna k'itwêchik, "Otah chi ê-tipeyêhtâkosêyin ôma nêhiyâw uskê?." N'itwân, tâpwe, ê mâmitonêhtâmân… Ni tâyân ôma otâh âschi pêyak'oskan, ikosi êtikwe ni tipeyêhtak'osêyin. Pukowê'yisi, ni pêhon uskooch nêya mêna ê'têpwatikaw'iyan tâ nâtamân mâskikun musinpayi'wina kâ otinâmihk sôwâpâchikun ochi.

Traditional Arts

The Métis are well known for our unique style of artwork; the main forms of this art being beadwork and silk embroidery. These art forms were important to the development of Métis culture, and became a key identifier for distinctively "Métis" artifacts. The Métis became known as the "Flower Beadwork People" due to our distinct style of creating vibrant, colourful, and floral patterns that adorn Métis clothing, bridles, saddle blankets and more.

Beatrice Demetrius: Mother embroidered tablecloths, pillowcases; she knitted socks and mitts. She taught me how to knit, my first pair of socks, but I missed the heel on one sock. I used to tell my children I invented the tube socks.

Ni mama kê kwâskwâsot wêyustaco'wêkina, uspuskwêsimowuta; wêya kê âpehkewet usikuna mêna ustisa. Wêya kê kiskino'hamowit tânisi t'âhpekewyân, ni nustum usikuna, mâka kê putamahan mahkwun ânta pêyak usikun. Ni kê wêhtâmakik mâna n'itawasimisa kê miskweyihtuman usiwachikunis usikuna.

Doreen Bergum: In the 1950s there were about 35 Métis families who worked and lived in the Sundre area. We were raised in our Métis Culture. My parents were also artists: sewing, beading, moccasin-making, working with leather and weaving.

Pechi 1950s êyachik nistomtano nêyânan li familles de Métis kâh âtoskechik mêna kê wêkichik ânihi Sundre tipahas'kanis. Nêyanân kê p'ohpikihe'wiyahk nêyanân li Métis nistum pimâchihiwin. Ni nêkê'hikowak wêstawâw nuspusi nuhikewahk; kwuskwâsowin, mêhkesêkatêwin, pahpêkinwêskisin k'âsehtahk, âtoskâtêwin âschi k'osehtâhk pâhkêkin mêna âtoskâtewin âschi pêmustehumowin.

Bertha Clark-Jones (as told by Gail Gallupe): The farm went under when times got difficult. Dad didn't have a lot of money to get a lot of machinery. He was always having to borrow. And then our farmhouse caught fire, which was very tragic because they lost everything. And that included a beautiful quilt that my mother had embroidered for me with, at least a twelve by twelve or eight by twelve squares. And it was all, a satin purple and, a light purple and a pretty yellow. Unfortunately, I lost it in the trunk she had in the closet. So that's a memory I'll never forget because she had just finished it, I put it in our farm fair and it won first prize for her work.

Kistikân pêko'payiwin tânispe kêsikâw kâ âyimi'payik. Ni papa nâmoya mistâhi sooniyâw kê âyat tâ kâchitinâhk mistâhi âpachi'chikuna uskêkoh kichi. Wêya mâna kâkikê nitâhta'mow. Mêna êkospê nêyanân kistikan wâskihikun suskisow iskotew, tâna mitoni mâyi'payiwin âyis kê wânihtâchik kâhkiyâw kekwîy. Êwuko mêna kuta'wusisin ispuki'wâches ânima ni mama kê musinis'tahikew kichi nêya usichi, nânto niso'sap ochi niso'sap âhpo âyinanew ochi niso'sap usaweyâwa. Mêna êkwa ânima kâhkiyaw sooskiwe'ekin sepeko meh'kwâw mêna, waseyâw sêpêko mêh'kwâw mêna kuta'wusisiw osâwâw. Miyâko'siwin ni wahnehtân ânta mistikowut kâkê âyât ânta âyâni'kamikos. Ikosi êkwâ'nima kiskisiwin nâmoya wêhkâch ni kâ wânkiskisin âyis wêya kê mwechi pooni osêhtât, ni tastan ânta puskiyâkêwin mêna otahowêt nustum kêspinatumâ'sowin kichi wêya âtoskêwin.

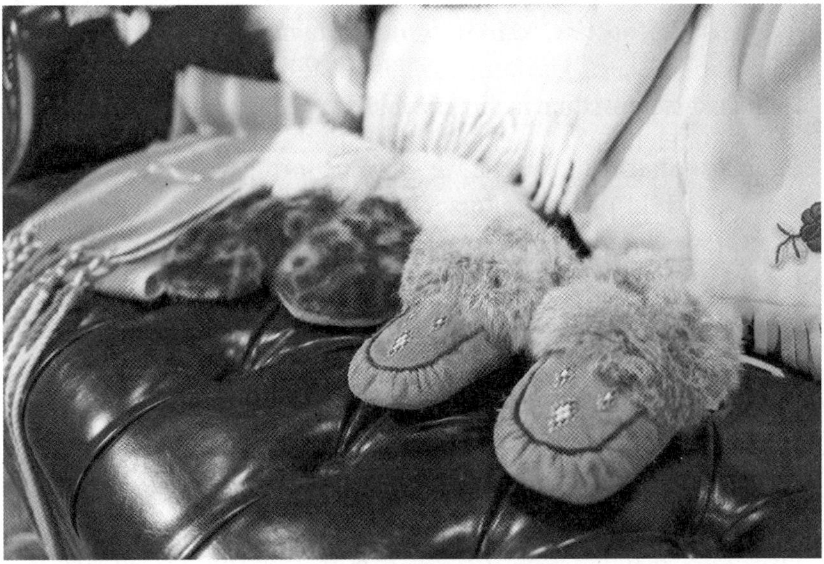

Mitts, mocassins, and Métis sash
Photo: Lisa Wolfe

Lisa Wolfe: My mom could make moccasins by hand. Like cut up and make moccasins and do beading and she can make necklaces and she could hand-bead a lot of things.

Ni mama kâsketaw tâ osetaht pâhpêkinwes'kisina môchôsetahk. Tâskoch tâ mansa mêna tâ osêtaht pâhpêkinwes'kisina mêna tâ mêkiseh'katam mêna wêya kaskêtaw tâ osêtaht tâpis kâ kuni'minak mêna kê kaskêtaht tâ mêkiseh'katahk mêchet kêkwîy.

My mom was a really good sewer, so she used to make my clothes. I got my jeans made, and all my outfits made right up until I was probably about fifteen. My mom would make a lot of my clothes, all my shirts and stuff. And I know she took personal pride in that and that's kind of neat.

Ni mama mitoni ê mêyo kwâskwâsowit, ikosi wêya ê'kê osêhtaht n'âyiwinisa... mitasaka êkê osêhtaht, mêna kâhkiyaw nitayâna ê-osêtaht iskô nêya nânto nêyânan'osap. Ni mama mêchet âyiwinisa kê osêtâw, kâhkiyâw ni pukowa'yân mêna kohtuk kêkwîya. Mêna ni kiskiten tipiyawe kiste'yimow êkwa ânima mêna êkwa ânima nâwach ê mêyosik.

Pearl Calahasen: I believe we have art forms that need to be recognized. In those lessons from my grandma are those art forms that were taught to us. They're the beading, they're the basket weaving, they're the moose hair tufting. It's all the art forms that I believe are historically based and give us the cultural component of who we are. It's ingrained in that.

Ni tâpwêhtên kêyanâw âyâyâhk musinpê'hikewna wêyawe'nâkuna tâ nistâwê'namahk. Âniki kiskino'humâkewina ochi n'ohkom âyâwahk êkonanhi musinpê'hikêwina wêyawe'nâkuna kâkê kiskino'humâkewiyahk nêyanân. Wêyawâw âniki mêkiseh'ka'chikêwin, wêyawâw âniki wuta'pêwat pêmuste'humikêwin, wêyawâw âniki mooswa mêchakâsa pêwâskêwin. Êwuko ânihi musinpe'hikewna wêyawe'nâkuna kâ tâpwêhtamân, ikonânhi kâyas'itotumowin ochi mêna ê'mêkawiyahk ânima nistum pimâchihiwin pâhki ochi awêna kêyanâw. It is ingrained in that.

That's how I believe our values and our mores get taught, is as we're being taught how to bead — this is how you're doing it. And then learn how to count, and we learn the colours. We learn everything on the art when we're dealing with those art forms.

Êkosi ânima êsi tâpwehtamân kêyanâw nistum pimâchihowin tâ kiskino'humâ'kêchik, mêna tâskoch kêyanâw kâ pê kiskino'humâ'kêyahk tânisi tâ mekiseh'kâ'tamahk – oma tânisi tâ itohtamân. Mêna êkospe ê'kiskino'humâ'kâwiyahk tânisi t'âkechikeyahk, mêna ê'kiskino'humâ'kâwiyahk ânihi tusinâ'steka. Nêyanân ê-kiskino'humâ'kâweyak kâhkiyâw kêkwîy ânima ochi musinpe'hikewna tânispe nêyanân k'âtoskâtâmahk êkonanhi musinpe'hikewna wêyawê'nâkuna.

And she used to be able to teach us, this is how it's done. This is why it's done this way. This is the reason why you are going to be

Floral fringed jacket
Photo: Lisa Wolfe

learning this progression. Because it's going to take you through life. That's the cultural component I think we sometimes lose. We have to bring that back, and we have to be able to bring those lessons from our Elders in and from the older people in our families, and from those have to come back to life in order for us to be able to get back those traditions and the lifestyle of who and how we were. That is the other part that I think that was so crucial to my teachings.

Mêna wêya kê kiskino'humâ'koyahk, oomsi ooma t'itotâmân. Ikohk ochi ooma oomsi kâ itotamân. Êkochi ooma iteyih'tum mami'skôtum tânehki kâ kiskino'humakâ'weyin ooma nise'kach yâhkohte'mâkun âyis êkwa ânima tâ wêchihikâwiyin kâ ti pimatisoyin. Êkwa ânima nistum pimâchihowin pâhki ni têhitên âskaw ê'wanihtayahk. Mêna puko tâ pêtayahk êkwa ânima kâwi mêna kêyanâw puko tâ pêtayahk ikonanihi kiskino'humâ'kuna ochi kêyanâw kêhtâyak pêchîyi kêyanâw kehte'hiya, pêchîyi nêyanân li familles, ikonanihi puko kâwi tâ pimâchihoyahk in order kichi kêyanâw tâ kâchitin'amahk ikonanihi ânisko'totumowina mêna ânima kâ pimâchihi'winân âwêna nêyanân, tânisi nêyanân kotuk pâhki ânima ê-têhtaman mitoni kêchiyi'wun ochi ni kiskino'humâ'kewina.

Dianne Ludwig: They (Dianne's daughters) had so much fun with my mom. and you know, being a Métis woman I think there's a lot of laughter and there's so much love. My mom used to come and stay with us for about a month in the springtime, and she would teach the girls how to make moccasins, she would teach my daughters how to make moccasins and how to sew.

Wêyawâw (Diane otânisa) kê mochikê'tâchik usichi ni mama. Mêna kiskêyihtên, kâ pimâtisiyak kêyanâw Métis iskwêwak, ni mâmitone'yihtên êkota mistâhi pâhpiwin mêna mistâhi sâkihitowin. Ni mama kê pêtohtew mêna otâ âyâ usichi nêyanân iskô pêyak pêsim ôma sêkwun, mêna wêya kiskino'humâkat ânki iskwewisak tânisi t'osetâchik pâhpêkin'weskisina, wêya kiskino'humâkat ni tânisak tânisi tâ osêtâchik pâhpêkin'weskisina mêna tânisi tâ kwâskwâsochik.

Language

Beatrice Demetrius: Grandmother Johnston was a descendant of Robert Johnston from the Orkneys, in Scotland. She was tall and slim and lived in a little house without electrical wiring. I asked why she didn't have electricity; she said, "Do you want to kill me?"

N'ohkom Johnston kê wâhkomatowin ochi Robert Johnston ochi ânihi Orkneys, ântê Scotland. Wêya ê'kinosit mêna sehkachiw, mêna kê wêkit ânta wâskihikunis mâkekwîy âyaw wâskote'pêyichikun. Ni kwêchimaw tânehki wêya mâkêkwîy âyât wâskote'pêyichikun; Wêya êtwew, "e'nohtê ni pahiyin chê nêya?"

She spoke only Cree and French when she kept my little brothers and me when my mother and father would take my sister Olive to Lac Ste. Anne, because she had eczema.

Wêya kê pêkiskwêt puko Nêhiyawêwin mêna la Fran☒ais, ispê kâkê kunâwêmat nistesa kâkê âpisâsichik mêna nêya ispê ni mama mêna ni papa kâ tohtahiyahk ni sêmis Olive ântê Lac Ste. Anne, âyis êkê âyât omikê'musakiy.

Grandmother would tell us scary stories about children who misbehaved and sometimes she would tell funny stories about Wisahkecahk. I don't know how I remember these stories because we didn't speak either language.

N'ohkom wêhtumâkoyahk costa âchimona âwâsisahk nâmoya kway-ustatisiw mêna âskow wêya kê wêhtumâkoyahk mohchikun âchimona âyâ ochi Wêsâkêchuk. Nâmoya ni kiskitên tânisi ê si kiskisiyân ôhi âchimona âyis nêyanân nâmoya kê pêkiskwêyahk puko'tânima pêkiskwêwina.

Delia Gray (as told by Bobbi): She knew how to speak Cree, French and English, thus, she was trilingual. From the way that she would make sure I behaved in a certain way I realize that her grandmother had taught her the things that she passed onto me.

Wêya kaskêtaw tâ pêkiskwêt Nêhiyawêwin, Fran⊠ais mêna Ânglais, itam, she was trilingual. Nantâwisi tâkê totâ wêyâhk ânima kâ kêchi-nahot nêya itâti'siwiyan tâskoch kêchina nantâwisi ni kiskêyihtên ânima okohma kê kiskinohumakot kêkwîya ânima wêya kâkê mêyet.

I always had very long hair and I'd get lice, every now and then. My mom would invite an old Indigenous woman over, my mom would make tea and bannock. The old lady would pick through my hair with a fine-tooth comb, she'd pull out the nits. Her and my mom would talk in Cree and laugh at all their stories. As negative as it is to have lice, the process of having nits pulled off my hair was comforted by listening to stories being told in Cree and the laughter of my mom and the old lady.

Ni tâhkê tâyân mitoni kinwâw mêschakâsa mêna ni kâchitenêt êhk-wak, tâhto êkwa mêna êkospê. Ni mama kê wêhkomat Indigenous kêhte'iskwew, ni mama kê osêtat muskêkê'wapoy mêna pâhk-wêsikan. Âna kêhte'iskwew kê mosâh'kina sâpo mêschakâsa usichi pêna hêhk'wan, wêya ochipitak âniki chêki'nâhka. Wêya mêna ni mama kê pêkiskwêchik âsichi Nêhiyawêwin mêna kê pâhpichik ânkê kâhkeyâw wêyawâw âchimona. Âniwê tumowin ânima t'âyâyâhk êhkwak, êsi tota'mihk ochi t'âyâyân chêki'nâhka ochipitak ochi mêschakâsa nâheyih'tumowin kê nâtohtâm âchimona kâ wêhtâmâkêchik âschi Nêhiyawêwin mêna ânima pâhpêwin ochi ni mama mêna âna kêhte'iskwew.

Doreen Bergum: My parents both spoke Cree. My mother spoke a high Cree which is considered a historic version of the Cree language. My mother's father, Daniel Vaness was an interpreter and Indian Agent at the Onion Lake Reserve in Saskatchewan. He spoke fluent Cree, French, and English. My dad spoke the northern Alberta Cree with bits of French. My grandfather Peter Dumont held Scrip Land in St. Paul, Alberta.

Ni nêkê'hikowak neswâyi kê pêkiskwechik Nêhiyawêwin. Ni mama kê pêkiskwew âyiwâk Nêhiyawêwin tâna mâmitone'yihtakêk kayâs ispayiwin iteyitumowin Nêhiyawêwin pêkiskwêwin. Ni mama son pére, Daniel Vaness kê twestamâkew mêna Êyiniw Okimâkaniwit ânte Onion Lake Reserve Saskatchewan. Wêya kê pêkiskwêt Nêhiyawêwin, la Fran⊠ais, mêna l'Ânglais. Ni papa kê pêkiskwêt ânima kêwitinohk Alberta Nêhiyawêwin usichi âpsis la Fran⊠ais. Ni moshom Peter Dumont kê tâhkonahk Uskê Kêchi Musinahikun ânte St. Paul, Alberta.

Doreen Poitras: Our Kookum Maggie, when I knew her, couldn't walk. She also couldn't speak English — only Michif, a mixture of French, English and Cree. As children, my brothers Gordon and Ernest, and myself could communicate with her. Now we have forgotten how.

N'ohkomnan Maggie, kâkê nistâwêmahk, moya kê pimohtêt. Moya mêna, pêkiskwew L' Ânglais - âyâ puko Michif, un mâmâwênikun Li Fran⊠ais, Li Ânglais mêna Nêhiyawêwin. Kâ wâsisoyahk, nistêsak Gordon mêna Ernest, mêna nêsta ni kê wêhta'matoyan wêya âsichi. Êkwa nêyanân ni wânkiskisinân.

We were typical Métis kids — we saw our father playing hand games and interacting with the reserve men, as Cree was his first language and the reserve kids were our friends. We grew up in transitional times, totally accepting the old with the new.

Nêyanân ôma mwechi Métis âwâsisâk – kê wâpimayahk ni papanân ê'mêtawêt michêchê'mêtawina mêna nukiskâtaht nêhiyaw uskênân nâpêwa, âyâ ochi Nêhiyawêwin nistum pêkiskwêwin mêna nêhiyaw uskênân âwâsisâk nêyanân ototêma. Kê ohpikêyahk âhtotêwin tipâhikuna, sôskwach otinânahk kâyâsiyahk ochi usichi oskîyi.

Lisa Wolfe: My parents didn't acknowledge in any way that we were even Indigenous. It was not a thing. My mom spoke Cree. I knew she spoke Cree, but it wasn't something that was spoken to us. So, my brother and I both don't have any Cree knowledge in that regard.

Ni kêhikowak nâmoya sooskwach istaweyih'tâkosiwak wêyâwak Indigenous. Êwuko nâmoya kêkwîy. Ni mama kê pêkiskwêt Nêhiyawêwin. Ni kiskêyitên kê nêhiyâwêt, mâkâ nâmoya kêkwîy kâkê pêkiskwâtoyak nêyanân. Iskô, nistes mêna nêya mâkêkwîy ni t'âyâyahk Nêhiyawêwin kiskêyitâmowin pisiskê'yihtâmân.

My dad, Rod, he, he came from a Cree family, but he didn't speak Cree either. So, they spoke English to us growing up, which is kind of interesting.

Ni papa, Rod, wêya kê pitohtêt ochi la famille Nêhiyawak, mâkâ wêya nâmoya pêkiskwew Nêhiyawêwin puko'tânima. Ikosi, wêyawâw pêkiskwêwâk L'Ânglais êkote nêyanân kâ ohpikêyahk, tâna pisis kâpu'mâw.

And there have been occasions where he (her grandfather) brought his mother down. So, I got to meet my great-grandmother, Veronique Ladouceur née, Cardinal and you know, she was a very interesting woman. She did not speak English. She only spoke French and Cree, so my grandfather could speak English and Cree and French.

Mêna êstiki ispayi'wina tânta wêya (omoshoma) kê pêsowat ômamawa. Ikosi ni nâkiskawâw n'ânskow nokominaw, Veronique Ladouceur, nee Cardinal, mêna kiskêtên, wêya mitoni pisis kâpu'mâw iskwew. Nâmoya pêkiskwew L'Ânglais. Wêya pohko kê pêkiskwêt La Français mêna Nêhiyawêwin, ikosi ni moshom kê pêkiskwew L'Ânglais mêna Nêhiyawêwin mêna La Français.

So she would always just kind of talk to us and she'd pet my head and she braid my hair and all these little things and my mom could speak to her, but that total relationship with language was just totally cut off from us. So, you kind of miss it now. You wish that you could have had more, more time to speak with them and learn and understand the language and kind of what life was like.

So wêya mâna kakikê mwechi ê'pêkiskwâtik'oyahk nêyanân mêna tâ yâyinew n'istikwân mêna wêya âpehkâta mêscha'kâsa mêna kâhkiyâw âniki âpsâsika kêkwîy mêna ni mama êkê pêkiskwâtat, mâka kâhkiyâw mâmâwe wâhkotowin usichi pêkiskwêwin mwechi kâhkiyâw mâmâwe munisakik nêyanân ochi. Ikosi, kêya kuskê yihtu'mahk êkwa. Âka'watum ânima kêya kêyapich kâkê âyâyin, kêyâpich âyiwak tâ pêkiskwê'tâchik mêna tâ kiskino'humakâwiyahk mêna tâ nistohtamahk ânima pêkiskwêwin mêna tânisi pimâtsiwin k'ispayêk.

Pearl Calahasen: On my mother's side my great-grandma and my grandma, they always told us what we needed to learn. And they taught us... they were trying really hard to teach us number of things. First of all the Michif language, which my father really spoke well. He did speak Michif. The Cree component was from my mother's side.

Ànima ni mama owâhkomitowin ni châpân mêna n'ohkom, wêyawâw kâkikê wêhtâmochik kêkwîy tâ kiskino'humâ' kâwiyahk. Mêna wêyawâw kê kiskino'humâ' kâwiyahk... wêyawâw mitoni ê'kochitachik tâ kiskino'humâ' kâwiyahk âkêhta'sowin kêkwîy. Nêkân ooma, Michif pêkiskwêwin, tânima ni papa mitoni kwayus kê pêkiskwew. Wêya kê pêkiskwêt Michif. Ànima Nêhiyawêwin ochi ni mama owâhkom'itowin.

Mary SkyBlue Morin: N'ohkom Lâpis was born in 1891 and had eight brothers and nine sisters. I knew only four of her sisters; Marie-Anne, Clara, Philomene and Octavie. They did not speak English but spoke Michif with Cree. N'ohkom Lapis's sisters were known as grandmothers as well. My mother and I had to speak

Michif Cree also to talk to our grandmothers. My cousin Josephine lived with n'ohkom Lâpis and she and I were the interpreters for our granny. We interpreted when n'ohkom Lâpis went to the Hudson Bay store to buy groceries, or to the doctor to get medicine, or to the Post Office to get mail or send mail and to the café to order lunch for us. In Green Lake the Mechif People spoke Michif Cree and everyone we met spoke Michif Cree including the town mayor. When we travelled and met Cree People, we understood each other's language even though the Métis used some French words. Sometimes, when speaking Michif, I can't find the Cree words because I learned it in French not in Cree. That is okay because that is my Michif language.

N'ohkom Lâpis ke pimâtiso 1891 mêna kê âyâw âyinanew ostesa mêna kêkâ mitataht osêmisa. Ni kiskê'yitâmân puko neyo âniki o'sêmisa; Marie-Anne, Clara, Philomene mêna Octavie. Nâmoya kâyasêmowak mâka kê pêkiskwêchik Michif usichi Nêhiyâwêwin. N'ohkom Lâpis osêmisa wêstawâw n'ohkomak mêna. Ni mama mêna nêya puko tâ pêkiskwêyâhk Michif Cree tâ pêkiskwâtâyâhkik n'ohkomak. Ni wâhkomâkun Josephine kê wêkit usichi nohkom Lâpis mêna wêya mêna nêya kê pêkiskwâtâmo'yâhk n'ohkomnan. Kê pêkiskwâtâmo'yâhk tânispe n'ohkom Lâpis kâ itohtêt ântê Hudson Bay âtâwi'kamik t'âtâwê'yâhk mêchiwin, âhpo muskêkê'eniw tâ nâtâmâhk muskêkê, âhpo post office tâ nâtâmâhk musinakunisa âhpo tâ sepwêtsâhamâk musinakunisa mêna ântê li café tâ nitotâmâhk mêchisiwin nêyanân kichi. Êkotê Green Lake li Mechif âyisêniwak pêkiskwêwâk Michif Cree mêna kâhkêyâwiyahk kâ nâkiskâw'iyâhk pêkiskwêwahk Michif Cree, âna mêna otênâsis mistikimâw. Misiwêtê kâ pâpâmâchi'hochik mêna nakiskâw'âyâkik Nêhiyawêwak. Ni'istotênân ohi pêkiskwêwina kêyâm âhpo li Métis âpâchêtâchik âtêht li Fran⊠ais pêkiskwêwina. Âskaw kâ pêkiskwêyan Michif, nâmoya ni kê miskên ânima Nêhiyawêwin pêkiskwêwina âyis kê kiskê'yitâmân en Fran⊠ais nâmoya Nêhiyâwêwin. Nâmoya nânto êkwâ'nima âyis êkwâ'nima ni Michif pêkiskwêwin.

Dianne Ludwig: At the age of about six, we went to school in Buffalo Narrows and we couldn't speak English yet at that time.

Nanto kotosik kê si piponyân, nêyanân kê tohtêyâhk kiskino'humâkew'kamik ântê Buffalo Narrows mêna nêyanân nâmoya k'âkâyâsimo'yahk chêskwâ, êkospê.

We spoke only Cree. I used to think we were very poor.

Nêyanân kê pêkiskwêyâhk puko Nêhiyawêwin. Kê têhtâmân nêyanân mitoni kê kitimâkisiyâhk.

When we went to school, we were poor, and the nuns would come there to the school as well.

Tânispe k'itohtêyahk tâ kiskino'humâkew'kamik, nêyanân kê kitimakisiyâhk mêna li soeurs kê pitohtiwâk êkotê kiskino'humâkew'kamik, mêna.

They would tell us not to speak Cree, that we had to speak another language now and I used to cry about that. They used to say I was a crybaby because I could not speak English.

Wêyawâw kê wêhtamâkoyâhk nâmoya tâ pêkiskwê'yâhk Nêhiyawêwin, ânima kotuk puko tâ pêkiskwê'yâhk êkwa mêna kê mâtoyân ochi êkwa'nima. Wêyawâw k'itwêchik ânima nêya mâto'âwâsis âyis nâmoya k'âkâyâsêmoyân.

Religion

The unique ethnogenesis of the Métis People has resulted in particularly complex religious practices. Historically, the Métis have followed Christian religious traditions, practicing traditional Catholic (and Protestant) weddings, baptisms, and pilgrimages. Historical accounts of the Métis buffalo hunts would regularly include the Métis practice of bringing a priest along to bless the hunt, and following Catholic tradition, the Métis would never hunt on the Sabbath.

However, just as is so common within Métis culture and history, Métis faith traditions are complex and multifaceted. The Métis' experience of religion is different to that of other Christian

Left: Church in Big Prairie (Prairie Echo) where Beatrice went to church
Right: Jobins going to church in winter. Photos: Beatrice Demetrius

based cultures. For the Métis, their religious practices are more focused on the lived experience of their faith and how it interacts with their understandings of the world and their relationship with their community. This was adopted from the Cree practice of *Wahkohtowin*, which refers to our interconnected relations to other beings, water, and the land. Despite one's personal spiritual belief, it is most important for Métis People to practice respect, reciprocity, and relationality. Innately, the Métis know to respect the land, to never take too much, and to take collective responsibility for the care of our communities and family. Today, Métis People practice a variety of different religious and spiritual beliefs, however the principles of good relations and kinship are still key to who we are and who we have always been as a People.

Beatrice Demetrius: We went to church every Sunday; our little church held about thirty parishioners, we were given a penny or two to put into the collection dish. Before Easter, the Catholic priest would bring the Virgin Mary statue to our house, each night we would have to kneel in front of Mother Mary and say the Rosary.

Nêyanânk'itohtêyâhkâyamihew'kamiktahtoâyimihew'kêsikâw; nêyanân k'âpisasik âyimihew'kamik eyâyâk nânto nistosap tipeyih'tâkosiw'iwâhk, ê kê mêkâwiyahk pêyak peyopiskos âhpo nêso t'âstayâhk pêchîyik ânima mâwâche'chikêwin oyâkun. Pâmweyês Easter, ânâ Catholic âyamihew'êniw kê pêsowât âna Virgin Mary âsinêwêkân yisi ni wêkinân, tâhto tipskâw nêyanân puko tâ chêhkwun'âpiyahk nêkân âna Mother Mary mêna tâ âyamihâwiyahk âna âyamihêminâk.

Doreen Bergum: Lac Ste. Anne — every summer in July, my parents would place willows and canvas over the box of the truck and load their family of ten, clothing, bedding, grub box, cooking supplies, and a trappers' tent, and we headed off to Lac Ste. Anne Pilgrimage. We would dress up, even wearing hats or scarves to cover our head when we entered church. Our parents made us attend all services held each day. Sometimes there were three or four services. We were taught to pray through the love of our parents. This was also a time of kinship as we lived in the south, we met new relatives every time we went to the lake. This was also a time for friends and relatives to fish and speak their language, share white fish and dried meat. Loving times as people would walk for miles to be with their own families and relatives. The people would come in huge farm trucks, 50 - 60 people to a load, bringing their tents, bedding, clothing and their prayer beads. To this day I have memories and visions of my parents walking in the healing waters of Lac Ste. Anne. I can still see my dad walking in the lake with his dress pants rolled up and his nice white shirt, his sleeves rolled up and praying for healing in the waters of Lac Ste Anne. I became a Eucharistic Minister in 2017. I attend the pilgrimage every year to give communion to our People at the Métis Mass and what a blessing this is to serve our People. The Spirit of Lac Ste. Anne will remain in my heart forever.

Lac Ste Anne – Tâhto nêpin ispê July, ni nêkêhikowak ê kê âstachik nêpisê mêna pukwâni'kwunêkin tâkoch la boite ânta âwâtâswâkun mêna pooséhtâchik wêyawâw la famille de mihtâhtâht, âyiwinisa,

Lac Ste. Anne pilgrimage, July 1913
Photo: Glenbow Archives PD-104-48

âkohpa, mêchiwin la boite, pinawaso mêchiwina, wunihikew la tente mêna nêyanân ê-tohtêyahk ântê Lac Ste. Anne Pilgrimage. Kê wawesewiyak, âhpo ê'potskâmâhk li chapeau âhpo tâpiskâkuna kwunahu ni mistikwân ispê kâh pêhtikwewiyak âyamihew'kamik. Ni nêkêhikowahk puminakowyak tâ mâmâwiyê'toyak kâhkiyaw âyamhewêna mâmâ'wâpowin tâhto kêsikâw. Âskâw nantâw êkota nisto âhpo neyo âyamihewena mâmâ'wapowin. Nêyanân kê kiskino'humakâwiyahk t'ayimhayahk sâpo sâkihitowin ochi ni nékéhikowak. Êkoma mêna mwechi êkota wâhkotowin usichi ê'wekiyâhk ântê sâwunohk, ê'nakiskawayakihk oskîyi wâhkomâkunâk kâhkiyâw tâhki nêyanân kâ itohtêyak êkotê yisi sâkuhikun. Êkoma mêna mwechi êkota mitotêmak mêna wâhkomâkunâk tâ kwâskwê'pichi'kêchik mêna tâ pêkiskwêchik wêyawâw pêkiskwêwin, tâ puhkwênuma'wêchik âtehkumêk mêna pâstew wiyâs. Sâkihitowin mwechi êkota âyisêniwâk wâhiyâw kê pimohtêchik t'âyâchik usichi wêyawâw li familles mêna wâhkomakunâk. Âyisêniwak ê-pê itohtêchik pêchîyi nipiymisaw uskê âwâtâswâkuna, nêyânan'omtanâw âhpo nikotwas'omtanâw âyisêniwak âwatâsowin, kê pêtâchik wêyawâw li tente, âkohpa, âyiwinisa mêna wêyawâw âyimhâwin'mêkisa. Iskohk ânoch nitayân kiskisiwina mêna wâpiwina âniki ni nêkêhikowak kê pimohtêchik ânta êyêniwiwa nipê ochi Lac Ste. Anne. Kêyâpich ni wâpimaw ni papa ê'pimohtêt pêchîyi nipê usichi wâwesêw mitas têhtipinam mêna ê'mêyosik wâpiskak pukowayân, unakwiy têhtipinam mêna âyimihat ochi êyêniwiwin ânta nipê ochi Lac Ste. Anne. Ni mâchi âtoskâtâmân âna Eucharistic Minister in 2017. N'itohtân âyimihâwin tâhto uskê tâ mêkiyân suskamowin nêyanân âyisêniwak ânta la Métis Mass mêna mitoni sâwêyihtâkwun tâ wêchihiyâkik nêyanân âyisêniwak. L'âchak de Lac Ste. Anne tayaw ni mitê kâkikê.

No one can take the spirit of God away from us. I have shared Ste Anne with my children and grandchildren, and it was my goal to give communion and share my spirit of God and Métis.

Nâmoya âweyâhk kâkê otinum Mânito âchak ochi nêyanân. Ni kê pâhkwê'numâwêyan Ste Anne usichi n'itâwâsimisak mêna ni châpânak, mêna êkwa ânima kê nohtê itotamân tâ mêkiyân suskumowin mêna tâ pâhkwê'numân nêya âchak Mânito ochi mêna li Métis.

Doreen Poitras: An event happened that kept me intrigued for 70 years. It occurred at the pilgrimage on the Mount St. Joseph which is held in mid-August on the Kehewin Reserve. It's a three or four-day event, attended by hundreds of people. Teams of horses and wagons would pass our place for days, heading to the pilgrimage. On this occasion, it was evening and hundreds of people were making the Stations of the Cross led by the clergy on the Mount.

Kêkwîy kê ispayik kâ kunêweyihi'koyân kâkwechekimowin ochi têpakohp'omtanaw ispayik antê âyamihâwin ânta Mount St. Joseph ki ispayêk âpehtâwiyi August ântê Kehewin nêhiyâw uskênân. Iko ânima nisto âhpo nêyo kêsikâw kêkwîy kê ispayik mâmâwê'ih-tochik mitahtaht'omtinaw âyisêniwak. Nêswapihsowak mista-timok mêyâskâtohk ni wâskihikanân iskô kêsikâhki sipwêtohtêchik ânta âyimhâwêwin. Ochi ispayiwin, mêkwâch otâkosin mêna mitâhtâht'omtinaw âyisêniwuk ê'osêtâchik ânihi Stations of the Cross nêkânêta âyimihawêniw êyinew tâhkoch mistâtim.

St. Joseph Pilgrimage, Kehewin, Alberta.
Photo: Courtesy of the Poitras Family (circa the early 1950's)

My parents had a concession booth and we were camped not far from the church and quite near the flats where the horses were staked. It was a neat time to be a kid. Anyway, on this evening, our Uncle Ben, our dad's younger brother, standing outside our booth said excitedly to our mom, Margaret, "look, look," and there, high up in the sky was a huge cross in the light. A minute, or minutes later, it turned into a long wavy ribbon that then rolled up into a ball of light, then disappeared. This event was seen by a lot of people, maybe hundreds, yet was, and is, rarely talked about. I have always wondered why.

Ni kêhikowak kê âyâchik mâmâwupi'wina mêna nêyanân kâpêsiyahk moya wâhiyo âschi âyimihew'kamik mêna nâwach chêki nâpukâw uskenânâ ântê mistâtimohk kâ chêsta'hikuniskaâchik. Kê mêyosik kêsikâw tâ tohtâhîyakik âwâsis. Pukowêyisi, mêkwach otâkosin, mon oncle Ben, ni papa oskîyi ostesa, ê'nêpawot wêyâwêtimihk nêyanân mâmâwupiwina k'itwew mêyotêhêhaw êkote êsi ni mamanân, Margaret. "Itape, itape" mêna êkota ispimihk kêsik k'âstêk nipiy misaw âyimihewêtihk ânta wasêyaw. Pêyak tipâhikunis âhpo tipâhikunisa mwestas, êmoko'chipayêk iskô êkinok wewhew sênipan ânima kê têhtipinan pêchîyi pukatowan ânta wâseyaw êkospe numatew. Oma kêkwîy k'ispayêk kê wapahtakik mistâhi âyisêniwak, âhpo mitahtaht'omtinaw, mêna chêskwa k'âskaw pêkiskwatiht. Ni mâmitohnitên kâkikê tânihkê.

Mary SkyBlue Morin: N'ohkom Lâpis was religious in the Catholic faith. When she got old, she went to church every day; early morning mass, evening benediction and Sunday mass. I think our family needed a lot of prayers. During mass, the nuns used clackers that clacked when we were to stand, to kneel and to sit. I learned later in life that I almost died at N'ohkom's house. My mother brought me to her mom when I was about three (1954) or four (1955) years old. I was malnourished with rickets and my grandmother sent for the Priest. The church was behind N'ohkom's house, a short walk through the trees. The priest gave me the Last Sacrament — they give it to a person when they are going to die to absolve them of all sins. I survived and from then on, three of my grandmothers; Lâpis, Otavie and Marie-Anne took turns taking care of me. I met my dad a year later, I think my grandmothers asked him to help them provide for me. The first time we saw a camera was when my dad took pictures of us, my mom, my cousin Josephine and me. My dad would give money to my grandmothers for food and he would buy me clothes, shoes and boots ordering from the Army & Navy and Sears and Eatons catalogues.

N'olkom Lâpis âyimihê'wâtisiw ânima Catholic tâpokeh'tumowi. Tânispe kâ kêhte'hiyitayowit k'itohtew ânta âyimihew'kâmik tâhto kêsikâw; wêpach kêkisepâ âyimihâwin, otâkosin âyimihâwin, mêna Âyimihewi'kêsikâw âyimihâwin. Ni têyihtên nêyanân la famille ni tâwê'yihtâmâhk mêchet âyimihâwina. Ka âyimhawêyahk, li soeurs ke âpâchêtâchik itêhta'kwun'âkâna tâ kisketâmâhk tânispe tâ nêpâwiyâhk, tâ chêkwun'âpiyahk mêna t'âpiyâhk. Ni kiskêyitên mwestus nâwach kâ kêhte'iyoyân ânima kêkach kê nipiyân ânte n'ohkom ânima wâskihikun. Ni mama kê pê itohtâhit ochi ômamawa nânto nisto âhpo neyo piponyân. Nêya mitoni nipâhâ'kâtosoyân êkoh kê wêhyâkatsêyân mena n'ohkom kê natsâhew âyimihew'eniw. Ânima âyimihew'kamik kê âstêk otâhk'ochi N'ohkom's wâskihikun, âpsis pimotêwin sâpo mêtosa. Âna âyimihew'eniw kê mêyit ânima Iskwêyach Suskamowin kâ êmêyâchik ispê âweyak kâ wi nipit tâ kâsêpehi'payêk kâhkêyâw pâstâ'howina. Ni pimâtisin mêna êkota ochi, nisto âniki n'ohkomak kê pâhkwê'numawêchik tâ kunawêmikawiyân. Ni nakiskawaw ni papa pêyak uskênan êkota ochi. N'iteyiten n'ohkomak kê kwechimachik tâ wechihachik tâ kunawêmêyit. Kâ nêkân wâpâtâmân ânima misini'payi'chikun ispê ni papa kâ misini'payi'koyahk, ni mama, ni wâhkomâkun Josephine mêna nêyâ. Ni papa kê meyew n'ohkomak sooniyaw kichi mêchowin mêna kê âtâwêstâmowit âyiwinesa, muskisina mêna mistiko'wuskisina kê nâtisâhak ochi Army & Navy mêna Sears mêna Eatons catalogues.

When my mother Suzanne died, her Wake was held at the Flying Dust Reserve in Meadow Lake, Saskatchewan as she had friends and relatives there. The priest, dressed in a black robe with prayers beads and a cross, said a prayer for my mom. They had an afternoon lunch of sandwiches. Then, the tables were cleared and everyone started playing cards; gin, rummy, etc. My mother loved to play cards, so in her honour, they were going to play cards until midnight. I left early as I wanted to take my daughter home to go to sleep. She was only two years old.

Ispê ni mama Suzanne kê nipit, wêya nipêpiw k'ispayik ânta Flying Dust Reserve antê Meadow Lake SK âyis wêya k'âyât mêchet ototêma mêna wâhkomakunak ikotê. Âyimihewi'eniw kê pohtskam ânima kaskitew la robe usâkiy usichi âyimihew'mêkisak mêna âyimihew'âhtik êtwêt âyimihâwin ni mama kichi. K'ayawak ânima mêchisowin ochi nêsoni'kuna. Ékospe, li tables kê kunâchi'tâwahk, mêna kâhkiyawiyak kê mâchi metawechik lis cartes; cribbage, hearts, gin, rummy, etc. Ni mama mitone kê mêyotâhk tâ mêtawêt lis cartes, ikosi kêchi'yimitowin, wêyâwâw kê mêtawêchik lis cartes iskô âpêhtâ'tipiskâw. Ni sipwehtân wêpach âyis nohtê kêweh'tâhak nitanis tâ nito'nipât. Wêya poko niso kêsi piponêt.

I did not know my grandmother Clara very well but her son used to babysit me. Something that bothered me since childhood. I didn't know why she was not allowed to be buried in the Green Lake church cemetery. She was buried on the other side of the fence, outside the grave yard. This has always been on my mind as a child because I could not understand that the Catholic church could do this. Maybe, when the cemetery needs to be expanded, my grandmother Clara could be included in the graveyard.

Nâmoya mitoni ni k'ikiskemaw n'ohkom Clara mâka okosisa kê kanawêmiyêt âskaw. Kêkwîy oma êka kê mêyo mamitone'yihtaman iskô kâ wasisoyan. Nâmoya kiskêyitâman tânihkê êkâ kê nayiniht ânta Green Lake âyimihew'kamik kêhka'hâskwân. Wêya kê nayiniht ohpimê'yisi mêni'kun, wâyâwêtimihk ochi kêhka'hâskwân. Êwuko oma mâna kê mâmâmitonê'tamân kâ wâsisoyân âyis nâmoya kê nisitotên êkwa ânima Catholic âyimihew'kamik kâh kê tohtahk oma. Âhpwetikwe, tânispe ochi kêhka'hâskwân puko nâwach tâ misak, n'ohkom Clara tâ k'âyâw êwuko wêsta mêna ânta kêhka'hâskwân.

In July 1961, we started our pilgrimages to Lac Ste. Anne to pray at that healing lake. We went each year for four years. The first year we went on a Greyhound bus, n'ohkom Lâpis and my mother and my cousin Josephine. The following year in 1962, we travelled there in a yellow school bus just n'ohkom Lâpis and Josephine and I. I wondered why my mother did not come. In 1963 & 64, I went with n'ohkom Marie-Anne. It was heartfelt gratitude for these pilgrimages to Lac Saint Anne, as they were a gentle transition from living with my mother to living with my grandmother Marie Anne and her daughter.

July 1961, ni mâchêtanan nêyanân li pilgrimage ântê Lac Saint Anne t'âyimihayahk êkote ânima mêyo mâchihiwon sâkihikan. Nêyanân ni k'itohtênan tahto nêwo uskênâna. Ânima nêkan uskênan ni posênân ânta Grey Hound tâpanis, Nohkom Lapis mêna ni mama mêna ni wâhkomâkun Josephine. Kotuk uskênân ânima 1962, nêyanân ni poosinan âna oshawasew kiskino'humâkewin tâpânis âya puko nohkom mêna ni wâhkomâkun Josephine mêna nêya. Ni mamtonê'yitin tânihkê ni mama êka kâ p'itohtet. 1963 & 1964, n'itohten usichi n'ohkom Marie-Anne. Êwoku mite'hi nânâskomowin ohi li pilgrimages ântê lac Ste. Anne, âyis êkwa'nima uspisêwin âhto'tewin ochi kê wêkiyân usichi ni mama iskô tâ wêkiyân usichi n'ohkom Marie-anne mêna otânisa.

The next time, I got to Lac Ste. Anne was when I moved to Edmonton, Alberta in 1994. It seemed like it was only half an hour drive to get there. I went a couple times before moving to Calgary in 1999. During the Truth and Reconciliation Commission events that took place in Edmonton, I got out to Lac Ste. Anne a couple times. More recently, the last couple times was in 2016 when I had cancer and in 2017 to ensure healing from the cancer. I went with my son as he lived in Edmonton. I wanted to go in 2018, but I was enrolled in the Canadian Indigenous Languages and Literacy Development Institute (CILLDI) at the University of Alberta.

Kâwi ni kê itohtân Lac Ste. Anne ispê k'âchipichêyan iskô Edmonton AB in 1994. Kê itayihtâkwak tâskoch puko âpehto tipahikun tâ pimpayiyuk êkote. N'itohtayân nêswâw pâmweyes k'âchpichiyan antê Calgary in 1999. Mêkwach ânima Truth and Reconciliation Commission kâkê ispayek ântê Edmonton, ni kâskêtan itohtêyân ântê Lac Ste. Anne nêswâw. Nâwach ânochchêkê, iskoyânihk ânima in 2016 kâ kâchitin'kâwiyân ochi cancer mêna in 2017 kê itohtêyan tâ kêchinâhoyân nâma'kêkwîy âyâyân cancer. Ni k'itohtên usichi ni kosis âyis wêya kê wêkit antê Edmonton. Ni kê nohtê itohtan in 2018 mâkâ mêkwach kê kiskino'humakâw'iyân ânta Canadian Indigenous Languages and Literacy Development Institute (CILLDI) ântê University of Alberta.

Olive Jobin with her daughter
Photo: Beatrice Demetrius

Employment, Lodging and Travel

Beatrice Demetrius: My father was a farmer, but he also trapped and would sell his furs at the HBC store in High Prairie; he gave me a rabbit fur which I sold for five cents, enough to buy an ice cream cone or some one-cent candy.

Ni papa kê kistikwê'wêyiniw, mâkâ mêna kê wânihêkêt mêna kê âtâwâket âhtiyak ânta HBC ântê High Prairie; wêya kê mêyit wapoos âhtiy tâna âtâwakiyan ochi nêyânan pêyopiskos, kwaykoh t'âtâwêyân muskwume munahikun wuskwetow âhpo âteht pêyak pêyopiskos sêwâchikana.

Doreen Bergum: My mother Mary worked as a cook with my dad in a logging camp outside of Sundre. They would leave Sunday night and come home from camp on Friday night. My mother was a great cook, pies, cakes, bannock, cinnamon buns, bread, buns, roast, stews, everyone loved her cooking.

Ni mama Mary âtoskêt kê pinawâsot âschi ni papa ânta mistik âtoskew'êniw okupêsi'win kâ kisipustêk ochi Sundre. Wêyawâw kê sêpwehtêchik ⌧yimhew'kêsikâw tipiskâw mêna kê pêkêwêchik âtoskêwin ochi ispê nêyânan kesikâhk tipiskaw. Ni mama mitoni kêchi pinawaso, nuputekusikina, wehkeh kusikuna, la galet, cinnamon pahkwêsikunisa, pâhkwêsikun, pâhkwêsikunsa, misiwêkusikan, pukachikewin, kâhkiyâw'iyak ê'sakitakihk opinawasowin.

Doreen Poitras: My parents started out owning only a dog team with a lead dog named Bruce but were very industrious and thrifty. By the time I was born, they bought land at Moose Hills where they mixed farming, raised some cattle, pigs and chickens. They built their own house, then mudded and whitewashed it. Our dad made a lot of our furniture: cupboards, tables, benches, and beds. We had a big kitchen and a big cookstove, wood box, a cellar and all the necessities. There was a round heater stove in the living room, and two bedrooms. Then an upstairs where the only heat was the stovepipe, so it was hot in summer and chilly in winter. Usually, the water pail was frozen solid.

Ni nêkêhikowak kê mâchitachik ê'tipêyichikit âtimohk nêswapih'sowak usichi nêkânew âtim Bruce ê-sêkasot, mâka wêyâwâw mitoni kâyawisew mêna mâwâchêchikew; mwestus kâ pimâtisiyân, wêyâwâw âtâwêchik uskê ântê Moose Hills tânta wêyâwâw kêkâwepayiw kâ kistikehk, ohpinakik carrel, kookosa mêna papahâkwâna. Wêyâwâw kê'chimatachik waskiyikun, êskope usiske êstachik mêna wapiskahumichik. Ni papanân kê'osehtaht mistaheh kesapowina: oyakuni'kumikana, li tables, tehtapowina, mêna nipewina. Nêyânan âyayahk ê-misahk pinawuso'kamik mêna ê'misahk pinawaso kotawanapisk, mehta li boite, un cave mêna kâhkiyâw âpuchichikuna. Ânâ wawiyêyaw kotâwânâpisk ânta apiw-kamik, mêna nêso nipewi'kamika. Êskope ispimihk tânta pohko kâ kisitek ânima kotâwânâpisk iskotakwân, ikosi kisitew kâ nêpin mêna tahkayasin kâ pipon. Mana, nipê uskihk miskawahkatin.

When starting school, my brother and I walked about one and a half miles to class. Held in a neighbour's living room, there were ten to fifteen students. Our curriculum was correspondence, and the instructor did enrollment and kept order. I can't remember the weather being an issue — but if it was extreme, our dad would pick us up with the team and sleigh, or our neighbour with a caboose.

Kâ mâchitayahk kiskino'humakewin, nistes mêna nêyâ ê'pimohtêyahk pêyak mêna âphetaw tantahto mistik êkotê yisi mâmâwikiskino'humatowin. Pimpayitâchik ânta wêtupimâkun âpiw'kamik, êkota kê mitahtaht'nêyânanosap kiskino'humakanuk. Nêyanân musinahi'kiyânân kiskino'humatowin musinahumâ'towin mêna kiskino'humakew mâmâwiyêtowak mêna âtoskewiyakun. Ni moya nikiskisin kâ siwepahk êka ê'meyo'yihtamahk - mâka kespin mamwayes, ni papanân pê mosahkina nêyanân nêswapihsowak mêna pipon tapanask, âhpo nêyân wêtupimakun âschi li kapos.

A year or so later, we had a proper schoolhouse hauled in and a teacherage. And now only about a half mile to walk, plus a real teacher's desk, a black board, a heater, stove, pencil sharpener, a water pail with dipper — we were so fortunate.

Pêyak uskê âhpo mwestes, wêyanân kê'âyayahk nuhinakwan kiskino'humato'kamik âwâtakihk mêna kiskino'humakew'kamik. Mêna, kêkwa âphetaw tântâhto mistik ê'pimohteyahk, mêna tâpwehtakwun kiskino'humakew'kamik musinahikewinahtik. Kuskitewahtik, kotâwânâpisk, opinawuso kotâwânâpisk, mohkochikun, nipi uskihk usichi kwâpâhikun – nêyanân mitoni wêyootsiyahk.

I was about grade four when we bussed to Elk Point in a weird little bus. The seat was sideways and I was car sick everyday. But when it snowed and the bus couldn't come, we had to walk about two miles to the highway. The snow would be very deep and drifts higher than the fence. But again, as a kid, weather was not an issue, we enjoyed the winter and our parents prepared well, cutting, and hauling wood. At home we swept and stacked wood. Our wood pile was high. Again, I don't remember feeling cold or deprived. Though I do remember getting frost bite now and then.

Nânto newo nâ âtikis'kino'humaht kâ poosiyahk kiskino'humakêwin'tâpânâs ântê Elk Point kostâchinâkwun âpisasin kiskino'humakewin'tâpânâs âpowin pemipayiwiki mêna êti âhkoseyan l'automobile kâ poseyan kâhkiyâw kêsikâw. Mâka kâ mispohk mêna kiskino'humakewin-tâpânâs moya êkê pihtohtêt, niyânan puko tâ pimohtêyahk nêso tântâhto mistik isi kêchi mêskanâw. Koona mitoni timew mêna papestiniwiw ispimihk mênikun. Mâka âsumena, kâ wasisoyan siwêpahk êka ê'meyoyih'tamahk. Ni mêyotênan pipon mêna nêyanân kêhikowak kwayachi'sêhtawahk mêyo âtoskêchik, kê'munsakihk mêna âwâtakihk mêhta. Chêki nêki kê nipayahk mêna wêstehkana mêhta. Niyânân mêhta âsusechikewina ispimihk âyahk. Âsumêna, ni moya kiskisin kê tâhkâyâyân âhpo muskâmâwiyânê.

For light we had a coal oil lamp and a lantern, eventually having a gas lamp that used gas and had mantles and had to be pumped. We kids were afraid of lighting it but it provided a much better light, especially for doing homework, catechism and reading.

Tâ waskotênâmahk ê'yâyâhk kuskitêhkan uskew pimê wâskotênikun mêna wâsitênikakun, pâmwayes âyâyâhk pâhkitewpimê wâskotênikun kâ âpachêtahk pâhkitewpimê mêna uschikêwin mêna puko tâ monayihikêt. Nêyanân âwâsisâk êkostâmahk tâ iskotenâmahk mâka nâwach ê'mekawiyahk mistâhi mêyo wâseyâw wâwâyes êkwa tâ âtoskatamahk kiskino'humâkêwin, âyimhew'kiskino'humâkêwin mêna âyâmichikêwin.

Lisa Wolfe: In those days, my grandfather would come in from up north somewhere and he would have big, great, big cases of furs. Like just laden with furs... just skins and furs and everything like that. And he would take them over to the Hudson Bay Company and sell them all. But I was still very young... I was probably about eight and that was kind of normal. Grandpa would be coming in every, you know, four or five months with a bunch of furs, and he'd sell it to the Hudson Bay Company. Everything would be good for a while and he'd visit for a few months and then he'd go back up north again.

Ikospê, ni moshom kê pêtakohtew ochi kêwe'tinohk nânto mêna wêya t'âyâw kâ misâk, mitoni misâki mus'kimota ânki âhtiyak. Tâskoch mistâhi nuyâhtam usichi âhtiyak... mwechi musâ'kiya mêna âhtiyak mêna kahkiyâw kêkwîy ikosi. Mêna wêya k'itohtatat ikonanhi ântê Hudson Bay Company mêna âtâwâket kahkiyaw. Mâka keyapich nêyâ âwâsis... Nêyâ oma nanto âyinânew ê si piponyân mêna êkwa ânima pêyakwun pimâtsiwin. Moshom kê pêtakohtew tâhto, kiskitên, neyo âhpo nêyânan pêsimok usichi mistâhi âhtiyak, mêna wêya âtâwâket ântê Hudson Bay Company, Kâhkiyâw tâ mêyosin âcheyaw mêna wêya kêhokew âteht pêsimok mêna êkospê wêya tâ yihtotew kêwitinohk kâwi.

Dianne Ludwig: I like to say we moved with the seasons. In the wintertime we would move to our cabin, and actually our transportation was a dog team. I'll never forget the sound of the snow and the way my dad would mush the dog team to get us where we were going. They would put a whole bunch of blankets in that toboggan and we would go to where we were supposed to and get to the cabin. And I can still remember my grandpa and them making a big fire in a woodstove and the fire was crackling and it was beautiful.

Nêya nohtê êtwan ânima nêyanân âchipichiyâhk usichi siwêpuna. Kâ pipohk nêyanân âchipichiyâhk ântê nêyanân wâskiyi'kunis, mêna nêyanân kê pimpayahk âna âtimok nêswapihsowâk. Nâmoya wêkach ni wânkiskisin ânima muska'wâw ânima kona mêna tânisi ni papa kê mush âtimok nêswapihsowak tâ itohtahikoyâhk tânte nêyanân kê tohtêyâhk. Wêyawâw kê âstachik mêchet âkohpa ânta soosko'chiwe'tâpânaskos mêna nêyanân itohtêyâhk tânte nêyanân k'ite'yihitumâhk itohtêyâhk mêna tâ itohtahikoyâhk êkotê kâmiskos. Mêna kêyapich ni kiskisen ni moshom mêna wêstawaw misi poonum ânta mêhta kotâwân'apisk mêna iskotew kê sêhko'sakun mêna mitoni kê mêyosik.

It would probably take us... probably just about the whole day to get to our trapline because our trapline was close to the Cold Lake bombing range. It was in that area that we were raised and we would stay there until springtime, and then when it was springtime my dad had a canoe and we would go back by canoe and go back into our little community of Buffalo Narrows.

Êwuko âhpo êtikwê mwechi.... Âhpo êtikwê mwechi nânto kâhkiyâw kêsikâw tâ tahkosiyâhk nêyanân wunêhikun tipahâskâna âyis nêyanân wunêhikun tipahâskâna k'âstêk chêki ânima Cold Lake bombing range. Êkote ânima uskês ê tipahâs'kâtamihk kê pê opikiyahk mêna kê wêkiyâhk êkota iskô sêkwun, mêna ânima ispê sêkwun ni papa âyât oosi mêna nêyanân usêtsa'wêyâhk usichi oosi mêna usêtsa'wêyâhk ânta nêyanân âpisis mâmâwi'e'âyâhk ânima Buffalo Narrows.

And during the wintertime they would take their furs.... You know what, to this day I'm not quite sure where they took their furs. I think they walked to Cold Lake. I really do. I think they walked to Cold Lake to sell their furs.

Mêna mêkwâch pipon wêyawâw k'itohtâhâchik âhtîyak.... Kiskêhiyitên kêkwîy, kêyâpich ânoch nâmoya mitoni ni kiskêhiyitên tânte k'itohtâhâchik wêyawâw âhtîyaka. Ni mâmitone'yiten kê pimohtêchik iskô Cold Lake. Ni tâpwêtên. Ni mâmitone'yitên kê pimohtêchik iskô Cold Lake tâ âtâwâkêchik wêyawâw âhtîyaka.

Family Life

Beatrice Demetrius: Grandmother Marie married Eugene Etienne Chalifoux. He died of the Spanish Flu in 1918.

N'ohkom Marie kê wêkimat Eugene Etienne Chalifoux. Wêya kê nipit ânima ochi Spanish Flu in 1918.

My paternal grandmother was Olive Dumas born 1875 at Fort St. John which was in the New Caledonia area. Her father Charlot aka Charles was postmaster for the Hudson Bay Company at Fort Dunvegan.

N'ohtawe nakisi n'ohkom kê Olive Duman pê pimatisit 1875 ântê Fort St. John tâna antê New Caledonia. Ôpapawa Charlot aka Charles kê musinahumato weyinew âschi Hudson Bay Company antê Fort Dunvegan.

She was a very quiet lady, she made beaded moccasins, I remember her many colours of beads on a white cloth.

Wêya mitoni ê kamwutun iskwew, wêya ê-osehtat mêkisikatum pâh-pêkin weskisina, ni kiskisin wêya mêchet tusinasteki mêkisikatuma ânta wâpiskahk âyânis.

Delia Gray (as told by Bobbi): There were expectations when going to visit relatives on reserve. When we would go to the reserve my mom would tell me, "Put on a skirt, tie your hair back, and then sit quiet with us women while we visit and drink tea with us." Then if we went to a Métis gathering, my mom told me wear a skirt, stay close to your brothers, and if anyone says something mean, don't be afraid to tell them to their face. I would never do this, I always enjoyed the music and watching people jig and square dance. When going to school in the city she would tell me, "Just go and get along with other kids." School in the city was pretty much all white kids. When we moved to Paddle Prairie and eventually High Prairie, I found it much easier, because there were a lot of Indigenous kids, it was more relaxing.

The farm hay wagon
Photo: Beatrice Demetrius

Usuwâpami'wêwin ispê k'itohtêyahk tâ kêwikêyahk wâhkomâkunahk ânta nêhiyâw'uskê. Tânispe nêyanân k'itohtêyahk ântê nêhiyâw'uskê ni mama wêhtamowit "âsta kêskusakas, tâhkopta usêyâpita ki mêschâkâsa mêna kêyâm'âpi usichi nêyanân iskwêwak mêkwâch kâ kêwikêyâhk mêna tâ minehkweyin muskêkê'wapoy usichi nêyanân. Êkospe kêspin ki tohtêyahk ânima Métis kâ mamawapik, ni mama âsta kêskusakas, ota âya chêki ki stasuk, mêna kêspin âwêyak êtwew kêkwîy muchîyi, kâya koosta tâ wêhtamwâchik yisi wêkwakun. Nâmoya wêhkach nitohtên ooma, ni tâhki mêyotên ânima kitochikêwin mêna wâpâh'tamâhk âyisêniwak kâ nêsosimochik mêna âyinâneyo kâ nêmêhitochik. Tânispe kâ tohtêyak kiskino'humâkêwin ântê otênâw, wêya kê wêhtâmowit "sooskwâch itohtê mêna tâ mêyo âschi kotuk âniki âwâsisâk." Kiskino'humâkêwin ântê otênahk nâwach puko mooniyâw âwasisak. Tânispe k'achipichi'yâhk yisi Paddle Prairie mêna pâmwayes High Prairie, ni miskên nâwach ê mêyosik, âyis êkote mêchêt Indigenous âwâsisâk , nâwach êkwa'nima âyiwêpiwin.

Many things were important to my mom and something that stands out for me even today is the people on the street. When she and I would be walking downtown, someone would call her name and she would stop to talk to them. She would introduce me to someone who might be quite inebriated, she would proudly say to me, "This is my cousin so and so, his mom and dad had a farm a few miles from the Cunningham farm." I could see that my cousin felt quite good about being recognized as a relative. She would say to me later, "Never be ashamed of any of your relatives that might be on the streets, they are still our relatives."

Mêchêt kêkwîy kêchi'yiwun ochi ni mama mêna kêkwîy kâ kêchi'yiwun nêya kichi kêyapich ânoch âniki âyisêniwak ânta pimohtê'skânâw. Tânispê wêya mêna nêya kê pimohtêyâhk antê otênaw, âwêyahk ê nitomkut owêhowin mêna wêya kê nâkew tâ pêkiskwatat êko'naniki. Wêya tâ nakâyas'kumohtahewit nêya âwêyahk âhpwetikwê kê kiskwêpêsit, wêya kê michimo, "êkwa âwa ni wâhkomakun so and so, ômamawa mêna opapwa kê âyawâchik uskênân tântâhto âtêht mistik ochi ânima Cunningham uskênân. Ni wâhpâtên ni wahkomakan êmeyotehitak âweyahk kê nistâwinamkot tâskoch owahkomakan. Wêya êtwet nêyâ mwestus, "kâya wêhkâch tâ nepewsiyin ki wâhkomâkunak ânima k'âyâchik ânta pimohtê'skanaw, wêyawas kêyapich kêyanâw wâhkomâkunak.

Delia Gray (as told by her granddaughter, Krista Leddy): This is one I tell when trying to describe my Kookum. This was in the summer or early fall of 1997. Kookum lived downtown and would call me up to take her places for meetings (she called it "going to a do") or go shopping. My first child was born earlier in the spring, and Kookum would find some really good reasons that would have me bringing the baby over. On that particular day, it was a really nice day, so we ended up going shopping in the City Centre Mall, right in the heart of downtown Edmonton. I was pushing the stroller with the baby in it and Kookum was fussing over the baby, very proud of

Delia Gray, in the middle
Photo: Cynthia Dunnegan

being out and about with her great-granddaughter, speaking to the baby in Cree and giving me advice. Up ahead, there was a man sitting on the sidewalk, leaning against a building, asking for change. He looked rough and most people were just walking by him. She elbowed me (she was quite a bit shorter than me, so it was a little jab to the hip) and told me to just keep walking. Don't look at the man, don't talk to him, just keep walking so that the baby wouldn't be bothered, she said. I told her I would do as she said as we got closer. She moved so that she would be between the stroller and the man sitting on the sidewalk. As we were about to pass, he looked up at us and began to ask for some change. Kookum looked at him and suddenly stopped. I stopped, thinking something was wrong but realized she had stopped right in front of the man she told me to ignore. She took a step towards him and asked if a certain person was his auntie. He looked startled. His glazed over look suddenly became sharp, and said yes. She then asked if another woman was his mother. He said yes and stood up. She started to tell him a story about his mom, then a great story about his grandfather. This man was so happy to listen and I remember his grin just lighting up his face. They chatted for a bit and then Kookum took out her wallet and started to pull out a ten-dollar bill. If you knew her, this was a big deal as she was very frugal. He said he didn't want to take her money and they talked back and forth for a bit. As the conversation began to become difficult for him, she made him promise to call his mother. He promised he would and she introduced the baby as her great-granddaughter and I as her granddaughter. He was so kind, saying hello to the baby and then me. Kookum then urged me on, helping to push the stroller down the sidewalk. I tried asking her about this, but she just returned to fussing over the baby. This wasn't the only time this sort of interaction would happen. She would see people and ask a few questions and then figure out who their relations are and tell them a great story, connecting them to a community and a place. She would give them pride in who they are and where they come from.

Êkoh oma pêyak âchimoyân tânispe kâkwe kochêtayân mâmiskotew n'ohkom. Êkoh oma kâ nêpik âhpo wêpach tâkwakin 1997. N'ohkom kê wêkit otênâw mêna kê sêwêptâmowit tâ tohtahuk ochi mâmi'wapi'waka (wêya ê sêkatahk êkwa'nima "going to a do") âhpo tâ tohte âtawiyâhk. Nêya nêkan apis'cha'wâsis kê pimâtisit wêpach sêkwun, mêna n'ohkom kê miskâhk âtêht tâpwe mêyosin iteyih'tumina tâ pesowiyâhkik âna pêpîsis êkote. Êkospe ânima wâwês êkwa, mitoni kê mêyo kêsikâw, iskô nêyanân ni tohtênân tâ âtâwêyâhk ânta otênâw âtâwâkew'kamik, mitoni otênâw Edmonton. Nêya kê yâkinaman âwâsis otupew tâpânâskos âschi pêpîsis pêchîyi mêna n'ohkom mikoska'tisit ochi âna pêpîsis, mitoni kistê'yimot tâ wâyâwêyâhk mêna pâpâmohtêyâhk âschi ochâpân iskwesis, ê Nêhiyâw pêkiskwêtât pêpîsis mêna kê mêyit wêhtâmowin. Ispimihk nêkân êkota nâpew kê âpit ânta pimohtêwin, sehka'chiwit uschîyi wâskiyikun, nâtotâhk sooniyâs. Kâspâw ê sinâkoso mêna mêchet âyisêniwâhk kê mwechi wêmâskâwewichik. Wêya châkinit usichi mitos'kwun (wêya mitoni nâwach chimisisiw êskohk nêya, ikosi êkwânima châkinit ânta mito'kwun) mêna kê wehtâmowit mwechi sooskwach tâ pimohtêyân. Kâya kitâpum nâpew, kâya pekiskwata wêya, mwechi sooskwâch pimohte iskô âna pêpîsis nâmoya âyimihew, itwew. Ni wehtamwaw ni kâ i toten tâskoch kâ itwet ispê kâ tahkoseyahk chêki . Wêya weyaskawew iskô ânima wêya t'âyât tusta'wihyâk ânima âwâsis otupew tâpânâskos mêna âna nâpew ê apit ânta pâpâmohtêwin. Usichi kekach kâ pimotêyahk chêki , wêya ê ki tapimkoyahk mêna mâchi kwechimkoyahk ochi ateht sooniyas. N'ohkom ki tapimew mêna sikoch nakew. Ni nakeyan, ê tihtaman kekwîy moya mêyo payek mâka kiskeyihtak wêya kê naket mitoni nêkân ânhi nâpewa kâ itwet êka tâ pêkiskwatak, wêya kâ wehtâmowit nâmoya tâ nakâte'yimak. Wêya otinâm takoskewin êkotê isi wêya mêna ê kwechimat kespin âweyak âyisenew kê wêya sa tante. Wêya sisiko'chihit isi'nâkosiw. His glazed over look suddenly became sharp, mêna êtwet tâpwe. Wêya kwechimew kespin kotuk iskwew ânâ ômamawa. Wêya êtwew tâpwe mêna nepawo. Wêya mâchi wehtamowew âchimowin âya ochi ômamawa, êkospê kêchi âchimowin âya ochi omoshoma. Êkwa âwa nâpew êkoh ê mêyotehitak to natotak mêna ni kiskehiten pahpehsewin mwechi lighting up his face. Wêyâwâw pekiskwewaw âchiyaw mêna êkospê n'ohkom otinanum sooniyas wates mêna mâchi otinanum mihtaht peyopis. Kespin kê kinstawemat, êkoh oma mistâhi kekwîy âyis wêya mitoni mâwi'chechi'kew. Wêya êtwew nâmoya ohti otinat o sooniyamsa mêna pekiskwechik mêna wêyâwâw kê pekiskwechik âsehte kahke'kwusk âchiyo. Iskô pekiskwatitatowin kâ mâchi âyimak wêya kichi, wêya wehtamowiw puko t'âsutamahet to seweptamowat ômamawa. Wêya âsutamahet ikos t'itohtak mêna wêya nakâyas'kumohtahew ânâ pêpîsis tapiskoch ochapanis-tanisa mêna nêyâ tapiskoch ochapan-tanisa. Wêya mitoni kisewatsit, êtwet tansi yisi ânâ pêpîsis mêna êkospê nêyâ. N'ohkom êkospê kê sêhkimit tâ itohteyan, ê wechihit tâ yakinaman ânima pêpîsis otupew tâpânâskos ânta pimohtewin. Ni kochitan tâ kwechimahk wêya oma ochi, mâka wêya mwechi kawi mêna tâ mikoskatisiw ochi ânâ pêpîsis. Nâmoya oma pêyakwaw oma itowahk nukiskumiwin kê ispayek. Wêya kê wapamat âyiseniwak mêna kê kwechimiw ateht kakwe chekemowin mêna kêseyihtam âwenâ owâkhomâkunak wêyâwâw mêna t'achimostawat mitoni mêyosik âchimowin, âniskohtaw wêyawas êkotê mâmâwi'e'âyâhk mêna nêta. Wêya kê meyat kiste'yimow ânima âwêna wêyâwâw mêna tanite ochi pê itohtechik.

Lisa Wolfe: Indigenous People have very large families, and they are very large, interconnected families. So, when you're a cousin of a cousin, you're like, "Hey you're family."

Indigenous âyisêniwak âyawak mitoni mishaki li familles, mâka ikonanhi mitoni mishaki aniskoh'tawichik li fammiles. Ikosi, oma kêya wahkomakan ochi ânâ wâhkomâkun, kêya oma tâskoch, "Hey, kêya oma famille."

It was great in that respect so that when we had family members that were out in the community, they can relate back to those community members and it creates a network, but it also creates a trust right with us. And, we might be policing, but we're also family. I think that is why I've always kept myself open.

Kê mêyosik ikosi ânima itam ânima tânispê, nêyanân âyâyâhk la famille oweche'hiwew anki âyâchik ânta mâmâwe'ê'âyâhk, wêyâwâw âtotom kawi ikonanki mâmâwe'ê'âyâhk oweche'hiwewak mêna êkwa ânima osehtâw mumesewin usichi nêyanân. Mêna, nêyanân âpwetikwe simâkunise'nahk, mâka kêyapich nêyanân mêna la famille. Ni tihitên êkochi ânima kâ kânâwemsoyan tâ mêyo nakiska'wâtakik âweyak.

Muriel Stanley Venne (as told by her daughter, Rachelle Venne): She (Muriel's mother) was a fantastic lady. Her name was Jessie Whitford and she apparently drove a red river cart and after being widowed quite young, she spent most of her time alone. My mother had a very close relationship with her grandmother and that's where she learned a lot of her Métis history and things like that. She does have a book written about her and her stories—

Wêya (Muriel ômamawa) kê mitoni mêyo'wâtisiw. Wêya owêhowin Jessie Whitford mêna wêya êsa kê puminat âna rivyer rooze karte mêna mwestes kâ pê moosiskwêwit mitoni kê oskîyit, wêya mêstinam tânito tipihikun kê yakwapit. Ni mama êki âyat mêyo wâhkotowin âschi ochapâna mêna êkote ânma kâ kiskêyitahk mistâhi ânma Métis kâyas âta'yohkun.

Mary SkyBlue Morin: We lived in poverty. There was no fridge and no electricity. We used a coal oil lamp when the sun went down. Heat for the main room was a heater stove and a cook stove. N'ohkom Lâpis and n'ohkom Marie-Ann kept a wooden grub box under the table. It was our job to pull it out to put the food on for meal time. The grub box usually had a paper bag of sugar, box of salt, berry sugar (jam) and bannock in a tea towel. We hauled our water from the lake and boil it on the stove for cooking and drinking. Sometimes we got water from a well and a water truck would come by. We caught rain in a barrel for washing and washing clothes.

Nêyanân mitoni kê kitimakisiyak. Nama'kêkwîy ânima fridge mêna makêkwîy wâskote'payi'chikun. Kê âpachitayahk kuskitehkan uskêw'pimê wâskotê'nikun ispê pêsim kâ pahkisimot. Kisitew kichi kêchi piski'kipahikun ânima iskotew kotawan'apisk mêna pinawaso kotawan'apisk. N'ohkom Lapis mêna n'ohkom Marie-Ann kê kanawehtawahk ânima la boite mehti mechiwin kichi sêpa la table. Nêyanân ânima âtoskatamahk tâ âchipitamahk ânima la boite mehti tâ âstayahk ânihi mêchowina mêchowin kichi. Ânima mêchowin la boite mana âyak ikota sewini'kun pechiyi le sac papier, âpsis la boite ochi sêwê'takun, menisa sewini'kun (jam) mêna pahkwesikun pechiyi muskeke'wapoy âkwuna'hikun. Nêyanân kê tahkonamahk nipi ochi ânima sakihikun kê pahkatamahk tâ pinawasoyahk kichi mêna tâ minekweyahk. Âskaw ânima kê kachitinamahk ochi moona'hipun âhpo mêna nipi tapanaskos pê pimpayew. Ni kachitinenan mêna kimowan nipi tâ sepekinsoyahk mêna tâ sepekinamahk âyiwinisa.

My three grandmothers all lived on the same half acre of land. N'ohkom Oktavie lived with her husband in a white house. Next to the house was a very small house where n'ohkom Lâpis and my cousin Josephine lived. Nearby was n'ohkom Marie-Anne's and Moshom Little Joe's log house. I think Octavie and her husband had lived in that log cabin before. The logs and mud plaster were covered in white paint. When you walked into the five foot door, we had to step down about a foot to reach the floor. Inside, there were no doors to rooms because the heat from the heater and the cook stove had to reach the rooms. There was always lots of blankets to use at night. I saw a picture of me in my first communion dress standing by the cabin but I don't know which grandmother had the picture.

N'ohkom Oktavie ânâ nâwach oskîyi ochi âniki nisto n'ohkomahk kâhkeyâw kê wêkichik ânta âpehto tipahuskan uskenan. Wêya kê wekit usichi onapema ânta kâ wapiskahk waskihikan. Chêki ânima waskihikan êsitek mitoni apisasik waskiyi'kunis tânite n'ohkom Lapis mêna ni wahkomakan Josephine kâ wêkichik. Kisiwak âniki n'ohkom Marie-Ann mêna moshom Little Joe mistik waskihikan. Ni iteyiten êkwa'nima Octavie mêna onapema ikota kê wêkichik. ânima mistik waskihikan. Ânihi misika mêna ânima uskê âkohpiso'win kê wapiskak sisopê'kahikatew. Kâ pêhtikewiyan pechiyi ânima la porte nêyânan kinwaw, nêyânan puko tâ tâhkoske'weyahk nanto pêyak tâhkoskewin. Pêchîyi, nama' kêkwîy li portes, âyis tâ kêsowak ochi kotawan'apisk mêna pinawaso kotawan'apisk puko kâhkiyâw êtê tâ ispayek. Mitoni mânâ mêchet âkohpa tâ apachitayahk kâ tipiskak. Ni kê wâpâhtên ânima musini'payiwina kê potskâmâk ni nêkan suskumowin usâkiya kê nêpâwiyan chêki ânima wâskihikunis mâkâ nâmoya ni kiskêyiten âwêna n'ohkom êkwa'nima êkê âyât.

In the fall of 1957, when I was 6 years old, I lived with n'ohkom Octavie, so that I could start school. She and her husband Toby looked after a cousin named Morris. He taught me how to catch the school bus. At the school, nuns wore black dresses with prayer beads and a cross. They were the teachers at the school. Sister Superior said I could not start school because I could not read and to wait until next year. I was confused as I had come to school to learn to read and write.

Kâ takwâ'kin ispê 1957, ispê nêya oma niko'twasik êsi piponyân, ni wêkin usichi n'ohkom Octavie, iskô tâ mâchitâyân ânta kiskinohumakew'kamik. Wêya mêna onapema kê kanawemâchik ni wâhkomâkun êsekasot Morris. Wêya kê kiskino'humawit tanis tâ kachitinat ânâ kiskino'humakew'tâpânis. Ânta kiskino'humakew'kamik, lis soeurs kê kiskiskamok ânihi kaskitew li robes usâkiya usichi âyimihew'mêkisak mêna âyimihew'âhtik, wêyâwâw kiskino'humakewak ântê kiskino'humakew'kamik. La soeur superior k'etew nâmoya kâkê mâchitayân kiskino'humakêwin âyis êka kê âyâmichikêyân mêna tâ pêhoyân iskô uskooch pêyak uskê. Ni wanêyihtên âyis kê pihtohteyân kiskino'humakew'kamik tâ kiskino'humakaw'iyân tâ âyâmichikêyân mêna tâ musinahikêyân.

Food, Harvesting and Traditional Medicines

Beatrice Demetrius: When the cranberries and blueberries were ripe, I remember going to the jack pines to pick. We slept in a tent; it was an adventure for us kids because other families would join us. It was common for us to look for spruce gum.

Tânispê ânihi wêsakêmina mêna êyênimina utsoki sâsiy, ni kiskisin ê-tohtêyahk antê minatika tâ mawasoyahk. Nêyanân kê nipîyahk dans la tente; êkwa'nima mêyo wahpatumowin kichi nêyanân âwâsisâk âyis kohtuk li famille âniskokunan. Êkwa ânima into nêyanân kichi tâ nâtonâmahk ochi sitah pikiw.

My grandmothers lived in High Prairie. My maternal grandmother Marie Magdeleine Johnston was born in 1880 at Lac La Biche. She made the best bannock in big slabs, then she would wrap it in tea towels and keep it in a larder. Sometimes when I visited she would make fish soup, I feared eating it because there would be bones sticking out of the pot.

N'ohkomahk kê wêkichik ântê High Prairie. N'ohkom âkawêwin Marie Magdeleine Johnston kê pimâtisit 1880 ântê Lac La Biche. Wêya kê osêhew mamweyes êmosit pâhkwesikun kê misaw napute puchikun, êkospe wêya wêwêkina ikonanhi muskêkê'wapoy âkwuna'hikuna mêna tâ kanawehtak ânta mêchiwin kamikos. Âskow ispê nêya kâ kêhokeyan, wêya kê'ositaht kinosew mêchimapoy, nêya kê kostaman tâ mêchiyan âya ochi miskuna kê chêpatastêki ochi uskihkos.

She knew some of the native medicines, she always had rat root, labonne tea and other herbs, I don't know what they were.

Wêya kaskêtum âhtit ânihi nêhiyaw muskêkêya, wêya tahki k'âyat wachusk mêchowin, labonne muskêkê wapoy mêna kotuk muskêkêya, nâmoya kiskeyitên kêkwîy anihi.

Delia Gray (as told by Bobbi): When she (Delia) was about four, her family was living on the Cunningham farm in St. Albert. She had many fond memories of the farm. At about age four, she was taken to the Mission School in St. Albert. She used to talk about this quite a bit and she said she had to leave school when she was in grade four, because she had tuberculosis. She didn't like the fact that she had tuberculosis, but she did like the fact that she then could stay on the farm and live in a teepee with her grandmother Sophie Chastellaine-Rowland.

Tânispe wêya (Delia) nânto newo piponit, wêya sa famille kê wêkichik ânta ânima Cunningham kistikân ântê St. Albert. Wêya kê âyâw mêchêt mamitonê'yichikun ochi ânima kistikân. Nanto newo piponit, wêya kê itohtâhiht ântê Mission School ântê St. Albert. Wêya kê pêkiskwatum oma mistâhi mêna wêya k'itwêt wêya puko kê nâkâtâhk kiskino'huma'kewin ikospe wêya kê âyât newo kâ ati kiskino'we'miwowat, âyis wêya kê âyât tuberculosis. Wêya nâmoya mêyohtam ânima tâpwêwin ânima ê âyât tuberculosis, mâka wêya mêhotam ânima wêya tâ kaskêtâht tâ âyât ânta kistikân mêna tâ wêkit ânta ânima têpê usichi ohkoma Sophie Chastellaine-Rowland.

Sophie (Delia's grandmother) took care of my mom and from what my mom always said Sophie knew how to work with traditional medicine. This is how her grandmother treated my mom's bout with TB.

Sophie (Delia ohkoma) kê kunâwêmew ni mama mêna ochi kêkwîy ni mama kâkê itwêt tâhki Sophie kê kiskeyitum tânisi tâ âtoskêt usichi kâyâs ochi muskêkê. Ikosi oma tânisi ohkoma êyêniwit ni mama âhkosêwin usichi TB.

Doreen Bergum: My father was an excellent hunter and would harvest deer, elk, and moose, only when we needed the meat. He would share the harvest with other Métis families in the area.

Ni papa mitoni méyo mâchéw mêna ké mâchet âpsimoosis, wâwâskesiw, mêna mooswa, puko kâ nitaweyihtamak wiyâs. Wêya ê-pâhkwenumât wiyâs mêchowina âschi kohtuk li Métis familles êkota.

My father and brother were out hunting and cutting wood, and my dad shot a moose out of season. He then covered the moose under the wood. The forest ranger stopped him and checked the back of the truck. A moose leg was sticking out of the wood in plain sight, but fortunately the ranger knew my dad and knew that my dad had shot the moose to feed his family, so let him go without charging him.

Ni papa mêna nistes wêyawâw kê mâchichik mêna munsâkihk mehta, mêna ni papa ê-paskisot mooswa moya mâchewin siwepun. Wêya kê kwunahat mooswa sepâ mehta. Ânâ sakaw kunweyichikew ê-nakinkot mêna k'itâpachikêt pechîyi âwâtâswâkun. Ânima mooswa miskat kê chepatâstek ochi ânihi mehta âweyâhk tâ wâpâtahk, mâka sakâw kunweyichikew kê nistawemat ni papawa mêna kê kisketachk ni papa êke machet t'âsumat la famille, ikosi pukitinew namoya âpachitaw okimaw tipahikewin.

Doreen Poitras: We were twelve miles from town so we did not go to the doctor. We used pioneer medicine. I remember our aunt showing us red willow bark and boiling it for breakouts on her face, then after use, pouring it back on a tree. I remember chewing a plant that we called Indian medicine, then applying it to cuts and abrasions. There were home cures for toothaches, for foot injuries. Seeing our dad roasting bark if he were out of tobacco, or roasting wheat to make coffee.

Nêyanân oma nesosap tânitahto miskik ochi otênaw nêyanân moya n'itohtênân muskêkê'weyinew. Nêyanân âpachitayahk kisêyiniw nistum kâ takosihk muskêkê. Ni kiskisin ni tosisinan wâpâhtihikoyahk mêhko nêpise wayukesk mêna kê pakahtat âya kichi kâ mooskipayek wekwakun, êkospê mwestas, niyânan sekinamayahk kowi ânta mêtos. Ni kiskisin mâmâ'kwah'tâman âna kistikew ânima kâ sêkatamak Nêhiyakân muskêkê, êskopê âstayahk kâ munsâhkik mêna pâhpakosiwin. K'âstikê ênikâhata ochi mêpitah'pinewin, ochi misit wêsukeyih'tumowin. Kê wâpimâyahk ni papanân misiwekusikun wayukesk kespin mâkêkwîy êstimaw âyaht, âhpo misiwêkusikun pâhkwêsikunimin tâ osêtaht pêhkatew'wâpoy.

Our mother grew a big garden and we picked lots of berries and canned a lot and we stored vegetables in the cellar — enough to last till the following year. Our dad was a hunter and trapper, so we grew up on wild meat — deer meat in particular, along with partridge, prairie chicken and duck. I watched our parents making dry meat, and skin and stretch hides. I remember having the living room filled with stretchers of drying muskrat, lynx and beaver hides. Or seeing our dad come home from hunting with a deer thrown over the horse in front of him. He had a real good horse, as most won't tolerate having a dead animal so near. I also remember watching them skin and butcher it on the kitchen floor.

Ni mamanan kê ohpikiw êkohk kê misahk kiskitikanis mêna kê mawisoyahk mistâhi mênisa mêna kaskapiskahikinana mistâhi mêna ustachikowin kichi kistikanisa dans li cave – ikosi iskô otahk kâkê uskewik. Ni papanân kê machew êniw mêna wunihikew êniw itam kê ohpikiyahk usichi pukwachiya wiyas – apsi moosis wiyâs wawês êkwa, wawês êkwa âya mêna pihew mêna âhkiskow mêna sêsêp. Ni wâpâmâwahk nêyanân kêhikowak kê osêtachik kahkewak wêyas mêna pahkonikêt mêna sêpêkipita uskêkina mêna ânta apiw-kamik sakuskinepuhew sêpahikuna ochi pastew wachusk, pisiw, âmisk uskêkina. Âhpo kê wapimiyahk ni papanân kê pêkêwêt ochi kâkê mâchêt âschi âpsi'moosis tâkoch âstew mistam nêkân weya. K'âyaht mitoni kê mêyosiyet mistâtim âya ochi mêchêt nâwach moya tâ pukitinuma'kêwin t'âyâchik kê nipêyet pisiskew kisiwak âhpo kê wapama'yakihk wêyâwâw pâhkonikêchik mêna mamunisum ânta pinawaso'kamik mochituk.

All summer we were barefoot or in moccasins – they would outline our feet on the paper and someone – I don't remember who

- would make them for us. I also remember [my brother] Ernest and I picking chokecherries, then smashing them on a flat rock with a small rock and having them with cream, no sugar, and [it was] so good. Life back then was great. We worked at helping our folks. We picked rocks and roots using a stone boat pulled by a team of horses. We cut wood, carried water used for the washing and sterilizing the [cream] separator parts, weeding the garden, and all other chores without too many complaints.

Kâhkiyâw kâ nêpik nêyanân sâsâkeh'tiyahk âhpo pâhpekin'weskisina – wêyâwâw kê musinpêhêwin misita sur li papier mêna âwiyuk – ni moya wânkiskisin âwêna – kê ositachik kichi nêyanân. Âhpo Ernest mêna nêyâ kê mâwâsoyahk takwahiminana, êkospê kê sikohtitawiyahk ânta nạpukaw âsine âya âschi âpisasik âsinêsis mêna âyâyâhk âschi munahikun tâkoch – makêkwîy sukaw mêna mitoni kê mêyosik. Pitmatsowin êkospê mitoni kêchi mêyosik. Nêyanân âtoskêyâhk kê wêchihî'yahkihk nêyanân âyisêniwahk. Nêyanân mosakinamahk âsineyahk mêna ochehpika kê pachitayahk oosi âsineyahk kichi ochipitak ochi neswapihsowak mistatmok. Nêyanân kê munsumahk mêhta, k'itahkonamahk nipi tâ âpâchêtachik ochi kisêpêkin'kewina mêna kunachita'yahk piskech pahkina puskopichi'kêyahk kistikanis mêna kâhkiyâw kotuk nêpa âtoskewina êka mistâhi misihkimowina.

Bertha Clark-Jones (as told by Gail Gallupe): I know a lot of women like my mom who could have absolutely —with very little staples within their cupboard — come up with this huge, fantastic meal to feed their families. We never went for food. We didn't have money and would have been considered borderline poor, but we always had a roof over our head.

Ni kiskêmawâhk mêchet iskwiwâhk tâskoch ni mama kuskapis'kiyikun mitoni... usichi mitoni âpsis pukoh mêchowina oyâkuni'kamik, mâka kê osêtachik oma mistâhi mêyo mêchowin t'âsumâchik wêyawâw li familles. Nâmoya wêhkâch n'itohtenân âsichi mêchowin. Nâmoya âyâyâhk sooniyâw mêna teyitamok tipaskêwin kitimaskisiwâhk, mâka kâkikê âyâyâhk waskihikan.

I grew up with the wild meat. Moose meat — no deer. There weren't a lot of deer up in Hawk Hills anyway, but moose meat was substantial. It could feed us and help others for quite a while.

Ni kê ohpikêyân âschi pukwachi wiyâs. Mooswa wiyâs - ma kêkwîy âpsi'moosis. Nâmoya mistâhi âpsi'moosisâk ântê Hawk Hills pukoweyisi, mâkâ mooswa wiyâs kê mistâhew. Êko âsumkâwiyâhk mêna wêchihâchik kohtuka âschi kinosês.

Mary SkyBlue Morin: When I was eleven and twelve years old, I was with my mom. We would go picking blueberries at Rabbit Lake and other places where we heard there was a lot of berries. A friend with a truck would drop us off and pick us up in a couple weeks. We lived in a tent for the summer putting cardboard on the ground for our floor. During the day, we rolled up our bedding which became our chairs. My job was to look after the camp while my mom and her husband would pick blueberries. My other job was to sell blueberries to people travelling on the road. I made a sign, "For Sale, blueberries 50 cents a pound" and staked it by the road side. When I would hear a car honk, I would run to the road to ask how many blueberries they wanted. The berries were in 10-pound boxes. What we did not sell at our camp, we sold at the grocery store in town.

Nêya oma piyakosâp mêna nêsosâp kê si piponyân, ni k'ayan usichi ni mama. Nêyanân k'itohtêyâhk tâ mâwisoyahk sêpêhkwâw eyênimina ânte Rabbit Lake mêna kohtuk uskêkânsa tânite kâ pêhtâmâhk êkotê âyâkik mêchêt eyênimina. Âna ni tohteminân usichi âwâ'tâswâkun kê nâkâtikoyâhk mêna kâwi tâ pê nâtikâwiyahk ispê nêso âyâmihew'kêsikaw. Nêyanân kê wêkiyâhk ânta la tente âyâ kichi kâ nêpin êti âstâyahk li boites carton ânta uskê tâskoch li plancher. Kâ kêsikâhk, nêyanân têhti'pinamâhk âhkopâh kâ pê tustêk ikonânhi li chaises. Nêya âtoskêwin tâ kunâwêhtâmân kâpêsi'win mêkwâch ni mama mêna o'nâpêma kâ mâwisochik sêpêhkwâw eyênimina. Nêya kohtuk âtoskêwin ânima t'âtawâkêyân ânihi sêpêhkwâw eyênimina ochi âyinêwak kâ pimpayêchik ântâ mêskânâhk. Ni k'osêtân ânima musinahikunis, "For Sale blueberries 50 cents a pound"

Mary Lapis Morin, Josephine Morin, and Mary SkyBlue Morin 1964
Photo: Mary SkyBlue Morin

mêna ni chêsta'hikên chêki ânima mêskânâw. Kâ pêhtâmân ânima tâpânâs otêpwê'win, ni pimpâhtân ântê mêskânâw tâ kwêchimakik tânimakoh sêpêhkwâw eyênimina ê ni tâwêhtâkik. Ânihi eyênimina âstêki pêchîyi mitahtaht kosikwun li boites. Kêkwîy êka âtawâkêyahk ânta kâpêsi'win, ni k'âtawâkêyâhk ânta mêchiwin âtawi'kumik ântê otênâw.

I would pick hazelnuts that I found around the camp. They were very tasty. One day, I came upon a big cat with pointed ears sitting in the branch of a tree. When I told my mom, her husband taught me how to shoot the rifle as the lynx was around our camp for food. When we were done working for the day, my mom would give me one of the cardboards and I would go sliding on the gravel mound that was nearby. I am happy with this memory when I see a gravel mound. My mother's husband also taught me how to snare rabbits when we were out at Rabbit Lake. When berry picking was done for the summer, we would come back to town in time for me to start school.

Nêya kê mosâkin'amân pakânak kâ miskâwakik wâsâ'kâmê kâpesi'win. Mitoni mêyo wêhkasina. Pêyak kêsikâw, ni nakiskawâw mitoni ê misikitit pisiw usichi chêpwâw mihtâwa'kiya ê chêpatapit ânta mêtos wutih'kwun. Tânispê kâ wêhtâmowak ni mama, o'nâpêma ni kiskino'humowit tânisi tâ pâskisâmân pâskisikun âyis âna pisiw kê âyât wâsâ'kâmê kâpêsi'win mêchiwin kichi. Kâ pooni âtoskêyâhk ânima kâ kêsikâk, ni mama ni kê mêyik pêyak ânima la boite carton mêna nêya ni to sôsko'chik'yân ânte yepe'yâmatin âsinêsahk ochi ânima kisiwâk. Ni mêyowe'yihtaman êkwa'nima mamitone'yichikun mânâ kâ wâpahtâmân ânima yepe'yâmatin âsinêsahk ochi. Ni mama o'nâpêma mêna kê kiskino'humâkiyit tânisi tâ tâpukwiyan wâpoos tânispê kâ âyâyâhk ânte Rabbit Lake. Kâ pooni mâwisoyahk ochi kâ nêpin, nêyanân kâwi ni kêwinân ântê otênâhk âyâ kichi nêya tâ mâchêtâyân kiskino'humâkêwin.

When my mother left Meadow Lake, I would stay with n'ohkom Marie-Ann and moshom Little Joe. I remember one winter, n'ohkom Marie-Ann's daughter's husband killed a moose hunting with his brothers. Since there was no fridge, we had to keep the moose meat on top of the house to keep it frozen and away from dogs. I love the good taste of fried moose meat.

Ispê ni mama kâ sepwetet ânte ochi Meadow Lake, nêya kê âyân usichi n'ohkom Marie-Ann mêna ni moshom Little Joe. Ni kiskisin pêyak pipon, n'ohkom Marie-Ann ânihi o'tânisa o'nâpêma kê nipahat ânâ mooswa kâkê mâchêt usichi wêya o'stesa. ⊠yis mâkêkwîy tâhkus'chikun, nêyanân puko tâ kunâwêhi'tâmâhk mooswa wiyâs tâhkoch ânima wâskihikun tâ miskâw'âhkâtin mêna âwâs ochi âtimok. Mitoni ni kê mêyohten ânima mêyo wêhkâsin ê nâwachehk'pimehk mooswa wiyâs.

Moshom Little Joe would take me to the garbage grounds to look for fruit thrown out by the grocery store and pastry and bread thrown out by the bakery. I always wore boots not to step on anything that could hurt my feet. The oranges were always good to bring home because we could slice off the section that was over-ripe. The bakery items were mostly bread and we just cut off the mould.

Ni moshom Little Joe mâna kê tohtâhit ânte iskwa'chikuna kâ sêki'wêpi'nakahk to nitonâmâhk mênisa kâ wayâweypin'âhkik âniki mêchiwin âtâwi'kumik mêna nupâtêku'sikêwin mêna pâhkwê'sikun kâ wayâweypin'âhkik âniki pâhkwê'sikun'ehkwêwâk. Ni tâhki potskên mistiko'wuskisina êka tâ tâkoskêyan ânima kêkwîy tâ wêsuskisina ni nisita. Âniki osawâsa mâna tâhki mêyosin tâ pê kêwê'tâhâyâkik âyis nêyanân kâkê munsâmâhk ânima kâ utsow'sâsîy. Ânihi kêkwîy ochi ânima pâhkwê'sikun'ehkwêwâhk ânihi nawâch pâhkwê'sikunâk mêna nêyanân ni munsênân ânima âkwâ'kohtin.

Dianne Ludwig: She (Dianne's mother) used to come, and she'd always bring me dried meat and muskrats. She'd bring us fish, she'd bring us dry fish and yeah, she'd really bring us a lot of good stuff. She used to bring us duck soup. The first time she put porridge in it and the kids looked at me and Sylvia looked at me and said, "Mom, are we having breakfast with our supper tonight?" Cause she put porridge in the duck soup! And then the muskrat... that was another thing, because when she cooked them, she cooked them with their backs down and it looked like the muskrat was lying like this... and with the teeth sticking out, you know how muskrats are? Their teeth stick out like this and the kids would say, "I'm not eating that."

Wêya (Dianne ômamawa) kê pêtohtew, mêna wêya kê pêmêyit pastew'kâhkêwâk mêna wâchuska. Wêya kê pêmêyikoyâhk kinosew, wêya kê pêmêyikoyâhk pâstew kinosew mêna yeah, wêya kê pêmêyikoyâhk mêchêt kâ mêyosiki kêkwîy. Wêya kê pêmêyikoyâhk sêsêp mêchima'poy. Ânima nistum wêya k'âstat kêkisipa'mêchiwin pêchîyi êkota mêna âwâsisâk ni kê tâpimkok mêna Sylvia kê kitâpimât mêna êtwew, "Mom, âyahak chê kêkisipâ'mêchiwin usichi kêyanâw otâkwun'mêchisowin ânoch'tipiskaki?" Âyis wêya k'âstaht kêkisipâ'mêchiwin ânta sêsêp mêchim'apoy! Mêna êkospe âna wachusk… êkwa ânima kohtuk kêkwîy, âyis tânispe kê opinâwâsot ikonânhi, wêya opinâwâsot ikonânhi usichi misokuna down mêna êsinâkwâhk tâpiskoch âna wâchusk kê pimisihk tâskoch oma… mêna usichi ânihi wêpita chêpatâstiki, kiskihiyitên tânisi k'âyâchik wâchusk ânki? Wêpitâyik chêpatâstiki tâpiskoch oma mêna âniki âwâsisâk kê itwêwak, "Nêya nâmoya ni wi mêchin ânima."

It's actually really good.

Êkwa ânima tâpwe êwuko mitoni mêyosin.

Pastimes/Games

Doreen Bergum: We had enough siblings to have our own softball team, as children we didn't have the luxury of electricity or running water, so we played cards, ball, aunty-I-over, tag, fox & goose, broom ball, swam in the Red Deer River and tobogganed down the Snake Hill. We played ball with Métis cousins and other Métis families in the Sundre area.

Nêyanân kê âyâyâhk êkwaykohk nisêmisak kichi pakahtowân mêchêtusowâk, mêkwach kâ âwâsisiyâk nâmoya âyâyâk wâskotêpayichikun âhpo kâ pimpayêk nipê, kê mêtawiyâk tênikunnak, pakahtowân, aunty-I-over, tag, fox & goose, broom ball, kê pâkâsimoyak ânta Red Deer River mêna nupukitapân êti posiyâk nêhtuchi Snake Hill. Nêyanân kê mêtâwêyâk pâkâhtowân âsichi li Métis wâhkomâknâk mêna kotuk li Métis familles ântâ Sundre uskês.

Poitras Family New Years Day
Photo: Poitras Family

Doreen Poitras: I grew up loving books and reading. I'm assuming it's because we didn't have access to books or a library, or a TV, and listening to the radio was rare as it ran off a battery.

Nêyâ kê ohpikiyan kê sâkihitâmân mâsinahikâna mêna âyimechikeyân. Nêyâ kê itihtaman êkwa ânima ochi âyis nêyanân makekwîy âyayahk musinahikuna âhpo musinahikun'kamik, âhpo kosapachikun, mêna kê nitohtamahk ânima pêhtumowâkân tâna kê nâmoya mwasi âyis kê pimpayêk ochi a battery.

Working on the farm. Sitting (R) Joseph Jobin (Beatrice's father), Back (L) Ambroise Jobin. Other men not identified.

Photo: Beatrice Demetrius

Chapter 3

Dark Times

February 29, 1880
Saskatchewan Herald

Mission Orphanages
Letter from Bishop Grandin
of St. Albert

I beg your permission gentlemen to the preservation and civilization of the poor Indians. That one hundred Indian, and halfbreed children be brought to the mission, when they leave, they will no longer be Indians, being able to become good citizens, earn their own living, and be useful to their country.

Should anyone doubt this, come to our orphanage at St. Albert, Lac la Biche, or Isle-a-la-Crosse, and he will see young men of Indian blood by birth, now quite civilized, and pretty good workmen. If instead of the one hundred orphans, I could receive a thousand. You will certainly confess, gentlemen, that it would be a great step towards civilization. I ask gentlemen that you sign the document I have handed to Rev. Father Le Duc Vital, St. Albert.

APPROVED

Letter from Bishop Grandin re: Residential Schools
Source: Métis Memories of Residential Schools, 2004

DARK TIMES

Residential Schools

> "There is no denying that the harm done to the children, their parents, and the Métis community was substantial. It is an ongoing shame that this damage has not been addressed and rectified."
>
> — *Canada's Residential Schools: The Métis Experience (2015). UK. The Final Report of the Truth and Reconciliation Commission of Canada, Volume 3*

Angie Crerar: (Note: this story comes from *"Métis Memories of Residential Schools"* published by the MNA in 2004.)

On January 15, 1948, that all came to an end. My mother had TB (tuberculosis) and she was on her death bed. So, the priest took us to the convent at Fort Resolution. I was nine, my youngest sister was six and the other one was three. We walked into that room on that cold day. We walked right into grey sheets hanging in the hall and the smell of fish. We went upstairs where all the girls were and we were introduced to about 115 children — girls at that time. That first week — my mother died two days after we got there — we only heard about it a week later. A man took us into a room and told us, "You are now orphans. Your mother is dead." I remember holding my sisters. I remember crying. I remember feeling so alone and so lost and so very lonely. Before we had left Yellowknife and my mother, we went to visit her and she told me at that time, "Angie, look after your family." I have done that till today.

January 15,1948, êkwa ânima kahkiyaw ispayen iskwa'yanihk. Ma mere k'âyâyât TB (tuberculosis) mêna wêya kekach pooni pima-chi'hot nipewin. Ikosi, âyamihew'eniw kê itohtahikoyahk ânta âyamihew'eniw iskewe'enahk ântê Fort Resolution. Nêyâ oma keka'mitahtaht, osemi'maw nisem wêya niko'twasik mêna ânâ kotuk kê nisto. Nêyanân kê pimohteyahk pechîyi ânima piski'kipa'hikum êkwa'nima tahkayaw kêsikâw. Nêyanân kê pimohteyahk sooskwach pechiyi wepi'nakwa âyukusk'ekina âkoteki pehtikwêwin'kamik mêna wehki'makwahk tâskoch kinosew. Nêyanân n'itohtênan ispimihk tantê kaykiyaw iskwesisak âyâchik mêna nêyanân kê nakayas'kumohta'hewiyak ovhi nanto 115 âwâsisâk – iskwesisak êkospê. Ânima nêkân pêyak âyamihew kêsikâw – ma mere nipiw nêso kêsikâw mwestus kâ tukohteyahk êkotê – nêyanân puko epihtamahk nânto pêyak âyamihew kêsikâw mwestus. Ânâ nâpew tohtahikoyahk pechiyi piski'kipa'hikum mêna whetamkoyahk "Keyawaw êkwa kewata'wasisak. Ki mere kê nipo." Ni kiskisin michi'minakik nisemak. Ni kiskisin êmatoyan. Ni kiskisin moosi'tayan êkohk epêyakoyan mêna êwansiniyan mêna mitoni pekis'kataman. P.amwayes kâ sepweteyahk Yellowknife mêna ma mere, nêyanân kê itohteyahk tâ kewikeyahk wêya mêna wêya ê-wehtâmowit êkospê: "Angie, kunawe'mok keya famille." Ni kê tohten êkwa'nima iskohk anoch.

It was brutal, it was humiliating. I don't have the words to express how I really feel about those years that I and my sisters spent behind those convent doors. It was surrounded by a fence and we were not allowed outside of it except Christmas and Easter when we all paraded to church. It was not easy when you are Métis and you are surrounded by First Nations. We were ridiculed, we were punished for things we didn't do. We were accused and the nuns themselves didn't believe or didn't listen or didn't hear a word we said. We were called — I was called savage — I didn't have a name I had a number — my number was six. The only time I was called by my name was when I got in trouble which I am sorry to say was quite often because I always stood up for myself and for the other girls.

Ékwa ânima mitoni âyiman, êkwa'nima ê nêpewi'hiht. Nâmoya n'itayan pêkiskwewina tâ nêhtawêyan tânisi êsi moositayan nânto ikonanhi uskêwina ânima nêya mêna nisemak âyâyak otachk'ochi êkonanhi âyamihew'êniw iskêwe'enahk li portes. Êwuko wâsâkâskâmik âschi mênikun mêna nêyanân nâmoya puki'tinam'awiyahk wâyâweyâmihk êkwa'nima âya puko Christmas mêna Easter tânispê

Angie Crerar (in front) at Fort Resolution Residential School
Source: Métis Memories of Residential Schools, 2004

nêyanân kâhkiyâw kâ mamawêti'chik êkote yisi âyamihew'kamik. Êkwa'nima nâmoya weh'tasin tanispê kêya li Métis mêna kêya wâsâkâskâm'kâwiyin ochi First Nations. Nêyanân kê nêpewi'hiht, nêyanân nochihâwiyak kichi kêkway êka k'itohtâmahk. Nêyanân âtame'yimawahk mêna âyimihaw'iskwêwak wêstawâw nâmoya ê tâpwemchik âhpo nâmoya n'itohtakik âhpo nâmoya pêhtam pêkiskwewin kâ itweyahk. Nêyanân kê sêhkatikâwiyahk – nêya kê sêhkatikâwiyan savage – Nâmoya wêhowin âyâyân, nêya âyâyân âkêhtâsowin – n'akêhtâsoyan ânima nikotosik. Ikospê puko kâ sêhkatikâwiyân ni wêhowin kê âyimpa'yiwin tânima ni mêhtâtên t'itwêyân mêchêtwâw êkwa'nima âyis nêyâ kâkikê stood up for myself mêna kichi âniki kotuk iskwêsisak.

Food, I could tell you the menu for the ten years that I lived there. For breakfast you had porridge and beans and cod liver oil. For dinner you had soup and buffalo meat. For supper you had hung fish. This only varied at Easter and Christmas when you got cornflakes and you got turkey. We all looked forward to those two days because they were so special to us. I hate rice pudding until today because that's the dessert we had. Rice pudding or bread pudding.

Mêchiwin, nêya kâkê wêhtâmâtin mêchiwina kâ kêsi'sumihk ochi ânki mitatâht uskêwina ânima nêya kâ wêkiyân êkotê. Ochi kêkisêpâ mêchisiwin kêya k'âyâyin kêkisêpâ mêchiwin mêna pêsweminak mêna cod liver oil. Ochi âpehtâ'kêsikâw mêchisiwin kêya k'âyâyin mêchimâpoy mêna paskwâw'mostos wiyâs. Ochi otak'wun mêchisiwin kêya k'âyâyin kê âko'tâw kinosew. Ooma puko mêsko'chipayew chêki Easter mêna Christmas tânta kêya ê kê mêyâwyin cornflakes mêna kêya ê kê mêyâwyin misihew. Kâhkeyâw nêyanân pukoseyimoyâhk êkonânhi nêso kêsikâw âyis mitoni êkonânhi mitoni kâchina nêyanân kichi. Ni pukwâtên wâpa'yoominâk kuskimo'têhkusikun iskô ânoch âyis êkwâ'nima wêhkikusina mêchiwin kâke âyâyâhk. Wâpa'yoominak kuskimo'têhkusikun âhpo pâhkwesikun kuskimo'têhkusikun.

And the way they dressed — we were not allowed to wear our own clothes, although my dad paid for us to be there. We were not attached to government in any shape or form though we were treated worse than the others.

Mêna kêkwîy kâ kiskiskamâhkik – nêyanân nâmoya pukitinkâwiyâhk tâ kiskiskamâhk nêyanân n'âyiwinisa, kêyâm âta mon père kê tipahâhk nêyanân kichi êkotâ t'âyâyâhk, nâmoya nêyanân government – nêyanân nâmoya ânis'kohpitamâhk ochi government in any shape or form âta nêyanân kitimahêkawiyak âyiwak ispêch kotukik.

As far as I can remember, the nuns and the priests and the Brothers, they were all hypocrites. One minute they'd tell us: "We come here to answer the call of Jesus. We were sent up here to educate you savages with the love of God," and then they treated us worse than dogs. I have witnessed many, many brutal things that happened to other girls and boys in those ten years. Some were beaten so badly that they couldn't walk. One lost an arm and some of them ended with humpbacks because of the brutal beating they got from a ruler with an edge. I myself had my hands cut and my sister was punished so severely one time that I got in a fight with the nuns. I had a whole world against me, and the other girls got involved — that was the first riot. I have nothing good to say about the nuns.

Tapiskoch usichi ni kiskisitotân, li soeurs mêna âyimihew'êniwak mêna ânki Brothers, wêyawâw kâhkêyâw ânki nanaspâch itotutakik. Pêyak tipahikunis wêyâwâw kê wêhtamkawiyahk: "Nêyanân kê p'itohtêyahk tâ nuskewese'tumowin têpwasêwin ochi Jesus. Nêyanân kê pê sipwê'tisaha'kawiyahk otê tâ kiskinohum'kawiyêk kêyawaw savages âsichi sakihitown ochi Manito," mêna kitimahêkawiyak âyiwak ispêch atimok. Ni wahpatên mêchêt, mêchêt mitoni âyimahk kêkwîy kâkê ispayikihk ochi kotuk iskwesisak mêna napêsisak êkospê ânima mitahtaht uskêwina. Atêht êkoh kê mayi wêsukata'whewchik ânima ni moya kê pimohtêwahk. Pêyak wanêhtaw ospiton mêna atêht ended with maskaw'ikuna âyis ochi wesukata'whewina kâ mekosichik âschi tipahikunis kasaw chekes'kwayi. Ney âni chechiya kê mansakik mêna nisemis mitoni ê nochihachik mistâhi pêyakwaw ânima ni notinkan âschi âyamihew iskwêwak . N'itayan misiwe uskê usichiyi nêyâ, mêna âniki kotuk iskwesisak involved – êkwan'ima nêkân keskwe'yahkumi'kisiw. Nâmoya ni kê itwan ochi ikonanki âyamihew iskwêwak.

I have nothing; no good memories except the memories that we made among us girls. We formed an alliance, we formed a friendship, we formed a strengthening. I don't know what we could call that now. I am trying to think what we called it: "You are my strength, you are my friend, you are my trust." We tried to look after the little ones and tried to avoid some of the beatings that were not necessary. There was no such thing as respect but we taught ourselves to have respect.

N'itâyân mâkekwiy, mâkekwiy mêyo kiskisiwina âhapoko ânihi kiskisiwina kâkê osetâyahk mâmâwi'ayak nêyanân iskwesisak. Nêyanân osetâyahk ânima wechita'towin, nêyanân osetâyahk ânima mitotem'owin, nêyanân osetâyahk ânima sokisiwin. Nâmoya ni kiskêhitên kêkwîy tâ sêkatamahk êkwa'nima. Ê kakwe kiskisiyân kêkwîy ê sêkatamahk ânima: "Kêya oma ni sokisiwin, kêya oma nitotêm, kêya oma ni uspeyi'mew." Nêyanân kê kochêhtayahk tâ kanawêmiyahkik âniki apisêsichik mêna kê kochêhtayahk tâ tapusetamahk atêht ânhi wêsukata'whawna nâmoya kâtâch. Nâmoya sooskwach kêkwîy tâskoch mêyo'totawew mâka ni kiskinohumakew'soyahk tâ âyâyâhk mêyo'totawew.

There are so many stories about that residential school. How many kids have died from beatings? How many girls were raped? How many children were born to these girls and given away? How many priests were taken out of there because they were found by another priest molesting the little boys and girls? They're all true. They're all true. I lived it. I saw it. By the grace of God it didn't happen to me. I guess I was too strong willed for them. But what I saw there will live with my memory forever because nobody, nobody has the right to treat you like you're not human. Nobody has the right to take away your identity. Nobody has the right to put pressures on you and say you are going to hell. They intimidated us and they tried everything to control us.

Nêta êkohk mêchet âchimona nântâw ânima residential school. Tânimakoh âwâsisâk kê nipichik ochi wêsukatâ'wâwna? Tânimakoh iskwesisak kê otêhtini'kewina? Tânimakoh âwâsisâk kê pê pimâtisichik oki ochi iskwesisak mêna kê mekichik? Tânimakoh âyimihew'eniwâk kê otinkechik ikota ochi âyis kê miskâwâchik ochi kotuk âyimihew'eniw mikoska'chihat ânki nâpêsisak mêna iskwesisak. Kâhkiyâw ânihi tâpwêwin. Nêyâ kê pimâtisiyân êkwa'nima. Nêyâ ni wahpaten. By the grace of God, nâmoya êkwa'nima nêyâ'espayek. Ni meskwe'yihtam nêyâ mitoni muskâwsiyan wêyâwâw kichi. Mâka kêkwîy kâ wâhpâtâmân êkota tâ pimâtâstiw ni kiskisiwin kâkikê âyis nâmoya'âwiyahk, nâmoya'âwiyahk âyaw tâ tipiyawe'wêya kitimahew'iyek tâskoch êka kêya âyisêniw. Nâmoya'âwiyahk âyâw tâ tipiyawe'wêya tâ mâkohawiyêk kêyawâw mêna t'itwet kêya oma are going to hell. Wêyâwâw sâseh'kimew'iyahk mêna kê koche'tâchik kâhkiyâw kêkwîy tâ tipêmikoyâhkwâw.

Many of them didn't make it. There are some very strong survivors. We still communicate and we formed a bond sixty years ago which is still working for us today. Many of us will not tell our stories. Many of us will not go in for the healing because it's not what they want. It's not what we want. We know what we want. All these healing foundations, all these workshops they are putting on, all the money being spent is spent wrong. I don't want anybody to tell me how I'm going to heal or bring me a psychiatrist or bring me a priest. Who put me there to begin with?

Mêchet âniki nâmoya kê pimâtisiwâhk. Atêht mitoni muskâwsiwak ânki kâ pimâtisichik. Kêyapich ni pêkiskwâtotâtowin mêna usitâyâhk âsotumâ'kewin niko'twâsomtânâw uskêwina uspin tâna kêyapich âtoskatamâhk nêyanân kichi ânoch. Mêchet nêyanân nâmoya t'âchimoyâhk nêyanân âchimowina. Mêchet nêyanân nâmoya t'itohteyâhk mêyo mâchihowin âyis moya êkwân'ima ê nitawêhtâkik. Nâmoya êkwâ'nima kê nitawêhtyâhk. Nêyanân kiskêtênân kêkwîy kâ nitawêhtamâhk. Kahkiyaw ohi mêyo mâchihowin wêyus'chike'wina, kahkiyaw ohi mêyo mâchihowin âtoskêwkumika k'astachik, kâhkîyâw sooniyaw kâ mêschinachik nâmoya kwayus âpachihachik. Nâmoya ni tawêmaw âwêyak tânisi nêya ooma tâ mêyo mâchihoyan âhpo tâ pêtamawit psychiatrist âhpo tâ pêtamawit âyimihew'êniw. âwêna âhit êkotê kâ mâchi payêk usichi?

Yes, I'm bitter, I admit it because I'm hurt, and I have a lot of pain. I don't usually bring stuff out, I bury it, but I know it's important, and I am doing it for the others, for the survivors of the forties, the fifties, and the sixties who walked that path and took the long journey that had no end, that had nothing, no goal at the end, there was nothing for us. There was no such thing as warmth. No hugs, no love except what we gave each other. We made ourselves survive. We gained strength from each other — in that world there was nobody, there was nobody.

Tâpwê, ni kisiwasin, ni tâpwêten êkwan'ima âyis ni wune'chikêwin, mêna ni tayân mistâhi wêsuke'yihtumowin. Nâmoya mâna ni wâyâwê'tatân kêkwîy, ni nayin'nên, mâka ni kiskihitên êkwan'ima kêchiyi'wun, mêna ê tohtâmân kichi kotuk ânika, kichi kâ pimatisochik ochi nêwomitanâw, ochi niyanomtanâw, mêna ochi nikotwasomitanâw âwêna kâ pimohtêchik ânima mêskunâs mêna k'otinâchik kinwâw pimohtêwin êka kâ poonipayêk, êkâ kêkwîy êkota, nâmâkêkwiy ispayiw wânuskoch, nâmâkêkwiy nêyanân kichi. Nâmakekwiy sooskwach kâ kunawe'yimiyahk. Nâmoya âkwus'kitinewa, nâmâkêkwiy sâkihitowin ânima puko kâ mêkoseyahk itoowak. Nêyanân kê pumihisoyahk tâ pimâtisiyahk. Nêyanân pihkotawiyahk mitotem'owin ochi kâ mekoseyahk – êkota ânima misiwe'uskê nâmâ'wiyak, êkota ânima nâmâ'wiyak.

Today I feel so hurt and angry and so much pain when I heard that the government was going to give the Catholic Church so many million dollars to help cure us. Cure us? That's a slap in the face. I really believe that if it wasn't for them my life wouldn't be what it is today. I struggled, and struggled and struggled for many years just to get back my Métis identity, to bring back my pride, to get my spirit going again and make sure my children will never have to go through what I went through. My children know my story and they have cried many times with me, and I am glad that I was able to share some of this story because it's important.

Ânoch ni moosihtân mitoni ni wunê'chikêwin mêna kisiwâsiyân mêna mistâhi wêsukê'yihtumowin tânispê kê pêhtâmân ânima the government kê wê mêyât âna Catholic Church mitoni mistâhi million dollars tâ wêchihâyâkik ênikahât nêyânân. Tâ ênikahât nêyanân? Êkwa ânima pukumêh'kweta'whew mâhkwa'kun. Ni tâpwêhtên ânima kêspin êka wêyawâw, ni pimâtisiwin nâmoya nohtê kêkwîy ânima ânoch. Ni wâwuska'wêyân, mêna wâwuska'weyân mêna wâwuska'weyân ochi mêchet uskêwina mwechi tâ kâchitinâmân kâwi li Métis istâwêyih'tâkosiwin tâ pekêwêta'tâyân kiste'yimowin, n'âchâhk tâ mâchipayitâyân kâwi mêna tâ kêchi'nâhoyân ni otawâsimsuk nâmoya wêhkâch tâ ispayik wêyâwâw tâskoch nêya kâkê ispayik. Ni tawâsimsuk kiskihtumok n'âchimon mêna wêyawâw kê mâtowâk mêchêt âsichi nêya, mêna ni mêyotên kê kuskêtâyân tâ pâhkwê'numawêyân âtêht oma âchimowin âyis êkwa'nima kêchiyiwan.

Angie Crerar (second from right) and her family
Photo: Angie Crerar

How many times, the government in its knowledge and wisdom said, "Oh, we're going to take children and we're going to give them better life, we know what's best for them." They take away — take us away from our family. Many children were just literally taken right out of their mother's arms. Many of them were born there, many of them came in there as babies and with never a touch of love, a touch of affection or the idea that somebody cares for them. So many have committed suicide. So many have lived a life of destruction. So many of them looked for happiness in the wrong places.

Tântâhtwâw tipâhikuna, the government kâke kiske'yihtâmowin mêna âyinese'win k'itwet "oh, nêyanân wi otinânâhkik âwâsisâk mêna we meyakewiyahkik nâwach kê mêyosit pimâtsiwin, nêyanân ni kiskihiyitenân kêkwîy mêyo mâchihochik." Wêyâwâw otinachik – otinatikawiyahk ochi nêyanân famille. Mêchet âwâsisâk kê mwechi otinachik ochi ômamawa mispitona. Mêchet âniki êkota kê pimatisichik, mêchet kê petakosechik kâ âwasisochik mêna moya wêkach sâkihitowin, usichi nâmoya wêkach sâkihitowin âhpo mêskweh'tamowin ânima âwiyahk kê sakihachik. Êkohk mêchet kê nipahisochik. Êkohk mêchet kê wêkichik mayi pimatisowin. Mêchet âniki kê nohtê miskakik mêyo'wechitowin ânta nâmoya kwayus places.

I cannot express in any language the horror that I lived. I cannot express or try to explain how I feel about the government, the Church and everybody who was involved. I thank God that there's no more and I realize that after they finished with residential schools, after they closed the doors they finally realized that it was not the answer. Then they created the child welfare —the welfare system that's the same thing — it's not helping.

Nâmoya ni kê wêhten mâkekwiy pekiskwewin ânima nipiy sêkisi'win kâkê pimâtisiyân. Nâmoya ni kê wêhten âhpo tâ kohchetâyân kwayus tâ wehtâmân tânisi nêyâ ê moosihtâyân nântâw the government, the church mêna kâhkiyâw'âwiyâk kâ âtoskâtâmâhk. Ni nânâskomâw Manito ânima nâmâ'kekwiy mêna ni kiskiyiten ânima mwestus uskoch kâ poonitachik usichi residential schools, mwestus kâ kipahâkik li portes wêyâwâw n'istohtâkihk kiskeyitâmok êkwa'nima nâmoya tâpwêwin. Êkospê osêtâchik ânima child welfare — ânima welfare system êkwa'nima pêyakwân — nâmoya kê wechihonân.

I don't know what the answer is for me. There's no answer for all the others. As far as my life and my memory goes, I love more now than I've ever loved before, because love is precious and if you lived the same kind of life that I did, it is the only thing you got to cling to. Thank you. That's it.

Nâmoya ni kiskihiten kêkwîy ânima nisitohtumowin nêyâ kichi. Namakêkwiy nisitohtumowin kichi anki kahkêkwiy. Iskô ni pimatisiwin mêna ni kiskisiwin êspayek, ni sâkihitowin nâwach mêchet êkwa ispêch kâkê sakihitoyan pamweyes, âyis sakihitown âyiwaki'teyihtâ'kwun mêna kêspin kê pimatisiyin pêyakwân pimatisiwin kâ k'itotâmân , êkwa'nima puko kêkwîy kêya puko tâ michiminuman. Merci. Ikosi ânima.

Lisa Wolfe: My mom grew up in the North. She lived a lot on trap lines. She literally cut it off (Métis culture) from her family for a reason. And it wasn't the same. And I didn't understand not wanting to be educated until actually, like I said, I was much older and then I thought, okay, I really need to be educated.

Ni mama kê pê opikihiht antê Kewetinohk. Wêya kê wêkit mistâhi ânta wunehikun tipahâskâna. Wêya sooskwatch ê-munisa (Métis nistum pimâchi'howin) ochi wêya la famille ochi iteyih'tum. Mêna moya êkwa ânima pêyakwân. Mêna nâmoya ni sitohten êkaw nohtê kiskino'hamasot iskô tâpwe ânima, tâskoch kâ itweyan, nêyâ nâwach êti ohpikeyan mêna ni tehten, okay, mitoni ni tawehten tâ ni to kiskino'humakâweyân.

So I took courses at the University of Alberta, but it was through talking with my mom — and in some ways not talking with my mom, because she would not talk about her past. And even to this day, she is very difficult to try to get information from about, you know, what was it like growing up, up North.

Ikosi, ni otenen kiskino'humakâwena ânta University of Alberta, mâka êkwa ânima âskâw êka pêkiskwatahk ni mama… mêna âteht nantâwesi êka pêkiskwatak ni mama, âyis wêya nâmoya wi pêkiskwatahk mêyas kumo'payiw. Mêna âhpo ânoch kêsikâw, wêya âyimsoo tâ kâkwe kâchitinâma âchimos'tâtowin ochi nântâw, kisketen, kêkwîy êspayek kâ pê pimâtisot ântê Kewitinohk.

And other than the fact that she loved her parents a lot, and her parents loved her, she didn't want to talk about it. And you know, until this whole thing with the reconciliation and restoration and everything that I actually even find out that she was actually part of a residential school system up North.

Mêna âhpo êtikwe tâpwêwin ânima wêya ê-sahketaht nêkê'hikowa mistâhi, mêna wêya nêkê'hikowa ê-sakihikot, wêya nâmoya ê-nohtê pêkiskwatahk ânima. Mêna kêya kiskiyitên, iskô oma kahkiyaw kêkwîy usichi reconciliation mêna restoration mêna kâhkiyâw kêkwîy ânima kawi pekiskwati'towak mêna kiwe meka'win mêna kâhkiyâw kêkwîy tâpwe êwuko êti kiskitamahk wêya kê pumihewikot ânima residential school system ântê kêwitinohk.

I didn't even know because she did not talk about it. And my aunts did not talk about it. Nobody talked about it. None of us knew that our moms were in residential schools. None of it, it was just totally cut off.

Nâmoya âhpo ni kisketên âyis wêya nâmoya kê pêkiskwatahk êkwa ânima. Mêna nitosisahk nâmoya kê pêkiskwatakik êkwa ânima. Nâmoya âwêyiyahk nêyanân kê-kiskitamahk ânima ni mamawak kê pumihewikochik ânima wêkêwin kiskino'humakêwina. Ma kêkwîy, êkwa ânima sookwach kê munisamok.

So it's kind of sad. Because you don't get that understanding. You don't know why your mom was so harsh with certain things and totally lacksey-daisy about some things. I didn't understand both extremes intellectually until about 10 or 15 years ago.

Ikosi, êkwa ânima pekiskatikwam. Ayis, êka instotamin. Nâmoya kê kiskêtamin tânihkê ki mama mitoni sohkipumenekit âchi kachina kêkwîya mêna kêyam êtehitaht nântâw kohtuk kêkwîya. Ni moya kê nistotaman neswâyi mamwayesa kâ mamitoni'taman iskô mitataht âhpo mitatht niyânan uskêya uspin.

Pearl Calahasen: My mother was apprehended early. She was kicking away from her parents to not go to residential school, and she did go, she and her family did go. And she was one of those individuals, a very strong woman, a very strong female.

Ni mama kê âstâsiwit oskâ'wâsis. Wêya tâhkis'kâchikew ochi nêkêhi'kowak êka tâ itohtêt residential school mêna kê itohtew, wêya mêna sa famille itohtêwak. Mêna wêya êkwatowahk âwiyâk, mitoni muskâwi'sew iskwew, mitoni muskâwi'sew iskwew.

Even though she was young, she would fight for the kids that were being beaten, or being taken away, or having to sleep in their own pee and things of that nature. And what she would do is she would fight, and she'd go to the priest and give them heck and she'd do whatever she had to do. And then because her parents were.... I don't know what it was, but there was something about her or her father and they might have been afraid of him. I'm not exactly sure.

Kêyam kêspin wêya oskâ'wâsis, wêya kê notinkew kichi âwâsisâk kâ wêsukata'whâw, âhpo kâ sipweh'tatâkik, âhpo kâ nipâchik ânta wêya sikiwin mêna kêkwîy êkwatowahk. Mêna kêkwîy kâ itohta kê notinkêt, mêna êtohtêt ânki âyamihew'êniw mêna êkêkamat mêna wêya kê itohtak puko kêkwîy. Mêna âyis ochi nêkê'hikowak... Nâmoya ni kiskeyihtên kêkwîy ânima, mâka kêkwîy nântâw wêya âhpo o-papawa mêna âpwêtikwê wêyawâw kê kôstâchik ânihi. Nâmoya mitoni ni kiskêyihtên.

She never did say but they would, they would say, "You gotta, you gotta get back there Mary, go into your room," and she would fight all the time. Then one day she decided that she wasn't gonna stand it anymore. She couldn't fight for everybody.

Wêya nâmoya êtwew mâka wêyawâw, wêyawâw k'itwêwak, "Kêya puko, kêya puko kâwi êkotê tâ ithohtêyin Mary, itohtê ki piska'kipa'hikun" mêna wêya kê notinkêt kâhkêyâw kêsikâw. Êkospê pêyak kêsikâw wêya kêse'yihtum ânima nâmoya puki'tinam êkwa ânima kêya'pich. Wêya nâmoya kaskêtâw tâ notinkêt kahkiyaw'yâhk kichi.

So, what she did was she ran away... she ran away and she took off from the residential school.

Ikosi kêkwîy wêya katotâhk kê tapasêt... wêya tapasew mêna wêya kê nakatâhk ochi residential school.

They found out the next morning that she was gone, and they sent a tracker after her. She had run away to go to her grandparents, so the tracker went looking for her and he must have found her tracks because there was a light smell.

Wêyâwâw kiskêyihtamok kotuk kêkisêpa ânima wêya kê sipwêtêht, mêna wêyâwâw sipwê'tisahakik âna kunawê'yichikew. Wêya kê tapasêt t'itohtêt ohêkê'koma'wak, ikosi kunawê'yichikew natona'wew mêna wêya pakâhkum kê miskâwat kê pimoh'têwêsa âyis âstew âpsis mêyachikew.

But she had made it to her grandparents, I think, overnight or something. I don't know, and I don't know where it was. And so anyway, the tracker knew that she was on her way and probably knew that she was safe. So, he goes back and he tells the priest and everybody else that he couldn't find her.

Mâka wêya tukohtew ohêkê'koma'wâk, ni tehtên, pêyako tipiskwew, âhpo kêkwîy. Ni moya ni kiskê'yihtên, mêna ni moya ni kiskê'yihtên tantê êkwa ânima. Mêna ikosi pukwayisi, âna kunawê'yichikêw kiskê'yihtum wêya kê sipwê'tet mêna âhpo êtikwê kiskê'yihtam wêya kê puspêw. Ikosi, wêya usetsawhêt mêna kê whêtamowat ânki âyamihew'êniw mêna kâhkâwiyahk ânima ê kâkê miskawat.

I think it was years later and I didn't know why my mom didn't know how to speak, or write, or read because she didn't learn. She didn't learn how to read or write, but she knew about the cultural ways. So, what she lost on the white man's way and the non-Indigenous way, she learned about the culture.

Ni têhyihtên uskêna mwestus mêna ni moya ni kiskeyihtên tanikeh ni mama êka kâ kâskêtat tâ pêkiskwet, âhpo tâ musinahikêt, âhpo tâ âyimechikêt âyis êkâ kê kiskino'huma'kawit. Wêya moya kiskino'huma'kawit tânisi t'âyimichekêt mêna tâ mâsinahikêt, mâka wêya kê kiskeyitam ânihi nistum pimâchi'hiwina. Ikosi, kêkwîy kâ wanêhtat ânima mooniyâw pimâchi'hiwin mêna ânima non-Indigenous pimâchi'hiwin, wêya êti kiskino'humâ'win nântaw ânima nistum pimâchi'hiwin.

On the other side, she knew so many things what to do, what not to do, how to do things, how to make medicines, how to trap. So she understood all that. But I never knew why she didn't know how to read. And that's the reason why, because she ran away from the residential school.

Kotuk, wêya kiskêyihtum mêchêt kêkwîy tâ itotak, kêkwîy êka t'itotak, tânisi tâ itotak, tânisi tâ osêtat muskêkêya, tânisi tâ wunê'hikunêt.

Ikosi wêya nisi'tohtum kâhkiyâw êkwa ânima. Mâka nâmoya ni kiskêtên tânikih êka kiskêyihta tâ âyimêchikêt. Mêna ikochi ânima kâ iteyitumik tânêhki, âyis wêya kê tupasêt ochi ânima residential school.

Years later the tracker came to apologize to her. He said to her, "I have to talk to you about this," because it bothered him. He said, "I knew you were safe, but I had come to apologize because I should have helped you and I didn't. I didn't help the kids. I went and tracked the kids and brought them back, and some of them died. Some of them got beaten, some of them, you know..." and he says, "I still have this regret and I don't know how to deal with it." He said, "So I come to talk to you about what I did or what I didn't do."

Uskêwina mwestus âna kunawê'yichikew kê pêhtotew tâ mêhta'tumowit wêya. Wêya itwêt, "Puko tâ pêkiskwatotawiyan kêya oma kichi, âyis âyimihew weya. Wêya itwêt, "Ni kiskêyihtên kê puspêwin, mâka puko tâ mêhtâ'tumowin âyis tâkê wêchêhitan mêna nâmoya wêchihitan. Nâmoya ni kê wêchihiyahk âwâsisâk . Nêya kê itonakik âwâsisâk mêna kê pêsowachik kawi mêna âtiht kê nipichik. Atêht ânihi wêsukata'wewichik, âtiht âniki, kêya kiskê'yihten..."mêna wêya itwew. "Nêya kêyapich ni tayân ooma mêhtatum mêna nâmoya ni kiskê'yihtên tânisi tâ totaman êkwa ânima." Wêya itwêt, "Ikosi nêya kê pêtohtêyan tâ pêkiskwatoyan kêya nantâw kêkwîy kâkê itotâmân âhpo kêkwîy êka k' itotâmân ."

He said, "Because I was really happy that you were gone, and I wasn't about to tell anybody about you making it, because I would have probably been, you know let go or whatever." And he said, "I just need to talk to you about this."

Wêya itwew, "Âyis nêya mitoni mêyowe'yihtaman ânima kêya kê sipwêtêhyin, mêna nâmoya âwêyahk kê wêhtamowahk êkê kuskêhowyin, âyis âhpo'êtikwê, kêya kiskê'yihten ni kâ pakitinakawon âhpo kêkwîy." Mêna itwêt, "Nêya puko kê nohtê pêkiskwatotân êkwa ânima."

And my mother was really quite emotional about it because, you know, she said, "You know, my parents, probably my grandparents would probably have not let you get back if you had tried to come and get me," because they were so incensed in terms of not allowing her to go back to that system.

Mêna ni mama mitoni moose'tawit êkwa ânima ochi âyis, kêya kiskê'yihtên, wêya itwew, "Kêya kiskê'yimowahk ni nêkêhikowak, âhpo'êtikwê n'ohêkê'komawak âhpwêtikwê nâmoya kạkê paktinikwak âwi tâ pê tohtêyêk kêspin kê kâ kwê tâ pê nâseyek." Âyis mitoni wêyawâw mitoni kê sohkisêchik êka tâ pâkitinachik wêya kâwi êkote tâ yi tohtêt that system.

And so, it was — it was a bad story, but you had a good ending.

Mêna ikosi, êkwa ânima.... Mayi âchimowin, mâka kêya ê mêyo pooni'payew.

Dianne Ludwig: When we started school was when we had to move back to our community because my dad didn't want us to be taken by the government. He didn't want us to be taken and put in residential school. I think he must have been warned or something because I know that I would have loved to stay out in the trapline as long as I could. But then he said, "No we have to go take you back so you can go to school."

Tânispe kê mâchê'tayahk kiskino'humâkêwin êkospe ânima nêyanân puko t'âchipichiyâhk tâ kêwiyâhk ânte nêyanân mâmâwi'e'âyâhk âyis ni papa nâmoya ni tawêhitâhk tâ kachitinkâwiyâhk mêna t'âstakoyak ânta residential school. Ni têhiyitên âwêyak kê wêhtamâkot âhpo kêkwîy âyis ni kiskeyihtên ânima nêya kê sâkihitâmân t'âyâyân ânte wunêhikun tipahaskana iskô kenoses kâ kasketayan. Mâka êkospê wêya êtwêt, "Nâmoya, nêyanân puko tâ kewitahi keya iskô kiskino'humatowin tâ itohteyin."

And my grandma, my Kookum was a prime example of being so scared of the priests, of the RCMP and whoever was there with the government agencies. She was very scared of anybody that had any authority in our community.

Mêna n'ohkom, n'ohkom wêya kesopikiwan kiskino'wapachikiwin ochi kê sêkisit ochi âyamihewinewak, oche RCMP mêna puko âwayak ikota k'ayat âschi government agencies. Wêya mitoni kê sekisit puko âweyak kâ puminê'kaweyahk anta nêyan mamawe'ayayak.

Without a word of a lie, you know what she used to do? She used to take us if she heard a plane. She would think that it was the government agencies coming to take kids and she would hide us in the bush. She would — any place she could hide us she would because she didn't want anybody to take us.

Nâmoya kê keyaskiyan, kiskihitên kêkwîy wêya kê itohta? Wêya kê itohtahi'kêyak kêspin kê pêhtaht ânima pimihâ'kun. Wêya mâna ête-hitak ikonanhi government agencies kâ pênatachik âwâsisâk mêna wêya kê kâsot ânta sakâk. Wêya.... Puko êwayitak tâ kê kasoyak wêya ikosi itotam âyis wêya nâmoya ê ni tâ wêmat âwiyak to oti-nayahk nêyanân.

And even a squirrel chirping in a tree — she'd tell that squirrel to be quiet in Cree and she'd tell that squirrel "Quit making so much noise, you're going to tell them where we're at." Yeah... she was really, really scared. So you know even us as children coming from the trapline, we used to be scared of the RCMP. And there was a lot of people that are still like that you know, older people anyways that are scared of authority and haven't gotten over it.

Mêna âhpo ânikwâchas kukêchimot âyat ânta mêtos... wêya kê wêhtamowat âna ânikwâchas tâ keyamapit ê Nêhiyawêt mêna wêya kê wêhtamowat âna ânikwâchas, "Pooni mitoni kweskwe'win, kâ wehtamwasak tanite ê âyayak." Tâpwe... wêya mitoni kê sekisit. Ikos, kisketen âhpo nêyanân âwâsisâk kâ pehtohteyak ochi wunêhi-kun tipahaskana, nêyanân kê sekiseyahk âniki RCMP. Mêna êkota mêchet âyiseniwak keyapich ikosi âyâchik tâskoch ikosi, kisketen, kehteyak kâ sekisichik âweyak kâ puminiket mêna nâmoya ê nakat-akik êkwa'nima..

Saskatoon Police shooting range poster featuring what appears to be an Indigenous woman
Photo: Muriel Stanley Venne

Missing and Murdered Indigenous Women and Girls (MMIWG)

> "Métis women are the heart of the Métis Nation, and they were equal partners in the development and life of Métis communities. They were fully engaged in the political, social, and economic life of the Métis Nation. Métis women have always held the honoured role of traditional knowledge keepers and have been accorded respect and held in high esteem by the Métis Nation. Yet outside of their communities, Métis women were not respected, their perspectives were devalued, and their voices were silenced. Métis People are often described as "invisible" within the general population," and this invisibility is even more profound for Métis women. This is because, as victims of the consequences of colonialism and patriarchy, Métis women faced and continue to face a unique form of marginalization and discrimination; first, as Indigenous peoples; second, as Métis—the "invisible" among Aboriginal people; and third, as women. As a result, Métis women have been uniquely vulnerable to violence and lack a great number of programs and supports, such as those provided to other Aboriginal peoples. The ongoing abuse, disappearance, and murder of Indigenous women ultimately results from the stigma and dehumanization brought upon these women by colonization."
>
> *— From Métis perspectives of Missing and Murdered Indigenous Women, Girls, and LGBTQ2S+ People. Women of the Métis Nation (2019). Les Femmes Michif Otipemisiwak.*

Muriel Stanley Venne (as told by Rachelle Venne): The work that has been done, and I'm involved in around the Missing and Murdered Indigenous Women and Girls, is so significant, because I think it's opening up people's eyes and recognizing that our history and the discrimination, the systemic discrimination that has happened to Indigenous People is not right and needs to be changed. Those cases that she (Muriel) worked on recently were very big for her because she figured that, you know, other women could identify.

Ânima âtoskewin kâkê tohtakik, mêna nêya âtoskatam ânki Missing and Murdered Indigenous Women and Girls. Êkwa ânima mitoni kêchiyi'wun, âyis ni mâmitone'yihten êwuko kê ôhtênâkik âyisêniwak oskêsika mêna nistâwinam ânima nêyanân kâyâs âtayokun mêna pêwê'yimitowin, puminêkiwin pêwê'yimitowin ânima k'ispayêk êkotê wêyâwâw Indigenous âyisêniwak nâmoya kwayus mêna puko tâ mêskotastêk. Ânihi musinahikuna'ânahawuschikêwin ânima wêya (Muriel) âtoskâtak ânochêhkê mitoni misâki wêya kichi âyis wêya êti kiskêtahk ânima, kêya kiskêtên, kohtuk iskwiwak kâkê wâpamisochik.

She has very deep connections to women of all cultures and did a lot of work over the years building that up, so you can share a little bit of what we're going through currently.

Wêya âyâw mitoni mite'hê âniskoh'pichikuna ânki iskwêwak kâhkiyâw ochi nistum pimâchi'howina mêna kê tohtâm mistâhi âstokêwin otuhk kâkê uskêwika osêhtayak êkwan'ima, ikosi kêya tâ pâhkwênumân âpsis kêkwîy nêyanân kâ kiskêyih'tumoyâhk mêkwach.

I think the discrimination she faced was pretty profound. When we would apply for funding, or we would look for opportunities for women and the government official would say...well they like to keep you hungry you know?

Ni mâmitone'yihten ânima pêwêyimitowin wêya kâ kênukiskawahk kê âtamukumikohk. Ispê kâ kâkwe kâchitinâma sooniyâw, âhpo kâ nâtomâhk kâ nâhipayiki iskwêwak kichi mêna ôkimâw nêkân k'itwêt... itâm wêyawâw kê nohtê kânâwêmis'koyêk tâ nohtê'katêyêk.

In 2005 she received the Alberta Human Rights Award and took the time to read 117 names of Missing and Murdered Indigenous Women who there were no convictions for. She read out their names when she received the award — the silence was deafening.

2005, wêya otihtikow ânma Alberta Human Rights Award mêna kê otinahk tipahikun tâ âyimichikêtat 117 wêhowina ânki Missing and Murdered Indigenous Women ochi nâmoya âwêyâhk ê kâchitiniht. Wêya kê âyimichikêt owêhowina ikonânhi ikospê kâ otihtikowit ânima kêchi mâsinahikun - kipiyo'wêwin ânima mitoni kipehtâwâ'ket.

There was a guy in the crowd and he's a community member. She did ask him later, "What did you think when I read those names all those years ago?" and he said, "Muriel, I thought you were grandstanding," and he said, "I'm sorry."

Kê âyat âna pêyak nâpew ântâ mamawê'yitowin mêna wêya mamawi'ê'âyahk owêchehiwew. Wêya kwêchimew mwestes, "Kêkwîy ê têhtamin ispê kâ âyimichikêyan ânihi kâhkiyaw wêhowina kâyâs ânima? Mêna wêya itwêt, "Muriel, kê têhtâmân ooma kêya mêchet wâpâhti'hiwewiyin." mêna, wêya itwew, "Ni mêhtâtên."

Because it seems like now people are a little bit more aware. They can't say that they haven't heard about it, you know? And those things, she's seen ... at so many different times and you just kinda keep getting up and keep coming back for more.

Âyis itêyihta'kwun tâpiskoch êkwa âyisêniwahk nâwuch âpsis kêyapich êkwa nisitotamok. Nâmoya tâ kê twêwak êka kê pêhtakik nântâw ânima, kêya kiskitên? Mêna ikonanhi kêkiwiya, wêya kâkê wâhpatâhk... chêki mistâhi pêtos tipahikuna mêna kêya mwechi tâpiskoch kê pâsikoyên mêna kêyapich kê pêtohtêchik ochi âyiwak.

So, that's the perseverance that a lot of Métis women have.

Ikosi, êkwa ânima âhkumê'yihtamowin mêchet Métis iskwêwak âyachik.

Muriel Stanley Venne (from The Alberta Order of Excellence video): I really wanted people to be equal; that there wasn't a hierarchy.

Ni tâpwê'stamân âyisêniwak pa pêyakwun âyawak ispêtêyih'tâkwun. Ânima êka âwêyak tâ nekânêt.

That was the right to be who you were and are, and that women needed to be respected.

Ânima mêyo tohtâmowin kichi kêya kâkê âyawak, mêna ânima iskwêwak puko tâ mêyo itohtâwêwak.

I got a call from the Friendship center and the person said to me, "We've got to support this woman."

N'otihtikowân sêwêpitamatowin ochi Friendship Centre mêna êkwa âna âyisêniw kê wêhtâmowit, "Nêyanân puko tâ wêchihiyâhk âwa iskwew."

When I phoned to see which courtroom, her case was being heard. The person on the line said, "And who do you represent?"

Ispê kâ sêwêpitaman tanima ôyusi wêwi'kamik, wêya musinahikuna'ânahawuschikêwin kê wê pêhtakik. Âyisêniw kâ sêwêpitamahk êtwew. "Mêna, âwina kêya ê-pêkiskwêyin kichi?"

And I said, "The Institute for the Advancement of Aboriginal Women. And it didn't exist at the time but that was the birth of the IAAW."

Mêna nêya n'itawan, "Ânima Institute for the Advancement of Aboriginal Women. Mêna nâmoya êhtaw ikospê mâka êkwa ânima kâ mâchi payêk ânima IAAW."

Our focus has been directed to what the courts do. Our first case that we were ever able to be involved in was the killing of Connie and Ty Jacobs. An RCMP officer shot them both. This wasn't an accident, this wasn't one time, just a mistake. It was a deliberate attempt to annihilate the Indigenous People of Saskatchewan. Somehow, we need to believe with all compassion and passion that we don't want our girls murdered and that something has to happen in our society to make it wrong.

Nêyanân kâ isi wâpâhtamik êkotê'yisi kêkwîy oyusi'wêwi'kamika kê itohtakik. Nêyanân nistum musinahikunâ'ânahawuschikêwin kâkê âtoskâtamâhk ânima nipâhâchik Connie mêna Ty Jacobs. Âna RCMP okimaw kâ paskisot ikoni nêso. Nâmoya oma pischi, nâmoya pêyakwâw puko, nâmoya mwechi chêsi'howin. Iko ôma tâpwehtâ'kwun kakwêtotum tâ nêsowachi'hachik âniki Indigenous âyisêniwak ochi Saskatchewan. Nântâwisi, kêyanâw tâ nitâwê'yihtâmâhk tâ tâpwêhtâmâhk usichi kâhkêyâw sâkihitowin mêna moosêhtâwin ânima nâmoya nitawêhtamâhk nêyanân iskwêsisak tâ nipâhâchik mêna nântâwisi puko tâ ispayêk ânta kêyanâw mamawê'hitowin tâ osêhtâhk nâmoya kwayus.

The Esquao Awards are to honour the strength and beauty of Aboriginal women; the beauty of it is we have no jury. The communities nominate the women, and we honour them.

Esquao Awards ânlki tâ kêchi'yimitowin ânlma sokisiwin mêna kuta'wusisiwin ochi Aboriginal iskwêwak ; ânma kuta'wusisiwin ânma nâmoya âyayâhk kêsi wêyusi'wêwak. Ânlki mamawi'ê'âyâhk owêchêhiwêna kâkwê nawusonâw ânlki iskwewahk, mêna nêyanân kêchi'yimitowin wêyawâw.

Rose Yellowfeet said, "As Aboriginal women we have mountains to climb. Rest if you must, but never give up." and to this day it sends shivers through my body when I think of that.

Rose Yellowfeet êkê itwêt, "tapiskoch Aboriginal iskwêwak kêyanâw âyayâhk li montagnes tâ âmuchiwê'ahta. ⊠yiwêpi kêspin puko, mâka kâya wêkach wâhkê'poomew" mênâ iskô ânoch kêsikâw ê-sipwê'tisaha nanumas'kuchiw sapo ni nêyâw kâ mâmiton'itamân êkwâ ânima.

Mary SkyBlue Morin: In 1960 or 1961 when I was about nine or ten, as I was walking home on the east side of the Stampede grounds, I saw two white guys walking, holding up a native woman on either side of her arms. The woman was one of my aunties. I hid in the grass so they would not see me. One of the guys was pouring alcohol down my auntie's mouth. The other guy led her to some trees and bushes. My heart started pounding and I ran for the roadway. I ran all the way home to our house and ran in the door. I yelled to my mom and her husband that two guys had my auntie and they were taking her into a bush by the Stampede grounds. Mom's husband ran very fast to the bush area I told him about. My mom told me to stay in the house. My mom's husband was gone for a while. When he came back later, he asked me what I saw. I told him I saw two white guys leading my auntie into the bush pouring alcohol in her mouth. I knew he saw something that a child was not supposed to see. I never saw my auntie again. I thought of her often, felt guilty that I could not have saved my aunt. I have lived with that for sixty years of my life, since I was nine or ten years old.

1960 âhpo 1961, tânispe nêya nânto kêka'mitâtâht âhpo mitâtâht, ê kê pimohtêyân tâ kêwiyân ânta east side ânima stampede grounds, ni wâpâhmâwak nêso mooniyâwahk ê pimohtêchik. Kê pâsêtâmok, ê michimnâchik nêhiyâw iskwewa putote'iyi tehko'kuna. Âna iskwew wêya pêyak âna ma tante. Ni kasôn ânta ânihi muskoseyâhk êka tâ wâpâhmichik. Pêyak âna nâpew ê sêkina ânima alcohol pêchîyi ma tante wêya mitoon. Kotuk âna nâpew sâkâpekinew ânte mêtosa mêna sakâhk. Ni mite mitoni sokêpayin mêna ni pimpâhtân ântê mêskânâw. Ni kiwi pimpâhtân iskô ni wêkinân mêna ni pimpâhtân pêchîyi. Ni têpwâtâw ni mama mêna o'napêma âniki nêso nâpêwak kê kâchitinâchik ma tante mêna ê tohtâhâchik ântê sakâhk chêki ânihi stampede grounds. Ni mama o'napêma mitoni sooki pimpâhtâw antê kâ wehtạmowâk ânima sakâhk. Ni mama ni wehtâmowit pêchîy waskihikuni t'âyâyân. Ni mama o'napêma kê sepwêtew kinawses. Tânispê kâ pê kêwêt mweschâses, ni kwêchimimk, kêkwîy kê wâpâhtâmân. Ni wêhtâmwâw kê wâpâhmâkik âniki nêso mooniyâwâhk ê michimnâchik ma tante putote'iyi tehko'kuna mêna ê tohtâhâchik ânte sakâhk mêna pêyak âna nâpew kê sêkina ânima alcohol pêchîyi ma tante mitoon. Ni kiskêyiten kêkwîy kâ wâpâtâhk nâmoya âwâsis tâ kê wâpâhtâhk. Nâmoya ni wâpâhmâw ma tante kâwi. Nêya mâna ni mâmtonêmâw, kê môsetâyân âtâmê'yimiht êka kê wêchihuk ma tante. Ni kê pimatison usichi êkwâ'nima iskô niko'twâsom'tanâw uskêwina ochi ni pimâtisiwin, tânispe nêya nânto kêkâ'mitâtâht âhpo mitâtâht.

In February 2018, I was asked to provide Elder support for the families that were attending a Missing & Murdered Indigenous Women (MMIW) Hearings meeting in Calgary. One of our teachings when we have done wrong is to make things right individually or working together as a community. Ceremony is one of the ways we do that. So, I helped the families with sage smudge cleansing. I sang an honour song for the women and girls who were missing or murdered. I did a sweetgrass ceremony and put offerings at the Bow River next to the hotel. I was an honor to help the families of women and girls who had been murdered. My prayer is "All My Relations"....

February 2018, ê kwê pê kwêchim'kâwêyân tâ wêchihiyakik tâskoch Kêchi Kehtaya t'âtoskêyân usichi li famille âniki kâ pêhtotêchik ânima MMIW Hearings mâmâwê'apowin ântê Calgary. Pêyak ânima keyanâw kiskino'humâkewin tânispe kâ mâyi'payek kêkwîy ânima kwayus t'istâhsoyahk pa'pêyak'âwiyak âhpo tâ mâmâwi'âtoskêyahk âna mâmâwi'ê'âyâhk. tâ âpachêtayahk sumân'êhkew ânima pêyak nântâwisi kêyanâw tâ itohtâmahk. Ni wêchihâwak li familles usichi wêhkus'kâhtikwa sumân'êhkew âpachêtâyân êsi kâhnâchêchikêyân. Ni nikamon ânima Kêchi'yimi'towin Nikamowin kichi âniki iskwêwak mêna oskîyi iskwêwak kâ wânêhtâ'yâkik âhpo kâkê nipâhewichik. N'itotên mêyâkâsikun sumân'êhkew mêna ni kê âstâyân mêkiwina ântê Bow River chêki ânima kâpêsew'kamik. Êkwa'nima kêchi'yimitowin tâ wêchihakik li famille ochi iskwêwak mêna oskîyi iskwêwak kâkê nipâhewichik. Ni âymihâwêwin ânima "Kâkêyâw ni wâhkomâkunak"....

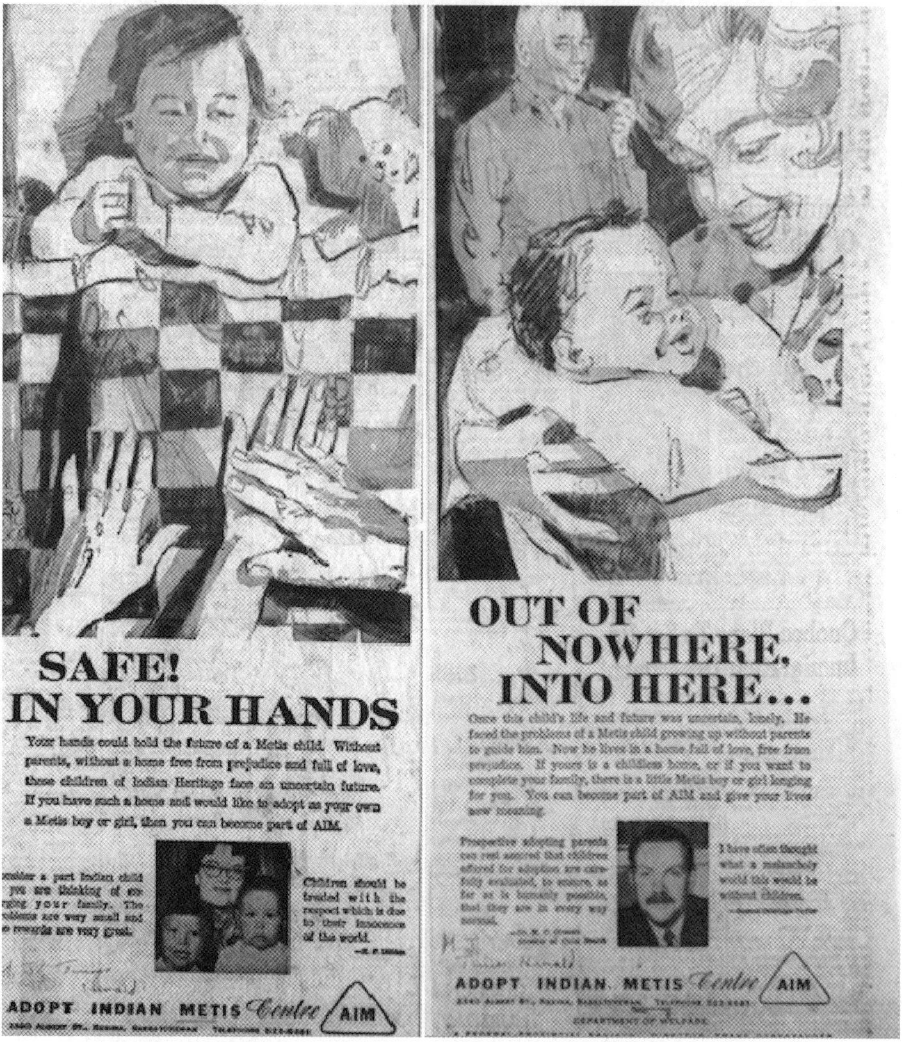

Selling the Sixties Scoop: Saskatchewan's Adopt Indian and Métis Project

Photo: Newspaper advertisements for the Adopt Indian and Métis Program, late 1960s, Saskatchewan

Sixties Scoop, Child Welfare System

Beginning in the 1960s a child welfare program was developed and implemented through the provincial governments. This program resulted in the apprehension of Indigenous children, whereby they were sent to foster homes or adopted outside of their communities. This most often led to Indigenous children ending up with middle-class white families, far away from their own family and community. While this program only officially began in the 1960s, the practice of taking Indigenous children from their homes was not a new one, as the Residential School system had been established in Canada since 1831 (the last one not closing until 1996).

As Tricia Logan writes in *A Metis Perspective on Truth and Reconciliation: Transforming the Legacy of Residential Schools,*

> The widespread practice of removing children from their Métis families and placing them in white, middle-class foster and adoptive homes was ideologically an extension of the residential school system, perpetuating the false image of the unfit Métis parent.

The practice of pulling these children not only from their family, but their community as well, resulted in many children experiencing culture shock, and the resulting psychological harm would go on to impact them years later. Many of these children completely lost contact with their family, their community, and thusly, their culture. Ultimately, they were robbed of their identity.

Approximately 20,000 children were taken from their families and placed up for adoption or moved into foster homes. The program ran until the 1980s, and while the official policy is now gone, Métis children are still highly overrepresented in the child welfare system today.

Pearl Calahasen: The apprehension policy of governments is really one of the worst possible because of what it does. It breaks down families. It breaks down the identity of children. It breaks down the strength of kids, you know, because kids have strength. I think the apprehension policy of any government is really wrong in my view. it needs to change.

Ânima âstâsew pima'tisew musinahikun ochi kêchi'okinmânâhka ânima tapwê pêyak ôchi mitoni moya mêyosik âyis ânima kâ tohtak. Êwuko pêkonam li familles. Êwuko pêkonam istawêyih'tâkosiwin ochi âwâsisk. Êwuko pêkonam muskâwsêwin ochi âwâsisâk, ki kiskêyiten, âyis âwâsis âyâchik muskâwsewin. Ni tehtên ânima âstâsew pimâ'tisew musinâhikun ochi kêchi'okimânâhk mitoni moya mêyosik kâ wâhpatamân... êwuko kwêtumawin tâ mêskotâstêk.

When I was in government, we tried to change that. We wanted the community to take over their children. We wanted them to be able to ensure that they were the ones who will determine the lives of the children.

Tânispê k'atoskâtamân ânta kêchi'okinmânâhk, nêyanân êkwakwe meskotonamâhk êkwa ânima. êyanân ni tâwehtamahk âna mamâwi'e'ayâhk t'otinâkik tâ pimpayihtachik kichi ôtawâsimsiwa. nêyanân ni tâwehtamahk weyawâw tâ kechinahochik ânima wêyawâw tâ êtwechik pimatisiwin kichi âwâsisâk .

The government is a bad, bad parent. They have never been good parents, whether it's through the whole notion of taking the kids from the parents, like my mother was taken away through the residential schools. That's really a horror.

Âna kêchi'okinmânâhk kê mayi, muchi nêkê'hikowak. Wêyawâw nâmoya wehkâch mêyosik neke'hikowak, mutwânche ikoht sapo iteyi'tomowin t'âstâsew pima'tisêwina ochi âwâsisâk ochi ni nêkê'hikowak, tâskoch ni mama kâke pê otiniht tâ sapoteht âniki residential schools êkwa ânima mitoni sooskwach nipiy'sêkisiwin.

However, the other part that we are carrying on, is this kind of institutionalization of children. That's wrong in my view, and I think we have to be able to do something, to be able to address the issue of how we deal with children.

Âtâwiya puko, kotuk kêkwîy kâ tâhkonamâhk, ânima nukayâsku'

mohikêwin âwâsisâk . Nâmoya kwayus ânima ni tehiyitên, mêna ni tehiyitên kêyanâw puko kêkwîy tâ totomahk, tâ âtoskatamâhk tânisi tâ âtoskatamâhk kichi âwâsisâk .

I think we have to help the parents. We have to help those who are struggling. We have to be able to offer them the possibilities. The intervention strategies need to be put in place in order for them to be able to take on their own children and to be able to help them as they start to bring up those kids so that our kids can feel number one, wanted.

Ni tehiyitên kêyanâw puko tâ wêchihiyâkik ni nêkê'hikowak. Kêyanâw puko tâ wêchihiyâkik ânihi kâ wâwuskâ'wêwichik. Kêyanâw puko mêkiwiyahkik kâ nâhi'payiki. Ânihi nakanumak puminê'kêwin putko tâ âstêkih âya kichi wêyawâw tâ ohtinachik wêyawâw ôtawâsimsiwa mêna tâ wêchihiyachik kâ mâchi ohpikinâwâsochik ikonânki âwâsisâk ikosi kêyanâw ôtawâsimsiwak tâ moosihtâchik ânima âkehta'sowin pêyak, tipê yêhtâk'osiw.

Number two, to feel like they belong to someone. Number three, to make sure that they have abilities to be able to challenge the world and to become the best that they can be.

Âkehta'sowin nêso, tâ moosihtâchik tâskoch tipê yêhtâk'osiw ochi âwiyahk. Âkehta'sowin nisto, to kêchi'nâhoyahk ânki wêyawâw âyâchik kuskêhtâwina tâ mâwinwe'hichik misiwe'uskê mêna tâ kuskitâchik mamwêyês êmêyosik kâkê tohtâkik.

People often wonder how come there's so much abuse. Well, because there's nothing now; destructors have broken down that family unit or of that tribal unit or of that nation unit. So, what happens now is there are no structures to be able to say you can't do that and that doesn't exist anymore.

Âyisêniwak mêchetwâw mamuskâtamok tânihki êkoh mistâhi kitimâ'hihkêwin. Ikosi, âyis mâkêkway êkwa; mis'wunâ'chê'wahk pêkonamok la famille pêyak'wâyi âhpo ânima ohtêmitowin pêyak'wâyi âhpo pêyako seht'wâwin. Ikosi, kekwîy k'ispayêk êkwa êwuko ma kêkwîy oyusi'wêwina tâ wêhtamkâwyik nâmoya êkwa kâkê tohtên mêna êkwa ânima nâmoya êhtâw.

As an example, one person told me when dealing with Children's Services and apprehending the children because they were abused by the father and the father said, what do you mean? That's not abuse. They taught us that at the residential school. The priest abused me, and it was okay. The organization abused me. That was okay. So how do I deal with this if that was wrong?

Tâpiskoch kiskino'wâpachikêwin, peyâk âyisêniw kê wêhtâmowit ânima kâ mâmisko'tâmwak âschi Children's Services mêna âstâsew pimâ'tisiwin âwâsisâk kichi, âyis wêyawâw kê kitimâhihtâw ochi ôpapawa mêna ânâ papanâw êtwêt, " kêkwîy êtihitâmin?" Nâmoya êkwa ânima kitimâhihtâwowin. Wêyawâw kê kiskino'hâmakâwiyak ikosi ântê residential school. Âna âyâmihew'êniw kê kitimâhit, mêna êkwa ânima kêyam. Ânima mamâwitowin ni kitimâhiht. Êkwa ânima kêyâm... ikosi tânisi tâ êsi âtoskâtamân oma kêspin êkwa ânima nâmoya kwayus?

The whole system itself created another situation, and I think that's where we need to be able to say, "How do we stop that? How do we stand that we provide people with what they knew, how they knew it and bring back those historical things, teach them about that and say, how do we support you as you move forward in your healing?"

Misiwêyâw puminikêwin wêya puko osȩhtâw kohtuk itapiwin, mêna ni têhyihitên êkota ânima kêyanâw puko tâ êtwêyâhk, "Tânisi tâ poonêtayâhk êkwa ânima? Tânisi tâ nêpawêyâhk tâ wêchihiyâkik kêyanâw âyisêniwak âschi kêkwîy kê kiskêyihtâkik, tânisi kê kiskêyihtâkik ânima mêna tâ pêkêwêtatâw êkonahi kayâs itotumowin kêkwîya, tâ kiskinohumakêyak êkwa ânima mêna tâ êtwêyâhk, tânisi tâ wêchiyâhk kêyawâw iskô wuskâwew yâhkotew tâ êti mêyoyayin.

Mary SkyBlue Morin: 1964, 13 years old, was an unlucky year for me, apprehended by Social Services and taken into foster care as my mother was in Hay River, NWT. N'ohkom Lâpis told the Social Welfare to come and get me. I hid under the bed behind cardboard boxes. N'ohkom Lâpis coaxed me out and I listened because I loved her. As the social worker took me away in her car, I was crying. I stood in the court room and my grandmother stood beside me. The judge said I should go to a foster home because my mother was not there. My granny was 74 years old, she died two years later. I was taken to a foster home that had five other foster kids, run by an elderly native woman. This was the first time I saw a different kind of stove, electric it was called, running water into a sink and a telephone on the wall. The heat for the rooms came through vents from a basement oil furnace. For 20 years, I wondered why N'ohkom had rejected me. A friend said, "She probably couldn't feed you" which made sense to me as we were poor halfbreeds. I stopped wondering why.

1964, nêstosap kê si piponyân, miyâkosiw pimâtisiwin nêya kichi, kê kâchtinkâwiyan ochi Social Welfare kê tohtâhichik ântâ âwâsisâk ohpiki'hewichik âyâ ochi ni mama kê âyât ântê Hay River, NWT. N'ohkom Lâpis kê wehtâmowat ânihi Social Welfare tâ pê nâsêyêt. Ni kâson sêpa nipêwin otâhk'ochi li cârton boites. N'ohkom Lâpis ni kus'kimik tâ pê wayâwiyân ikota ochi mêna ni nâtohtawâw âyis ochi kê sâkihak. Âna Social Worker ni sipwêh'tâhik pêchîyi o'tâpânâs, nêya ê mâtoyân. Nêya mêna n'ohkom kê nêpawinan ânta court room. Âna oyusi'wew k'itwew ânima nêya t'itohtêyân foster home âyis ni mama nâmoya ikota âyâyat. N'ohkom âna tipahohp'omitanâw'nêwosâp ê si piponit, kê nipo nêso uskêwina mwestes. Ni tohtêhikwak ânta foster home, ânima neyanan kotuk foster kids, êkwâ'nima ê puminikêt ochi kehtayâ nêhiyâw iskwew. Êkospe oma nêkan kâ wâpâhtâmân pêtos kotâwânâpisk, electric ê sêkâtêk, nipi kâ pimpayêk ânta kosâpew mêna ânima sêwêpchikun ânta ânima nâkeh'tuk. Ânima kisitew piski'kipa'hikuna kê pê ispayek sâpo yoht'êni'kunisa ochi ânta wâtêh'kân pimê'kisisikun. Iskô nêstânâw uskêwina, ni mâmuskâtêyimâw n'ohkom tânike kê âtâwe'yihmit. Pêyak nitotêm k'itwew, "Wêya êtikwê nâmoya kuskêtâht t'âsumisk" tâna kâ mâmitoni'yichikun ochi nêya âyis nêyanân kê kitimâkisêyâhk âhpêto'kosisânâhk. Ni pooni mâmiton'yihitên tânehki.

Scrip, Land Displacement, and Road Allowance

To address Métis claims to the land, the federal government devised a system using Métis Subscription Certificates, "Métis scrip" or "Half-breed" scrip as it was officially known. The government decided that instead of conducting Treaty negotiations as they had with the First Nations Peoples, they would negotiate with the Métis on an individual basis, which created a barrier by attempting to separate our communities and kinship ties.

Scrip was issued as either money scrip ($160/$240) or land scrip (160 acres/240 acres) and was ultimately used to extinguish the Aboriginal title of the Métis. The process of applying for scrip was a long and incredibly difficult one which was filled with an abundance of paperwork, procedures, and lengthy wait times between each phase. Families would also often receive land scrip claims that were situated long distances from their current homes, and communities. This kept a vast majority of Métis People from being able to obtain their scrip. Additionally, this was a grant system laden with fraud. Scrip served to further dispossess Métis Peoples of the lands they occupied and with it, our Indigenous rights.

As described in *Métis Scrip in Alberta,*[1] life in these communities was difficult and communities were often disbanded due to government and police interference. A new land base for Métis opened in St. Paul (in what is now Alberta), but eventually, the Catholic Oblate missionaries had deemed that this was a failure and that the land should be opened for French settlers.

This is just one of the many examples of the Métis People being marginalized, dispossessed from our lands, and forced to the outskirts of society. Because of this, the Métis became known as the "Road Allowance People" in the early 20th century. Due to facing discrimination and being dispossessed from our land due to Métis scrip fraud, some Métis moved to road allowance communities which consisted of small, Métis-built shacks and log cabins. The road allowances were Crown land on the side of the

1 L. Hrycun, F. Tough, N. Kermoal, J. Rossiter, J. Madden, and Z. Davis (2018). *Métis Scrip in Alberta* [Pamphlet]. Rupertsland Centre for Métis Research.

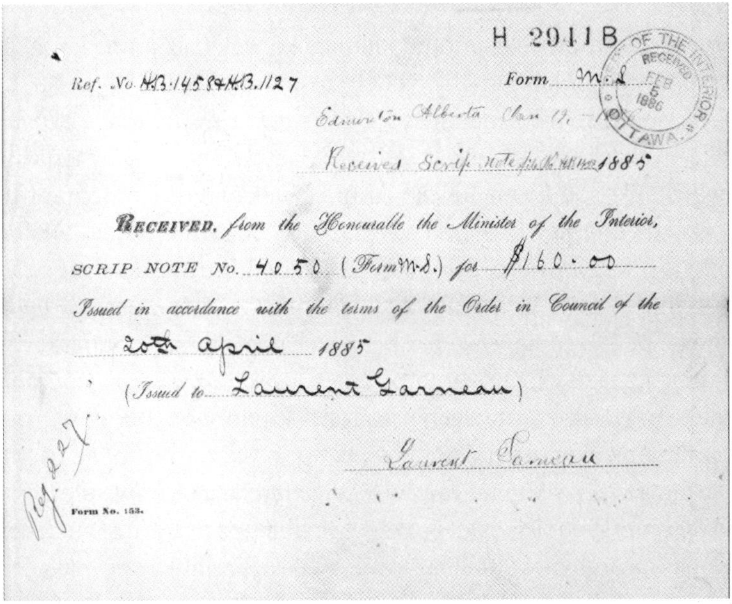

H 2941 B

Ref. No. HB. 1458 HB. 1127

Form M.S.

DEPT OF THE INTERIOR RECEIVED FEB 5 1886 OTTAWA

Edmonton Alberta Jan 17, 18

Received Scrip note ... 1885

RECEIVED, from the Honourable the Minister of the Interior,

SCRIP NOTE No. 4050 (Form M.S.) for $160.00

Issued in accordance with the terms of the Order in Council of the

20th April 1885

(Issued to Laurent Garneau)

Laurent Garneau

Reg. 227

Form No. 153.

Scrip number 4050

Source: Library and Archives Canada

road where some claimed that the Métis were living illegally (although many would argue that the Métis had the right to live on the land).

Doreen Bergum: The Mary and Ambrose Dumont family lived on what was called the road allowance, Crown land in Alberta, between the ditch and Red Deer River. We were known as squatters living off the land and the ruling back then was if you lived on this land for ten years you could claim this land as 'Squatters Rights.' I cannot remember if was two weeks or two months before we could claim the land and a town person did not want us to live there and claim the land, so he tried to burn our house down. It was then that my parents bought an old schoolhouse and moved it onto an acre of land and built it into a home for their family. The funny part of this, there was still the maps with the chocolate bars on the corners and the blackboards were still on the walls. They had so many children they had to buy a schoolhouse.

Mary mêna Ambrose Dumont la famille kê wêkichik ânma kâ sekâtek mêskanâw kâ pukitinumâhk, kehchi okimâw uskê ânta Alberta, tustawâyik sepêsisehkân mêna Red Deer sepê. Nêyanân kê kiskêyihtuma'kawiyâk chêpatapewiwâk êti pimatsoyâk ânta uskê mêna weyisewêwin êkospê ânima kêspin ikohta ê'wêkêyin iskô mitahtaht uskê kêya kâkê otinâskewiyâk oma uskê tâskoch 'Squatters Rights." Nâmoya ni kiskisin kêspin nêso âyimihaw kesikâw âhpo nêso tahto pesimiwak pâmweyes kâ k'otinâskewiyâk ânima uskê mêna otenâw eyinew nâmoya ni tâwêmkawyâk ikota tâ wekiyâhk mêna t'otinâskewiyâk ânima uskê, ikosi kochitâw tâ poona ni waskihikanân. Ikospê ânima ni nêkê'hikowâk kâ âtawêchik kayâsiyi kiskinohumâto-kamik mêna âchiptamâhk êkwa ânima ânta pêyak tipuhaskân uskê mêna osehtâw êkwa'nima wâskiyikun wêyawâw kichi la famille. Kâ wâwiyate'takosiw kêkwîy oma, kêyapich êsteki uskê wasinahikuna âschi kuskitê osâwâki sêwinikuna ânta okwêhtakâhka mêna kuskitêwâhtika kêyapich êstike ânta meyaw eh'kâna. Wêyawâw êkohk mistâhi âwâsisâk k'ayawachit wêyawâw puhko âtâwechik kiskinohumâto-kamik.

Doreen Poitras: The Garneau's remained in the St. Paul area even though they, like all the Métis, were taxed out of business and all prosperity through the intervening of the Catholic Church. Francois Poitras carried this injustice near for the rest of his life. He would not attend church, but he would hook up the team and take us (his grandkids and our mother) to Mass. We would come out and there he would be, sitting on the wagon pole. He and my father are both buried at the Mount of St. Joseph at Kehewin Reserve.

Li Garneau êyachik ântê St. Paul uskês kêspin âhpo wêyawâw, tâskoch kâhkiyâw li Mêtis sâm mistaheh kâ tipahikêhchik ohkimânahk tipahikan mêna wêyootsiwin sapo nâkunum puhkwayumihâwin ochi âyamihew'kamik. Francois Poitras kê tahkonam chêki oma mayi tohtumowin iskoh kâ pimatisit. Wêya nâmoya nohtê itohtew âyamihew'kamik, mâka nukwasow nêswapihsowak mistatimok mêna êtohtahat (osisima mêna ni mamanan) âyaminhawin. Nêyanan kâ pê wayawêyahk mêna ikota âyâht, ê-chipâtâpit otapânâsk uskihk. Wêya mêna ni papa nêso kê nayihihtchik âstew Mount St. Joseph ântê Kêhêwin nêhiyaw uskê.

Pearl Calahasen: Some of the dark times I believe for my father was when he and his family — they had land, they had everything that was given to them through scrip and it got taken away. We tried so hard — so hard to get that back and it was almost impossible.

Âteht ânihi kuskitêwâw âyimi'payiw kêsikâw ni tâpwehtên ochi ni papa tanispê wêya mêna sa famille... wêyawâw âyâchik uskê, wêyawâw âyâchik kâhkêyaw kêkwîy kâkê mêkosichik usichi Uskê Kêchi Musinahikân mêna muska'towân êspayêk. Nêyanân kochêtayâhk mitoni... mitoni tâ kâchitinamâhk tâ pêkêwêtatâyâhk mêna mitoni nâmoya'ta'êhkin.

In fact, we never did get the entire portion of what he was owed to him and his family, and so as a result, they lost that. They lost... they lost the land that was theirs, and they worked so hard for that land. That was, yes, it was part of the scrip, but it was theirs and it was taken away and there was nothing... nothing that can be done on that respect. And I think that was one of the reasons why many of the Métis People had lost their scrip. They had lost all the stuff that they had built towards.

Oma tâpwêwin, nêyanân nâmoya wêkâch ni kâchetinênân kâhkêyâw pâhki kêkwîy kâkê musina'hikêtâstek kichi wêya mêna sa famille, mêna ikosi ispayiw, kê wânitâchik ânima. Wêyawâw wunêhtâchik... wêyawâw wânitachik ânima uskê kâkê âyachik, mêna kê sookih âtoskêchik êkwa ânima uskê. Êkwa ânima, tapwê, êkoh pâhki ânima Uskê Kêchi Musinahikân, mâka wêyâwâw êkwa ânima mêna kê muskâmkâwichik mêna êkota mâkêkwîy... mâkêkwîy ânima kâkê tohtâkik ekwa'nima pisiske'yihtam. Mêna ni têhiyitên êkwa ânima pêyak itêyitum tânikê ochi mêchêt li Mêtis âyisêniwak kâkê wanêtâchik wêyawâw Uskê Kêchi Musinahikâ. Wêyawâw kê wanitâchik kâhkêyâw kêkwîy kâkê osêtâchik êkote.

They had lost everything.

Wêyawâw kê wunehtâchik kâhkêyâw kêkwîy.

The presbytery at St. Paul des Métis
Source: Library and Archives Canada

Father Lacombe
Source: Library and Archives Canada

The History of St. Paul des Métis

Distinct Métis communities developed along trade routes throughout the Métis Homeland in the 19th century. Several of these communities were established throughout Alberta, and many remain to this day. Communities such as Lac Ste. Anne became well-known for their historic pilgrimage that would take place each year, where in late July, Métis, and First Nations families would travel to the site to celebrate the pilgrimage. The pilgrimage still happens to this day and has become an important marker for many Métis across the Province.

Other historic Métis communities in Alberta include, but are not limited to St. Albert, Lac La Biche, Fort Vermilion, Fort Chipewyan, Dunvegan, Peace River, Jasper House, Buffalo Lake, Tail Creek, Pakan, and Grouard. Communities such as this became a landing-place for Métis moving westward. While many Métis did live a somewhat nomadic lifestyle, most often when they moved, they were moving towards something. They were not just moving anywhere; they were moving towards their kin who had already established these communities across the Homeland.

In 1934, the Ewing Commission, an Alberta Royal Commission was established to respond to the problems of health, education, and the general welfare of the Métis population in Alberta. In 1938, Alberta passed the Métis Population Betterment Act which set aside colonies for Métis People and in doing so, Alberta became the first Province to enact legislation specific to Métis. This allowed for the establishment of a land base within Alberta, which at the time included twelve settlements, or "colonies" as they were called at the time. These include: Buffalo Lake, Cold Lake, East Prairie, Elizabeth, Fishing Lake, Gift Lake, Kikino, Marlboro, Paddle Prairie, Big Prairie (now Peavine), Touchwood and Wolf Lake. However, four of the original settlements — Cold Lake, Marlboro, Touchwood, and Wolf Lake were later dissolved.

Prior to the development of the Métis Settlements, St. Paul des Métis was developed as a federally operated Métis settlement in Alberta. The history of St. Paul des Métis, while vitally important to understanding the Métis story, is one that's largely been forgotten until recently. Today, work is being done within the town to bring this story to the forefront, however there is still some resistance to reconciling with the true history of this place.

To shed light on this history, we have included the story of Caroline Charlebois (Poitras). Caroline was born in 1892, she was a Métis woman with her roots in the Red River Settlement. Her father was Elzear Poitras, and her mother was Marguerite Dauphinais. Her family was one of the first to settle in St. Paul des Métis in the late 19th century. She later married St. Paul's first doctor, Jean Baptiste Charlebois. Before her death, she spoke on tape with Gordon and Audrey Poitras. She recounted memories of growing up in St. Paul des Métis and shared her recollection of what had happened there. In her story, she recounts her memories from growing up on the settlement. Throughout the interview she discusses her memories of Father Therien and the other priests who resided there. She recalls the injustices her family faced, and the strength of her mother who had to fight to get what was rightfully hers.

We included this case study of one Métis community as an example of what had happened to the Métis repeatedly throughout the Homeland. With this history, alongside Caroline Charlebois' interview, we hope to highlight how the Métis were forced from their land, and cheated of their rights time and time again.

History of St. Paul des Métis

Following the 1885 Resistance at Batoche there were few established places for the Métis to settle (Devine, 2004). As a result, many went into hiding, fearing for the safety of themselves and their family. Others were forced to hide their culture and heritage and quickly adapt to the changing world of western Canada. St. Paul des Métis was the only and last attempt to develop a substantial Métis settlement following the events of

1885 where many of the founding families reported participation in the Resistance (Dobbin, 1981).

The St. Paul des Métis colony was established through the efforts of Father Lacombe in 1895. He leased a tract of land and had the first mission building erected in 1896. For the next 13 years, Métis settled on these lands. Many Métis experienced remarkable successes and were relatively well to do, possessing large herds of cattle, horses, and other livestock as evidenced by last wills and testaments (Brady, n.d.).

In 1908, a report was issued to the Dominion Government by Father Therien which claimed that the farming colony was a "failure" and would therefore have to be disbanded (Brady, 2004). Therien, angered by the destruction of a boarding school by the Métis students who went there, had started a quiet campaign to have the Métis evicted from their lands, attributing what he termed a lack of growth in the colony to the laziness of the Métis (Sawchuk, 1981).

The Métis observed the implications of this damning report during the summer and fall of 1908 as white squatters arrived and started to squat on their established homesteads. Several Métis had their homes invaded and their lands taken through a variety of fraudulent schemes, enacted by the clergy with the help of local influential priest, Father Therien (Brady, n.d.). The Métis were facing displacement, and dispossession of their lands once again.

The failed colony report outraged the Métis who were living in St. Paul at the time. They organized and signed a mass petition, which demanded that their settlement remain under Métis control. However, the petition was ignored by the Dominion of Canada who, when later questioned, claimed they never received the document (Brady, n.d.).

The Métis attempted to maintain control of their settlement lands, but the Church defended their actions by claiming that the Métis had failed to adapt to agricultural life. There were varying levels of economic stature throughout the settlement; however, many Métis families prospered as recorded by Jim Brady in his later capacity as a Métis historian:

> The results attendant upon this [agricultural] venture were remarkably successful. Many Métis were comparatively well to do. Many possessed large herds of cattle and horses and other holdings of a comfortable nature... Some opinion can be derived from the following figures:
>
> Dion Laboucane: 1200 cattle;
> Elzear Poitras: 400 cattle, 300 horses, chain of trading posts;
> Lawrence (Laurent) Garneau: 400 cattle, 135 horses, chain of trading posts, timber birth and saw mill;
> Louis LaFramboise: 160 extra grade cattle, threshing machine;
> Jean Lariviere: 100 acres of cultivated land;
> John Ross: 125 cattle, *etc.*

Many of the more educated Métis, including Laurent Garneau, tried to negotiate with both the Catholic Church and the federal government to acknowledge Métis rights to the land. These efforts, however, fell on deaf ears. The constant intimidation and attacks against the Métis resulted in devastating effects on their morale and soon many of the Métis families relinquished their efforts and moved away. Within a few years, St. Paul was dominated by incoming Quebecois; few Métis families remained, and for those who did, they endured ongoing racial abuse on the streets and in the classrooms. Brady characterizes this moment in Alberta history as a "mass violation of government regulations."

The events that took place in the St. Paul des Métis settlement were by no means unique to the Métis experience. As author Murray Dobbin (1981) notes, "St. Paul was a microcosm of the [wider] Métis dilemma after the turn of the century." Much of the Métis story is one of displacement and dispossession of their lands and their livelihoods, just as much as it is a story of their perseverance and resilience. Still, the events that took place in St. Paul des Métis changed the lives and experiences of these founding Métis families in a profoundly negative way.

—Written by Bailey Oster and Dr. Yvonne Poitras Pratt

Caroline Charlebois (Poitras)

An interview with Audrey and Gordon Poitras

Left: Elizear Poitras and Marguerite Dauphinais (Caroline's parents)
Right: Caroline and her sister
Photos: Audrey Poitras

Caroline Charlebois: They had no money to pay. He lost all that too and one of them was going to hit him because he sends this bill to pay. Oh yeah, my father had a lot more money than that but then he lost lots on that one. Then he sent a horse, one time he never gets any money.

Nâmoya âyâchik kêkwîy sooniyâw tâ tipahikêchik. Wêya kê wânihtâw kâhkiyâw êkwânima mêna pêyak âna kê pukamihat âyis êtsahâhk musina'hikêwin tâ tipahâhk. Tâpwe, ni papa k'âyâw mêchet sooniyâw ispêch êkwâ'nima mâka wêya wânihtaht mêchêt êkwâ'nima. Êkospê wêya kê itsâhew mistâtim, pêyakwâw wêya nâmoya kachitinew sooniyâw.

He doesn't get fed nothing. Yeah, he lost lots of money on that one, on top of everything and then that man comes with Father Therien, and he takes everything away. Everything, from my mother... [he] put my mother out. That's terrible.

Wêya nâmoya kê âsamiht kêkwîy. Tâpwe kê wanihtaht mêchet sooniyâw êkwânima, takoch kâhkiyâw'kêkwîy mêna êkospê ânâ nâpew petohtew usichi Father Therien, mêna wêya otinahk kâhkiyâw'kekwîy. Kahkiyâw'kêkwîy, ochi ni mama… [wêya] wayawe'ahi ni mama. Ânima kostate'yihtâkwun.

Gordon Poitras: Who was this man? Hopkins? What was that man's name? Hopkins?

Âwêna ânâ nâpew? Hopkins? Tânisi ânâ nâpew kê sêkasot? Hopkins?

Caroline Charlebois: Yeah. That's him.

Tâpwe. Ânâ wêya.

Gordon Poitras: Did he work for your dad... your father to start with?

Kê âtoskêt chê kichi ki Papa… ki papa tâ machêtaht usichi?

Caroline Charlebois: Yes, yes. He was surveying and him and Father Therien took everything. They locked him in a room, and they had a jar of wine and they got him piped and they signed everything and what do you call it, a power of attorney or something.

Tâpwe, tâpwe. Wêya kê oti'pahaskew (tipaskatum) mêna wêya mêna Father Therien otinâkik kâhkiyâw'kêkwîy. Wêyawâw kipo'piskâhat ânta piska'kipahikun, mêna âyâchik usiwa'chikun ochi soomin'apoy mêna wêyawâw got him piped mêna wêyawâw tipiyawe'wêhowichik kâhkiyâw'kêkwîy mêna kêkwîy kâ sêhkâtâmin, power of attorney âhpo kêkwîy.

Gordon Poitras: Power of attorney, yeah.

Power of attorney, tâpwe.

Left: Caroline and Gordon Poitras
Right: Caroline Charlebois, 1958
Photos: Audrey Poitras

Caroline Charlebois: And got everything, everything. Put my mother out and everything. Father Therien did that.

Mêna kâchitinâhk kâhkiyaw'kêkwîy, kâhkiyâw'kêkwîy. Âstaht ni mama wêyawêtimit mêna kâhkiyâw'kêkwîy. Father Therien êkwa'nima itohtahk.

Audrey Poitras: So, then what did your mother do?

Ikosi, êkospê kêkwîy ki mama kê totum?

Caroline Charlebois: Well, she had some money too, you know. So, she had to get a lawyer, and she had to come to Edmonton. Where [she] hired a lawyer... to get her home back. So much... yeah. It cost her a lot of money.

Well, wêya k'âyâw atêht sooniyâw too, kiske'yihtên. Ikosi, wêya puko tâ kâchitinat oyusi'wew, mêna wêya puko tâ pêhtohtêt otê

Edmonton. Tânite [wêya] tipa'humwew oyusi'wew... tâ kâchitinâhk kâwi wêki. Mitoni mistâhi... tâpwê. Mistakêh'tew wêya kichi mistâhi sooniyâw.

Audrey Poitras: And that's all she got was her home?

Mêna êkwâ'nima puko wêya kê kâchitinahk kê wêki?

Caroline Charlebois: That's all — just so much. So much, got the, the house and the chicken coop and the chicken and everything. She got all that, and so much, ah, the...

Êkwa'nima puko — êkoh kahkêkwîy. Êko mistâhi, kê kâchitinahk, waskahikan mêna ânima pâpâha'kwân waskahikunis mêna ânâ pâpâhâ'kwan mêna kâhkiyâw'kêkwîy. Wêya kê kâchitinahk kâhkiyâw ânima, mêna êkoh mistâhi...

Audrey Poitras: Land?

Uskê?

Caroline Charlebois: Yes. Got that.

Tâpwe. Ni kâchitinên ânima.

Audrey Poitras: And what happened to the rest of it?

Mêna kêkwîy ispayêk ânima kotuk kâhkiyaw'kêkwîy?

Caroline Charlebois: Well, Father Therien had the money and sold everything. And Hopkins, he built some houses with that money, you know. Then he was married quite late, you know. And Father Therien, he had some relations in Montreal, they were poor. He sent some... he sent for them all. All these relations.

Ikosi, Father Therien kê âyât ânima sooniyâw mêna atâwâkêt kâhkiyaw'kêkwîy. Mêna Hopkins, wêya osêhtâw âteht wâskihikâna âschi êkwân'ima sooniyâw, kiske'yihtên. Êkospê kê wêkêtow mitoni mwesis'kum, kiske'yihtên. Mêna Father Therien, wêya kê âyât atêht wâhko'makunahk ântê Montreal, weyâwâw kê kitimaksichik. Wêya kê tisahâm... wêya kê tisahak ochi kâhkiyaw âniki. Kâhkiyaw oki wâhko'makunahk.

Audrey Poitras: To come to St. Paul?

Tâ petohtechik ântê St. Paul?

Caroline Charlebois: And he bought them houses and everything, land, he put them in there. That's how much money my dad had. Oh, my mother was mad. I don't blame her.

Mêna wêya âtâwêstamwat wêstawâw wâskihikâna mêna kâhkiyâw' kêkwîy, uskê, wêya kê âhât ikota. Êkwa'nima êkoh sooniyaw ni papa kê âyât. Oh, ni mama kisowâso. Nâmoya âtâme'yimaw.

Hopkins said to me. "Oh you better shut up or I will take even your chairs or shoes," And I told the preacher, I said "I hope there is a Hell for you when you die." I told him. "You talk about Hell when you are preaching in front of God. You both are going to Hell. I'd like to see you there when you die," I told him. He run away.

Hopkins itwet nêya. "Oh, puko tâ kipahaman kitoon âhpo ni otinên kêya êwuko li chaises âhpo muskisina." Mêna ni wehtamwâw âyami'hewêniw, n'itwan "Ni puko'seyi'mowin muchi'manito'nâhk kêya kichi kâ nipiyin. Kêya ê pêkiskwâtâmân ânima muchi'manito'nâhk kâ kêskih'kemowin nêkân ochi Manito. Kêyawâw tâ nêsoyek kâ tohtêyêk muchi'manito'nâhk. N'ohte wâpâmitinêk kêyawâw ikotê tânispê kâ nipiyêk." N'itwâw. Wêya tâpâsew.

He did not listen to me, you know. He run away. Oh, that priest, you know. You can't believe he is a priest. No sir.

Wêya nâmoya natohtam nêya, kiskihitên. Wêya tâpâsew. Oh, ânâ âyamihe'wêniw, kiske'yihtên. Kêya nâmoya kakê tâpwehtâmân wêya ânâ âyamihe'wêniw... Namoya, sir.

And I find out one of Johnny's, he said, "I'm not the same kind of Priest as you." That was a good one. You know he was always preaching, that Father Larose you know. Oh, what's his...oh,

Father Therien. My mother wouldn't let us dance a waltz when we happened to go a wedding or something. We could not waltz, we could not dance waltz, because Father Therien said so, it was a sin to waltz, to dance the waltz. Only quadrille, that's all we were allowed.

Mêna ni kiske'yihtên pêyak ochi Johnny, wêya itwet, "Nâmoya nêya pêyakwân tâskoch âyamihe'wêniw tâskoch kêya." Êkwâ'nima mêyo puko. Kiske'yihtên wêya tâhki kêskih'kemowit, ânâ Father Larose, kiske'yihtên. Oh, kêkwîy ânima wêya… oh, Father Therien. Ni mama nâmoya pakitinkoyahk tâ nêmihitoyahk ânima nêson'towin tânispê kâ toteyahk wêkih'towin âhpo kêkwiy. Nâmoya kê nêson'towin, nâmoya kê nêmihitoyahk nêson'towin, âyis Father Therien k'itwet ikosi, êkwâ'nima pastahon tâ nêson'towin, tâ nêmihitoyahk ânima nêson'towin. Âya puko quadrille, êkwâ'nima puko nêyanân kê pukitinkawiyahk.

My mother would allowed you, us to waltz, to dance a waltz, and he was going out with this Mrs. Paquette, hey, you know? He was, my sister Laura, he caught her in his lap,

Ni mama kê pakitinkoyêk, nêyanân tâ nêson'towin, tâ nêmihitoyahk ânima nêson'towin, mêna wêya nêso wayawêchik âsichi âwa Mrs. Paquette, hey, kiske'yihtên. Wêya ânâ nisêmis Laura, wêya kachitinew t'api nêchikwunihk.

And he is the one that don't want to dance? Oh, you can't believe him. I feel like, when, one nurse said it, "You can't believe nobody," not even a priest, nobody. It's true you know.

Mêna wêya ânâ êka'noti nemihitot? Oh, nâmoya kâkê tapeh'tamot wêya. Ni moosihtan tâskoch, tânispê, pêyak muskêkê iskwew itwet ânâ, "Nâmoya âweyahk kâkê tâpweh'tâmtâwâw, " moya âhpo âyami'hewêniw, nama'wiyak. Tâpwêwin oma, kiske'yihtên.

Audrey Poitras: What was so bad about dancing a waltz?

Kêkwîy êkoh mayatahk ooma tâ nêmihitoyahk ânima nêson'towin, ni mutwanche?

Caroline Charlebois: I don't know. I know, ah, you know, ah you wanted to [to know] about our father, he was a Poitras though, wasn't he?

Namaoya ni kiske'yihtên. Ni kiske'yihtên, ah, kiske'yihtên, ah kêya kâ nohtê [tâ kiske'yihtamêk] ooma ni papanân, wêya ânâ Poitras kêyam'kispin, kê chê?

Well, anyway, I think she's too old for a priest one time, something like that — anyway, what was I going to say about this priest anyway. He was going out, this priest was going out with a woman again. And the sister told me, this sister, this nun, another sister that just came out — some nun, you know.

Ikosi pukowe'yisi, ni kiske'yihtên wêya nâwach kêhtehiyiwew kichi ânâ âyami'hewêniw pêyakwaw, kêkwîy tâskoch êkwanima — pukowe'yisi, kêkwîy ooma tâ itweyan âwa ochi âyami'hewêniw pukowe'yisi. Wêya nêso wayawêchik âsichi, âwa âyami'hewêniw kê nêso wayawêchik âsichi iskwew âsumena. Mêna ânâ la soeur wehtâmowit, âwa la soeur, âwa la soeur, kotuk la soeur kâ pê way-awêt — âwiyahk la soeur, kiske'yihtên.

She said don't kid yourself that the priests hasn't got their own friend. That's what she told me. Every priest has their own friend. I guess so — it looks like it after that, to me. Father Therien had this Mrs. Poitras, Father Larose had Mrs. Poitras; there's a Poitras there in St. Paul and he was going out with that woman, Mrs. Poitras, Father Larose. That's the one that Johnny said not the same kind of priest like you. I said that was a good one, on Father Larose, he was always preaching. That was a good one. And no, you can't trust every priest.

Wêya itwet kâya tâ moch'wenisoyin ânima âniki âyamihew'êniwahk kâya ê yachik wêyawâw ototêma. Êkwa'nima ê wehtâmowit. Tâhto âyami'hewêniw âyâw wêya ototêma. Meskwe'yihtâm ikosi — êkwâ'nima ê sinakwak mwestes ânima, nêya ochi. Father Therien kê âyât âwa Mrs. Poitras, Father Larose kê âyat Mrs. Poitras; êkota ânâ Poitras antê St. Paul mêna wêya nêso wâyawêchik âsichi ânâ iskwew,

Mrs. Poitras, Father Larose. Wêya ânima ânâ Johnny k'itwêt, nâmoya nêya pêyakwân tâskoch kêya. Nêya n'itwan mêyo nuskwêstumowin êkwa'nima, ahchi Father Larose, wêya tahki kêskih'kemowit. Êkwa'nima nuskwêstumowin. Mêna nâmoyaka kê mumisew tahto âyamihew'êniwahk.

Like me now, I went to see my Jean [her husband] you know, in Hobbema. When I come, when I used to at that time, I was kind of afraid when I sat alone. I didn't want to sleep in a hotel, I was scared, I don't know. So, I phoned the sisters hall, ah, there is a sisters of Métis or the Chief. The girls that got no home, or they were looking for a job. The sisters had that kind of a place.

Tâpiskoch nêya êkwa, ni tohtên tâ wâpamahk Jean [onapema] kiske'yihtên, antê Hobbema. Kâ petohteyan, tânispê kakê tohtaman ispê, nâwach ni sêkisin kâ pêyakwapiyan. Nâmoya nohtê nipâyan ânta kapêsew'kamik, kê kostaman, nâmoya ni kiske'yihtên. Ikosi ni sêwêptamowahk ânima li soeurs petekwewin'kamik, ah, êkotê kê âyawak li soeurs ochi li Métis âhpo okimahkan. Âniki iskwesisak êka ê yachik wêki, âhpo kâ intonahkik âtoskêwin. Ânikê li soeurs kê âyâchik itowahk petekwêwin'kamik.

So, I began to know them. I phoned them [to see] if they would find a home for me. So, they said, "Yes, we will find a room for you." So, I went there instead of the hotel. And the priest at Hobbema, he was half drunk. And he said that he would phone a ride for me to come back to St. Paul. There was some, these people from Bonnyville and they knew me so they would stop for me in St. Paul, for going home to Bonnyville. So, he found a ride for me, so he find me where I was, he knew where I was, I guess. So, the sister said "there's a priest here to see you." she said to me. The Sister said, after I was, she found me a room.

Ikosi, ni mâchi kiskêmawâhk. Ni sêwêptamawâhk mâhti kêspin wêyawâw tâmskâmâchik wêkih nêya kichi. Ikosi, wêyawâw êtwêwâhk, "tâpwe, nêyanân kâmiskâmâtinan piski'kipahikun kêya kichi." Ikosi, ni tohtân êkote mêskoch ochi kapêsewkâmik. Mêna âyâmihew'êniw ântê Hobbema, wêya kê kêskwê'pet âpehtaw. Mêna êtwêt ânima wêya tâ sêwêptâmawot poosêwin nêya kichi tâ kêwêyân yisi St. Paul. Êkota âtêht kê, oki âyisêniwak ochi Bonnyville mêna wêyawâw kiskêmichik ikosi wêyawâw kê nakinkêchik nêya kichi ânta St. Paul, ochi êti kêwêyâhk yisi Bonnyville. Ikosi, wêya miskum poosêwin nêya kichi, ikosi wêya ni miskâwik tânta kâ yâyân, kê kiskêtâhk tânte ê âyâyân, n'itê'yitam. Ikosi, la soeur itwew "Êkota âyâmihew'êniw ota tâ wapamis." wêya k'êtwêt nêya. Âna la soeur k'itwew, mwestus nêya kê, wêya kê miskak nêya kichi piski'kipahikun.

So, I came down in the sitting room, he was there, this priest from Hobbema. He said, "I found you a ride." "Did you?" but the door was open, you know, I was still scared. He grabbed me, and puts me and a big bag up to my room. He grabs me and and starts to carry me around the hall and if you think I was not scared, haha!

Ikosi, ni pê nehtachowan ânte apew kamiskos, wêya êkotê âyaw, âwa âyâmihew'eniw ochi Hobbema. Wêya êtwew, "Ni misken keya tâ poosiyin.' "Kêya che?" mâka iskwatem kê tawow, kiske'yihtên, keyapich ni kosten. Wêya kê kachitinik, mêna âstahit nêyâ mêna ê mishak muskimot ânta ni piski'kipahikun. Wêya ni kachitinik mêna… wêya ê ohpinit mêna ê mâchi tahkonit pa pami petekwewin'kamik mêna kespin kite'yihtên nâmoya êkostaman, haha!

Oh, I was scared, the sisters could come in any time, or past there, you know. Oh, I tried to pull his hands away from me. If you think I was not scared of what the sister would see there.

Oh, ni sêkisin, li soeurs tâ pê tohtêwak pokwêspê, âhpo tâ mêyâskamchik êkota, kiskêyihtên. Oh, ni kochitan tâ ochipitâmân ochichêya âwâs ochi nêya. Kêspin kitêyihtên nâmoya kê kostâmân kêkwîy la soeur tâ wâpâhta êkote.

That's a priest for you. But he was a joker, I suppose... Oh, those priests, you know, you can't trust them either.

Ikonânima âyâmihew'êniw kêya kichi. Mâka wêya âna wuwêyutwe'wiw, n'ite'yitam… Oh, ikonâniki âyâmihew'êniw, kiskêyihten, kêya nâmoya kâkê mumisew wêstawâw puko'tânima.

Doreen Poitras and her siblings near Elk Point
Photos: Poitras Family

Racism and Discrimination

> In reference to his first year at school in 1915 at St. Paul des Métis, Jim Brady noted in his Journal:
>
> "My first contact with racial discrimination. The unending ordeal of daily combat."
>
> *—From One-and-a-Half-Men: The Story of Jim Brady and Malcolm Norris by Murray Dobbin*

Doreen Poitras: We didn't realize what the world was like out there. So, upon busing to school in Elk Point, we faced a new world that looked at us as different. Called us halfbreeds, dirty halfbreeds and treated us as inferior and stupid.

Nêyanan moya kiskêtamahk kêkwîy misiwe uskê ê-sipayek wêyawê'tumow. Ikosi, tapiskoch kâ kê sipayahk kiskinohumato-kamik ântê Elk Point, nêyanan kê nawakiskamahk ôskîyi misiwe uskê kâ wapamkawyahk tâskoch pêtos. Ê'sehkatikawyahk âpehtaw-kosisanak, wepatisiw âpehtaw-kosisanuk mêna mayi-totawewiyahk êyuskoch nâmoya nêkânew mêna tâskoch makêkwîy kê kisketmahk êka kâkê patisiwiyahk.

Then as we grew older our mosom [grandfather] and Gordon [Doreen's older brother] told us of going to town with a team and having the Ukrainians along the way throwing stones at them, so even to this day, I feel that ostracism and never want to move back or return in that community.

Êkospe kâ êti ohpikiwiyâhk ni moshomnaw mêna Gordon kê wehtakâmkakâwyakâhk otenâw êtohtechik âya usichi neswapi-hsowak mêna ânkih Ukrainians êkotê yisi wêpinakihk âsinêyak, itam kêyapich anoch kêsikâw, ni moositan kâ wunkiskisitohtaht kipawhakun mêna moya wêhkâch tâ apichêwiyahk ikote kowi âhpo tâ pêkêwewyahk êkotê ânima kâ mamawi'e'âyahk.

So though all that occurred there many years ago, the Poitras family now, as then have great loyalty to the Métis Nation of Alberta.

Ikosi, sapo kahkiyaw kêkwîy oma êkotê kâ ispayek kâyas ochi, li Poitras famille oma êkwa, tapiskoch ikosi âyâchik âsota mâkew tapwin âschi Li Métis Nation of Alberta.

Pearl Calahasen: I was a Minister of the Crown at that time. I went to shop at Safeway and there was this little older lady that was ahead of me, and she was an Indigenous lady. I don't know what nation she was from. And she was in front and she had... I forget what it was, she had a certain amount of money, I guess.

Nêya oma Minister of the Crown ikospê. Ni tohtân t'âtâwêyân nêta Safeway mêna êkota âyâw nâwach apisesi'sit kehte iskwiw nêkânew nêya, mêna wêya ânâ Indigenous iskwew. Nâmoya ni kiskiyitên kêkwîy nation ochi. Mêna nêkânew mêna ê âyât... Ni wânkiskisin kêkwîy ânima, wêya kê âyât mwechi âkechi'kêwin sooniyas, ni mêskwê'yihtên.

And she had bought all this food and I think she was short like five dollars or something. And the lady was just berating her, and I thought holy mackerel, this is not right. So anyway, I said, "Excuse me, I'll pay for her."

Mêna âtâwêt kâhkêyaw ôma mêchowin mêna ni têhiyitên wêya nâmoya êkoh âyâyat nântâw niyânan pêhikun soonias âhpo kêkwîy. Mêna ânâ iskwew kê kêhkamat wêya, mêna ni têhiyitên holy mackerel, moya oma kwayus.

She was so embarrassed.

Wêya mitoni nepewi'keyimow.

And I said, "Listen," I said, "stop it." And she (the cashier) says, "Who the heck do you think you are?" and I just said, "Well, first of all, I'm an individual paying for my stuff and I'm willing to pay for her stuff. That's number one."

Mêna n'itweyan, "nâtohta, n'itweyân, "nâki," Mêna wêya (sooniyaw pumi'nikês) itwew, "Awêna the heck êtihtâmân kêya?" mêna ni mwechi n'itwêyan," Ikosi, nistum, nêya oma âyisêno ê tipahamân nêya ohi kêkwîya mêna nêya nohtê tipahamân wêya âna kêkwîya. Êkwa ânima âkêhta'sowin pêyak."

"Number two," I said, "You have no right to treat her like that. She's an elderly lady. You have no right."

"Âkêhta'sowin nêso," ni itwân, "Kêya nâmoya ki tâyân tâ kitimâhât wêya ikosi. Wêya âwa kehte iskwiw. Nâmoya."

And I said, "Number three," I never do this. But I said, "I'm the Minister of Aboriginal Relations in the Province of Alberta." And she (the cashier) just about died. "I want to talk to your manager right now."

Mêna n'itwêyân, "Âkêhta'sowin nisto," Nâmoya wêhkach ni tohtên ôma. Mâka n'itwan, "Nêya oma the Minister of Aboriginal Relations in the Province of Alberta." Mêna (ana sooniyaw pumi'nikês) kêkach nipiw. "Nohtê pêkiskwâtâw kâ'tipê'yichikêt sêmak."

I said "Call please. Immediately. Otherwise, I'll make a scene right here and that's not what you want."

N'itwan "Call mâhti. Sêmak. Âhpo êtikwe, ni kisopayin mêna moya êkwa ânima k'intâwehten."

And so, she did and this poor little lady... and I just felt so sad for her. I said, "Just go ahead and I'll pay," and she ran. She... she didn't want anything to do with... she took her stuff and she took off. I didn't even get her name.

Mêna ikosi, wêya itohtum mêna âwa kâ kitimaksit apisesi'siw iskwiw... mêna sooskwach ni moosetan êkoh pekiskatuman wêya kichi. N'ititwan, "sooskwach sepweti nêkân mêna nêyâ ni tipahen", mêna wêya tapesew. Wêya... wêya mamoya kêkwîy ê nohtê tohtak êkwanma.... Wêya otinum so mêchowin mêna wêya sepwe tapisew. Nâmoya âhpo nêyâ ê kachitinaman owehowin.

And so, the manager comes, and I said, "I'm just really disgusted by what happened here." and I proceeded to explain.

Mêna ikosi, katipê'yichikêt pehtohtew, mêna n'itwan, "Nêyâ mitoni ni pukwaten oma kekwîy k'ispayek ôta." Mêna ni mâchi mamiskotum.

This guy who was the person in front of me was like, "Holy, I've never seen this before," and he said, "Sir, I was standing here and the way this lady treated that little old lady was really unacceptable."

Awa nâpew âweya âyisêniw nêkân nêyâ êtwew, "Holy, nâmoya wekach ôma ni kê wahpahten," mêna êtwew, "Sir, nêyâ nepawiyan ôta mêna tânisi âwa iskwew kâ totawat ânihi apisesi'siw kehte iskwiw mitoni tâpwe moya mêyosit."

And I thought, Well, why didn't you step in? You know?

Mêna ni tehiyiten, ikos, tânihkê ê kâ tahkos'kewin? Ki si kehiyiten?

And then I said, "So I want this woman to be reprimanded and to be taught about Indigenous People." And he was like, "Okay."

Mêna êkospe n'itwan, "Ikosi, ni tawemaw âwa iskwew tâ kehkamaw mêna tâ kiskinohamakewat ochi Indigenous âyseniwak." Mêna wêya tapiskoch, "Okay."

And I said, "I want to write you a letter." And I did write him a letter. I said, "I need your address. I need your card please."

Mêna ni itawn, "Ni nohtê masinahen keya musinahekan," Mêna ni kê masinaheken ânima masinahekan. Ni itawn, "Ni intawehten keya tânta kâ wekihk. Ni intawehten keya masinahikunis mahti."

So, I did and I cc'd Safeway Canada. But, you know, those kinds of things... we have to step in. If we don't have the intestinal fortitude to step in in times like that, when people are being berated, people are being embarrassed and they don't have their wherewithal to be able to deal with that because they are poor and they don't understand the system and they think that they have to ignore that. No, it's wrong. It's so totally wrong. And we have to be able to step in and those times to be able to help anybody, anyone who needs our help.

Pearl Calahasen seen as Minister of Aboriginal Relations
Photos: Métis Nation of Alberta

Ikosi, ni tohten mêna nêyâ cc'd Safeway Canada. Mâka, kis kehiten, êkwa itowahk kekwîy… keyanaw puko kâ tahkos'kewina. Kespin nâmoya âyayahk ânima sohkite'hewin tâ tahkos'kewin ikosi, tânispê âyeseniwak kâ kehkamichik, âyseniwak kâ pê nepewi'keyimow mêna weyawâw nâmoya kasketachik tâ deal with that âyis weyawâw êkitimaksichik mêna nâmoya ê nistotachik the system mêna êtehtakik tâ pakitinakik êkwa ânima. Nâmoya, nâmoya kwayus êkwa ânima. Mitoni nâmoya kwayus êkwa'nima. Mêna keyanaaw puko tahkos'kewina mêna âniki times tâ wechihîyakik âweyahk, âweyahk kâ nitawetahk wechihowin.

So, yeah, it was really interesting because… It worked out very well actually. I mean, those kinds of things you have to do, if you don't do them, who are you? Who are you standing for? What do you stand for?

Ikosi, yeah, êkwa'nima mitoni pisis kapu'maw âyis... Mitoni kwayus êspayew âtawyak. Ni tâpwêtên êkwa'towahk kêkwîy puko tâ tohtamin, kêspin ê kâ totamin, âwêna kêya? âwêna êsi nêpawêyin kichi? kêkwîy kêya ê nêpawêyin kichi?

If you're not willing to be able to do that — step in when the need is there... I don't think that's being human.

Kêspin, nâmoya kê nohtê tohtên êkwa ânima — tâ tâhkos'kewina tânispê nitawê'yihtam êkota êstek... Nêya nâmoya ni têhiyitên êkwa'nima âyisênihkan.

Mary SkyBlue Morin: In Green Lake, Saskatchewan, the racism I saw was when the L.I.D. office said the halfbreeds had to live across the lake and moved my granny's house there. In Meadow Lake, some kids at school called me a "dirty Indian." Those were fighting words. I may have been part Indian, but I was not dirty! Kids learned to respect this halfbreed Indian. They learned too that I would not back down from a fight. To keep my dignity, I told myself, they did not know what it was like to be a halfbreed.

They didn't even know the difference between a Halfbreed and a Cree Indian. In my adult life, I experienced racism from native people because they saw a pale face. They would say; "I thought you were a white woman," which was hurtful because I knew what that meant. I quit government jobs because of redneck war whoops, people telling Indian jokes: Indians as wagon burners, circling the wagons, lazy Indians not wanting to work.

I heard "let's pow-wow" or "let's do a rain dance", not knowing these traditional ceremonies or celebrations took four days. They called Indian and Halfbreed women by a derogatory name because they could not say "iskwew" and calling children white or Indian bastard. Many times, I have walked away in shame, the judgement harder to take from my own people.

Ântê Green Lake SK, ânima mâyi'wêchêtowin kâ wâpâtâmân ispê L.I.D. kâ wêhtâmâchik âhpêhto'kosisânahk tâ wêkichik âkâ'mihk sâkuhikun mêna kê âchipichitik ânima n'ohkom's wâskihikun ikotê. Ânte Meadow Lake SK, âtêht âwâsisâk ânta kiskino'humâkêwin kê itwêchik oma nêya "wêpatisiw êyinew."

Ikonânhi notinkew pêkiskwêwina. Âpwêtike nêya âpehto'kosisan êyinew mâkâ nâmoya ni wêpatisin! Âwâsisâk êti kiskitomok tâ mêyo'totâwêmâchik ohi âpêhto'kosisan êyinew. Wêyawâw êti kiskitomok ânima nêya nâmoya êka tâ notinkêyan. Tâ kânâwêyitâmân tâ mêyo itêmkoyan, ni wêhtâmâson, wêyawâw nâmoya kiskêtamok tânisi oma êkê si pimâtisiyahk âpêhto'kosisân. Nâmoya âhpo kê kiskitêchik ânima pêtosiwin ochi Âpêhto'kosisân mêna Nêhiyâwak Eyinew. Kâ opikêyan, ni kiskêtên mâyi'wêchêtowin ochi êyinêwahk âyis kê wâpâtâkik wâpinewi'siwiyân. Wêyawâw k'itwêwak; "Etêhtâm oma kêya mooniyas iskwew" tâna kê wune'chikêkâwiyân âyis kê kiskêtâmân kêkwîy ânima. Ni pooni âtoskân usichi mistikimâw âtoskêwin âyis ochi redneck war whoops, âyisêniwâk kê wêhtâmâkichik Indian jokes: Indians as wagon burners, circling the wagons, ê kê timichik nehiyâwak nâmoya nohtê âtoskêchik.

Ni pêyiten, "let's pow-wow" âhpo "let's do a rain dance", nâmoya kiskêtâchik ikonânhi traditional ceremonies nêwo kêsikâkik êsi spayêkik. Wêyawâw kê mâchiyi sêkâtâchik nêhiyâw mêna âpêhto'kosisan iskwêwak âyis nâmoya ê kâskêtachik tâ itwêchik "Iskwew" mêna ê sêkâtâchik âwâsisâk mooniyaw âhpo Nêhiyaw bastarde. Mêchêtwâw, ni sêpwê'pimohtân kê nêpêwisiyân, ânima wêyusi'wêwin nâwach âymimak tâ otinâmân ochi ni wâhkomâkunak.

Loss of Culture and History

> Métis parents encouraged their daughters to marry white men if they could, for marriage was a sure escape — if not for the Métis woman, at least for her children. Métis women who married white men commonly denied their Indian ancestry as a duty to their husbands' careers. Métis men were not so fortunate. It was a rare occasion for a Métis man to marry a white woman. That social taboo was one of the strongest in white society.
>
> — *From One-and-a-Half-Men: The Story of Jim Brady and Malcolm Norris by Murray Dobbin*

Following 1885, many Métis were relegated to the outskirts of society. Faced with daily discrimination, displacement and shame, some Métis families chose to hide their identity as a survival tactic. Because of this, many Métis lost their culture, language, customs, and community. Some practiced their culture in private, behind closed doors, while others chose to hide their identity even from their own children. Now today, many Métis People are discovering these cultural and family ties. They are learning about their history and connecting to their communities once again to reclaim that which has been taken from them.

Juanita Marois: I don't have memories of being on the land with my Kookum or anything like that. And I guess that's part of the story. I guess I didn't start to identify until I was a young adult.

Nâmoya ni tayân kiskisiwina ê-pimâtsoyahk ânta uskê n'ohkom âschi âhpo kêkway ikosi. Mêna ni miskwêyitumân êkwa'nima pâhki âchimowin… kê ni miskwêyituman êka êmâchitayân istaweyih tâkosiwin iskô nêya kê oskîyi âyiseniw.

And at that point, that was kind of the last recollection I had of, of having a Métis history or identity. So, we grew up very non-Indigenous. We didn't identify as Métis growing up at all. As I reflect back on it now, I realize though that things like going to the Lac

Métis Crossing Staff (Juanita far right)
Photos: Métis Nation of Alberta

Ste. Anne pilgrimage was a very Métis thing to do, but we never identified as Métis.

Mêna iskope, êkwa ânima iskoyanihk kiskisiwin âyâyân ochi, ochi ê-âyâyân Métis kâyas âchimowin âhpo isyaweyih'takosiwin. So, êti opikeyâhk mitoni nâmoya Indigenous. Nêyanân nâmoya isyaweyih'takosiyahk tâskoch li Métis kâ êti opikeyahk sookwach. Kâ mâmitonitâmân êkwa ânima ânoch, ni kisketên kêkwîy tâskoch kâ tohteyahk Lac St. Anne Pilgrimage ânima mitoni li Métis kâ tohtakik, mâka nâmoya wêkach isyaweyih'takosiyahk li Métis.

So it wasn't really until I had graduated from university, I had finished my master's degree. And I was asked by a professor to go into northern Saskatchewan. I had done a very successful master's degree in northern Thailand, and I was very successful integrating with the community. And they asked if I would go into northern Saskatchewan to work on a project that they had been doing up there.

Ikosi, nâmoya iskô kâ kesi kiskinohumakawyan ochi university, nêyâ kê poyoyan ânima Master's Degree. Mêna ê kwechimkawiyan âya ochi kiskinohumakew tâ tohteyan ântê kewitinohk Saskatchewan. Nêyâ kâ poyoyan ânima Masters degree ântê kewintinohk Thailand, mêna mitoni kaskitamasoyan mamawi'tatisiwin usichi ânima mamawe'e'âyachk. Mêna kê kwêchimchik kêspin nêyâ nohtê tohtêyan kêwêtinohk Saskatchewan tâ âtoskêyan ânima kâ mâmâwi'osêtâhk kâkê âtoskatamihk êkote.

I went up to northern Saskatchewan, which, at the time was almost as much culture shock to me as I'd had when I went into Thailand and I spent the best year of my life interviewing Indigenous hunters and trappers.

Ikosi ni tohṭen iskô kewetinohk Saskatchewan, tâna, ikospe kekach ânima nistum pimâchihowin pukamis'kakow kichi nêyâ tâskoch kâkê âyâyân kâ tohteyan Thailand mêna metinaman pêyak uskê oma ni pimatsowin pekiskwatawahk Indigenous mâchiwahk mêna wunihikewiwahk.

So, I interviewed First Nations hunters and Métis hunters, Dene and Cree. And I was in an area of the province at the time that had only had roads come in in the last five years. So, there were people there when I was doing the interviews, I was using an actual interpreter because many of the people I was interviewing — Dene, Cree or Michif was their first language. So, they couldn't speak to me in English, and they took me out onto the land, and they took me hunting and they made me wait while they skinned moose. And they showed me their trap lines and, wild rice harvesting and all sorts of things. And it was during that year that I realized — holy crap, this is who I am. This is a piece of me that I've been missing. And it's something that I can be very proud of. So when I came back, I went to the MNA and I started filling out the genealogy and I had a very clear linkage to the Red River, to the scrip. And it was something that I started pursuing at that time.

Ikosi, ni pêkiskwatawak First Nations machêwak mêna Métis machêwak, Dene mêna Cree. Mêna âyâyân anta uskês ochi the province ikospê kâ âyâchik mêskana âya puko iskôyanihk nêyânan uskêwina. Ikosi, êkotê âyâchik âyiseniwahk êkota ispê nêyâ kâ âtoskataman pekiskwatawina, nêyâ âpâchehak twesta'mâkew âyis mêchet âniki âyiseniwâk kâ pekiskwâtâkik – Dene, Cree âhpo Michif wêyawâw nêkân pêkiskwêwin. Ikosi, nâmoya kê pêkiswêchik English, mêna kê tohtahichik ânta pukwachuske, mêna wêyawâw kê tohtahichik tâ machêyahk mêna wêyawâw kê itohtahichik tâ pêhoyân mêkwach wêyawâw pâhkonikechik mooswa. Mêna kê wapahti'hichik weyawâw wunehikun tipahaskana mêna, pukwachiya wapa'yoominak kâ mawoso'konamihk kistikana mêna kâhkiyâw kêkwîy. Mêna ikospe ânima uskenan kiske'yitaman – holy crap, oma âwêna nêyâ ooma. Ooma pâhki nêyâ kâkê nâmoya âyayan. Mêna êkwa ânima kêkwîy ni kuskêtan mitoni tâ mumichisewa. Ikosi kâ pêkêwiyan, ni tohtan ântê MNA mêna ni mâchitan sakukina'haman ânki âniskôtapana mêna ni tayan mitoni tâpwêwin wawiye'yaspiskos ânta Red River, ânima uskê masinahekan. Mêna êkwa ânima kêkwîy kâ mâchi nawusi'wataman ikospe.

And now twenty years later I'm the executive director of Métis Crossing, leading what will be Canada's first major Métis cultural destination.

Mêna êkdwa neso- mistanaw uskêa mwestus nêyâ oma Executive Director ochi Métis Crossing, ê-nêkânêstâmân ânima Canada's nêkân kêchi sêmakanêkahn Métis nistum pimâchihowin tântê tâ pêtohtêchik.

Beatrice Demetrius, at two or three years old
Photo: Beatrice Demetrius

Beatrice's brother Fred Jobin
Photo: Beatrice Demetrius

Beatrice's aunts Louise and Alice after fishing
Photo: Beatrice Demetrius

Chapter 4

Resiliency and Celebration

Upper: (L) Lucy Jobin (Beatrice's grandfather's sister) and Lucy's nieces Wihlemena and Lisa
Lower: Beatrice's aunts (L-R) Helen, Louise, Alice, and Liza
Photos: Beatrice Demetrius

RESILIENCY AND CELEBRATION

SINCE THE FORMATION of the Métis Nation and of Métis Peoplehood, Métis women have been, and continue to be the heart of the community. Historically, communities and hunting brigades most often consisted of family units connected through maternal kinship ties. These matrilineal connections and systems helped to nurture and preserve the Métis culture.

Against challenges, sexism and discrimination, Métis woman have been strong and resilient. There is a well-known story of the legendary Annie Bannatyne, a Métis woman who was born around 1830 in Red River. In 1869, the Toronto Daily Globe ran a disparaging and belittling article about the Red River Métis and focused particularly on Métis women. About one month later, Annie had occasion to confront the author of said article, Charles Mair, wherein she proceeded to publicly horse whip him while admonishing him for insulting Métis women. Just as Annie Bannatyne and the many strong Métis women who came before her, these Métis women have never lost their spirit despite facing adversity.

In a Métis household, the heart of the home is the kitchen. Furniture would be moved and dances, now known contemporarily as "kitchen parties" would take place. Young and old would participate. Intergenerational visiting and storytelling would take place at the kitchen table. This 'knowledge transmission' was necessary to keep the culture alive. Women played a central role in this. It is through the knowledge and pride in our culture that we, as Métis People have been able to overcome the effects of colonization. While colonization, discrimination and marginalization in many instances served to sever connections and spirits, Métis women remain the matriarchs of our Nation. Whether it is formally recognized or not, within the Métis community, women continue to be regarded as role models and leaders. Knowing and feeling pride in who we are and celebrating the Métis culture is what holds the Métis People together. Regaining and retaining those strong kinship ties and bonds are integral to our personhood and culture.

The Métis People have elected a remarkable woman, Audrey Poitras, as the President of the Métis Nation of Alberta an unprecedented eight times. Under her leadership, the Métis Nation of Alberta has grown exponentially. The MNA now has a variety of Departments and Affiliates, all of which are dedicated to improving the lives of Métis citizens across Alberta. The MNA also owns Métis Crossing which is the first major cultural interpretive centre in Alberta; it is located along the banks of the North Saskatchewan River, near Smoky Lake, Alberta. This centre serves to preserve the Métis language and culture for current and future generations. The development and operation of this facility mirrors the core values of the Métis community including self-sufficiency, respect of Elders, participation of youth, and pride in our culture.

The Métis Nation has specific representation from women as well. Les Femmes Michif Otipemisiwak, Women of the Métis Nation (LFMO–WMN), advocates specifically for women's rights. The mandate is to "ensure that Métis women from across the Homeland are safe, connected, empowered to help create the conditions for healthy, vibrant, and productive communities throughout the Métis Nation." Under the leadership of Melanie Omeniho, LFMO-WMN, has been involved in Provincial, Territorial, Federal, and United Nations-level consultations for the Status of Women, as well as giving a voice at Child and Family Services summits, creation of a "Trauma Informed Toolkit," facilitating conferences, and raising awareness about Missing and Murdered Indigenous Women, Girls and 2SLGBTQQIA+ community members.

Although there are far too many Métis women to honour in one book, we also honour Melanie Omeniho's mother, Marge Friedel, who was one of the founders of the Women of the Métis Nation, as well as a founder of Amiskwaciy Academy in Edmonton (the first Indigenous public high school of its kind). Sheila Genaille is also notable for her work with the National Métis Women of Canada. Thelma Chalifoux was the first Métis woman in the Canadian Senate. Today, another Métis woman, Patti LaBoucane-Benson serves as the Director of Research at the Native Counselling Services of Alberta, as well as a sitting Canadian Senator. Marilyn Dumont has changed the literary landscape with her expressive and evocative poetry, which often focuses on her Métis identity and culture. Margaret Froh is a lawyer and the President of the Métis Nation of Ontario, and Maria Campbell is a prolific Métis author, playwright, and filmmaker whose pivotal memoir *Halfbreed* has inspired generations of Métis People across Canada.

This is only a small sampling of the many accomplished Métis women across the Homeland. There are now Métis women who are doctors, lawyers, academics, athletes, and above all, proud matriarchs to their Métis families and communities.

It is through the knowledge of culture, through the ways of knowing, through respect, reciprocity, and relationality, that the women are strong and resilient. We celebrate their stories as we present how far they have come, what they are doing now, or how they are remembered by their family and community.

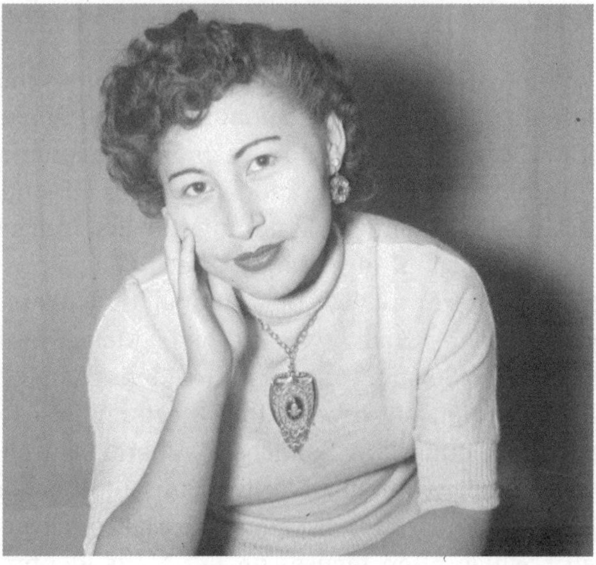

Young Angie Crerar
Photo: Angie Crerar

Angie Crerar: Angie is currently the President of Métis Nation of Alberta Local 1990 in Grande Prairie, AB. She has become an active supporter of Métis and First Nations students, knowing the first-hand pain and loneliness as a survivor of the residential school system. She was even personally invited by Prime Minister Justin Trudeau to attend the annual Crown-Métis summit in 2017 where she conducted the opening prayer on Parliament Hill. Now in her 80s, Angie is a mother of eleven children and a grandmother to twenty-three.

"It was Grande Prairie and the people I met at the Friendship Centre who taught me my self esteem and how to acknowledge who I am. I never knew I had skills! We all have special gifts; I found mine were giving and kindness. I still feel like I have lots to give. I got so much help when I got here, and it is now my turn to help others reach their goals and vision.

"Êkwa'nima Grande Prairie mêna âyisêniwahk kâ nakiskawakik ântê the Friendship Centre kâ kiskinohumakichik nêyâ sakihitown mêna tânisi nuskwesih'tamsoyahn âwêna nêyâ oma.

Angie Crerar waving a Métis flag
Photo: Métis Nation of Alberta

Nâmoya kê tehtaman kê âyâyân kuskihiwona! Kâhkiyâw kêyanaw âyayahk kechi kuskihiwona; ni êti kiskeyihtaman ânhi tâ mekosoyan mêna kisewatisiwin. Kêyapich ni moositan tâskoch nêyâ âyâyân mistâhi tâ mêkêyan. Nêyâ kê mêkawiyan mistâhi wêchihowin tânispê kâ pêtakohteyan ota, mêna ânima êkwa nêyâ tâ wêchihakik kotukik tâ cachitinakik wêyawâw kâ nitawehtakik pimatisiwin ochi.

It took me 64 years to regain my identity, my family, and my community. I thank God for the opportunity to help those out there, to hear their stories and give them a voice so they can take control of their lives and their self-esteem."

"Êkwa'nima 64 uskêkewina tâ kachitinaman kawi la famille mêna ânâ mamawi'e'âyahk. Ni nanaskomon kichi manito kê mêkiwiyahkik kâ nahi payik tâ wêchihakik wêyawâw êkote, tâ pêhtamahk wêyawâw âchimona mêna tâ mêyakik wêyawâw pêkiskwêwin ikosi wêyawâw tâ kê otinakik puminekwêwin ochi weyawâw pimatiswin mêna wêyawâw sakihitowin."

Family Gravestones at Batoche
Photo: Beatrice Demetrius

Beatrice Demetrius: A friend from the Métis Nation said they were looking for a researcher to do Métis genealogy; I applied and got the job. I retired after fifteen years it was such a rewarding time helping people do their family trees, especially at the beginning. It was so new to them, and they were so excited to know about their ancestry.

Ni tohtem ochi la Métis Nation ê-twechik ê nantonakêt nutonikêwiniw tâ âtoskatakit Métis ânisko kumakêwin; ê-nitotâmân mêna ni kachitinên êkwa'nima âtoskêwin. Ni poona putisiw mwestus nêyân fifteen years êkwa'nima mitoni tipahumakosiwin nahêyikok kê wêchihakik âyiseniwak tâ osêtachik wêyawâw la famille mêtosa, wawes êkwa kâ mâchipayêk. Sooskwach oskayi wêyawâw, mêna wêyawâw mitoni ê-wahke koskweyatisiwahk tâ kiskehtachik wêyawâw wahkomêtowin.

I believe in respecting my white grandfathers as I respect my First Nations grandmothers, for we wouldn't be Métis without them. We fought many battles to be recognized as a distinct

Norma Spicer, Beatrice Demetrius, and Doreen Poitras at 2019 MNA AGA in St. Paul

Photo: Beatrice Demetrius

group of people, we are the Bois Brules, Half-breeds, or Métis. Don't mix our culture with any other group.

Ni tâpwêhtên tâ mêyo tohtawêyan ni moshomahk moniyawahk tâskoch kâ tohtawêyan n'ohkomahk nistum pêyako sehtwawin, ochi nêyanân nâmoya nohtê kâkê pimâtsonân li Métis êka wêyawâw ochi. Niyanan ê notinkêyahk mistâhi tâ nistawinawêw'yahk tâskoch pechâw mêchetiwak âyinewâhk, nêyanâw oma li Bois Brules, Apihtâwkosisânâhk, âhpo Métis. Kâya tâ kêkawena nêyanân nistum pimâchihowin usichi kohtuk mêchetiwak.

Delia Gray: Delia Gray passed away in 1999. These are the teachings she left her daughters, granddaughters, and great granddaughters.

Daughters

Bobbi: It's good to know that my mom is important to the Métis community, as this was always important to her. As well as her ancestral line, this is why I felt it was important to identify the families that her Indigenous and Scottish blood flows from and that we, the next generation, carry on the bloodline.

Mêyosin tâ kiskêhitâmân ni mama kêchîyi'wun ochi li Métis mamawi'e'âyâhk, âyis oma tâhki kêchîyi'wun wêya kichi. Tâpiskoch usichi wêya wâhkomitowin tipâhaskân, êkosi oma kê moositâmân ânima kê kêchîyi'wun tâ nista'wey-imiht lis familles âna wêya Indigenous mêna Scottish mêh-koh pimichiwun ochi mêna nêyanân, kotuk ânisko'tapân, tâ tâhkonâkik ânima mehkoh tipahâskân.

Anne: My mom was in charge at home, and she ran a tight ship. If her children were squabbling about anything, her response (after discerning the cause of the altercation) was always: "Now shake hands. Kindness starts at home." When it came time to choose her epitaph, my siblings and I agreed those four words were it. As an adult, I fully appreciate the meaning of those words and I strive to live by them. Another directive from my mom was: "Never sink to a person's level." Together with "Kindness starts at home," all of life's challenges can be met with dignity, compassion, and empathy.

Ni mama kê tipinkêt ânta ni wêkinân, mêna kê puminâhk a tight ship. Kêspin otawasimisak kêsiwâsichik puko kêkwîy, wêya nuspimowin (mwestus kâ kiskêyihtamâk tânêhki ochi kâ notinkêchik) kê tâhki: "Êkwa pâhpâwina kichêchêya, kise'wâtisiwin mâchipâyin ni wêkinâk." Êkospê kâ mâchi-payek tâ nâwâsonayâhk wêya epitaph, ni sêmisak mêna nêyâ ikonanhi neyo pêkiskwêna. Tapis'koch kê kesohpi'ki-win, mitoni meye'yihtam itwemu'kâhk ikonânhi pêkisk-wêna mêna n'âtoskâ'tâmân êkosi tâ pimâtisiyan. Kohtuk nâtotum ochi ni mama ke: "Kâyâ wêkâch kosâpew kotuk âyisêniw kumikohk." Mâmâwi usichi "kise'wâtisiwin mâchipayin ni wêkinâk," kâhkiyâw pimâtisiwin mâwin'wê-chi'wina kâke nuskiska'wew usichi kiste'yimowin, kitimâke'yimi'wewin mêna moosihtâ'win.

Delia Gray
Photo: Cynthia Dunnigan

Elizabeth (Betty): My grandmothers both passed away before I was born, but I would like to pass on a story about my mother. She passed away 20 years ago and what I miss is that she was always in my corner. This does not mean to say that she always agreed with my choices, but she stood by me. One year I was about to leave to run my first marathon.

Nohkomâk kê pooni'pimâchisi'wâk pâmweyês nêya kâ pimâtsoyan, mâka nohtê mêkiyân âchimowin ochi ni mama. Wêya kê pooni'pimâchisiw nânto nêstanâw uskêwina uspin mêna kêkwîy ni kwetâwe'yihten ânima wêya kê tâhki in my corner. Nâmoya oma itwemu'kâhk ânima wêya kâkike tâpwehtumit nêyâ nâwasona'mâwina, mâka wêya kê nêpawot usichi nêya. Pêyak uskê nêyâ mekwach kê we sipweteyan tâ pimpahtayan nêyâ oma nistum kakwe pimpahtawewin.

I was leaving early in the morning and the phone rang about 4:30 a.m. It was my mother who said, "I don't understand what you are doing, but good luck!" I still draw strength from that moment.

Nêyâ êti sepwêtêyan kêkisêpa mêna sêwêpchikun kê sêwêpchikunêk nanto 4:30 a.m. Êkwa'nima ni mama âwêna k'itwêt "Nâmoya nisitohtên kêkwîy kê tohtamêk, mâka good luck!" Kêyapich ni maskawsêwin êkota ochi kunaskês.

Granddaughters

Cynthia: My Kookum sent me out into the world full of her teachings about everything from Cree to lipstick and short skirts to saying the Rosary twice a day. If I had to summarize what she stood for I would say the Cree language, her Catholic faith and prayer, family — not just her own family but the extended family of the Métis community, and service to the Indigenous community. She was always volunteering and on boards. With her combined teachings on those things, she sent me into the world wrapped in confidence to be Métis, to never ever think I was anything else. It never occurred to me to be anything but proud. She had a way of giving me confidence without making me prideful. She'd say, "My girl I'm so glad you're not afraid to wear red lipstick. But I can't tell you that, I don't want it to go to your head." She did not like to talk about people behind their back, she would say "I won't say anything behind someone's back that I wouldn't say to their face," and she meant it. I saw her do it many times and the funny thing is, people were always okay to hear what she had to say to them.

Nohkom kê sipwe'tisâhit ântê misiwe'uskê usichi wêya kiskino'humâkêwina âyâ ochi kâhkêyâw kêkwîy ochi Cree yisi mêhko'tonêhon mêna chimâsina kêskusâ'kâs êkote kê pêkiskwâtamân âna âyamihêminâk nêso ânta pêyak kêsikâw. Kêspin tâ mâmu'wusina'hikêyân kêkwîy wêya tâpwêhtâhk nêyâ kâke itwân ânima Nehiyâwewin, wêya Catholic tapohke'tumowin mêna âyimahewin, li famille, nâmoya puko wêya la famille mâkâ kotuk mêna wâhkomâkuna ochi li Métis mâmâwi'e'âyâk, mêna tâ wechihat ânihi Indigenous mâmâwi'e'âyâk. Wêya kâkike nosohkum'âkew mêna âyât âtoskâtewina kâ pumina'mihk. Usichi wêya kiskino'humakewina âniki kêkwîya, wêya ê tisahot misiwe'uskê wewekina usichi sohke'yimowin to be

Delia Gray with members of the Aboriginal Veterans Society of Alberta
Photo: Cynthia Dunnigan

Métis, nâmoya wekâch t'itehtaman oma nêyâ kotuk kêkwîy. Nâmoya wekâch ni tehten êka tâ kiste'yimoyan. Wêya ê âyât tânisi tâ meyit sohke'yimowin kwetamaw tâ mechimoyan. Wêya k'itwew "n'iskwesis ni mêyoten êka ê kostâmân tâ putskâmân mêhko'tonêhon. Mâkâ nâmoya kâkê wehtamatan êkwa'nima, nâmoya ni tawehtaman kistikwan t'ispayek. Wêya nâmoya nohtê pêkiskwâtew âyisêniwak otâhk'ochi ospis'kwun, wêya êtwew "Nâmoya kêkwîy n'itwan âwêyahk âyisêniw otâhk'ochi ospis'kwun ânima n'itoyan ochi wêyawâw mêhkaw'kun" mêna wêya kêchi'nâhow. Ni wapamaw ikosi êtohtahk mêchetwaw mêna wâwihate'tâkwun kêkwîy, âyisêniwak kê tahki tâ pehtakik kêkwîy wêya t'itwet yisi weyawâw.

Krista: The most important thing she taught me was to be proud that I am Métis, and to make sure my children learn this as well. She taught me that no matter what happens in our lives, we still belong. Even if we end up far away from our communities and the places we once called home, we are still Métis, we are still loved, and we still have people who claim us as family. I have spent a lot of time working with families and individuals who are on their journey to reconnect with the Métis community and the lessons Kookum taught me included that there is no shame in not knowing the stories or where you are from. There is only joy in coming back and rebuilding relationships that were lost or taken. And those of us who know the stories, the art, the ways of our people — we have a responsibility to share this with those who are just learning, without judgement.

Kâ mitoni kêchîyi'wun kêkwîy wêya kê kiskino'humawit tâ kê kiste'yimoyan ânima nêya oma Métis, mêna tâ kêchi'nahowyan ni chiwasimsak kiskino'hum'akêchik êkw'ânima mêna. Wêya kê kiskino'humowith ânima nâmoya mêyêwin kêkwîy ispayêk kâ pimatisiyahk, kêyanaw kêyapich tipe'yêhtak'osiw. Kêyam kêspin wunuskoch wahiyaw ochi keyanaw mamawi'e'âyahkana mêna nêta pêyakwaw kitotamahk kêkinaw, kêyanaw kêyapich li Métis, kêyanaw kêyapich ki sahkihokinawahk, mêna kêyanaw kêyapich âyayahk âyisêniwak âwêna otinewyahk tâskoch li famille. Ni kê apachitan mêchetwaw tipahikun âtoskêyan usichi li familles mêna âyisêniwak kâ pimohtêchik oma pimatisiwin tâ ânishkotaw kawi usichi li Métis mamawi'e'âyahk mêna ânhi kiskino'humake'wina n'ohkom kâ kiskino'humowit êwuko'mêna nâmoya tâ nêpewsitchik êka kiskitiyichik ânhi âchimona âhpo tanite ochi kêya. Êkota puko mêyo'watamowin kakê pê'itohteyêk kawi mêna âchi'sêtaw wâhkotowin kakê wanêhtayahk âhpo otinamakawiyahk. Mêna âniki kêyanaw kâ kiskiyihtamak ânihi âchimona, ânihi musinêpê'hike'wina, nântâwisi ochi kêyanaw âyisêniwak – kêyanaw puko âyayak nêpawêstum'iyahk tâ pahkwênumawê'yahk oma usichi ânihi mwechi kâ mâchi kiskino'humasochik usichi makêkwîy wêyusiwêwin.

Great Granddaughters

Josephine and Sullivan: The stories from our (câpân) great-Kookum, have been passed to us through the women that she raised. Our mother, our Kookum, and our aunties have all raised us, and through them we have learned the lessons that our câpân instilled into them. Our mother, Cynthia, was essentially raised by her Kookum and this instilled a great respect and love for grandparents within her. Because of this, we grew up with our grandparents as major influences and caretakers because our mother, due to the time spent with her Kookum, learned the importance of family in a child's life. We should note that our Kookum is Bobbi but because we were so fortunate to still have Delia, for us great grandchildren she became Old Kookum and Bobbi was Young Kookum.

Ânihi âchimona ochi ni châpânân, kohkomnân, kê pê mekâwiyâhk sapo âniki iskwewak kâke ohpikihat. Ni mama, nêyanan n'ohkom, mêna mes tantes kâhkiyâw kê pe'opikihiyakik, mêna sapo weyawâw nêyanan kê kiskno'humakew'iyahk ânâ nêyanan chapanan kâ kiskeyih'tumoyahk. Ni mamanan, Cynthia, kê pe'ohpikihatikot ohkoma mêna êkoma kê kiskeyih'tumoyahk kechi mêyo'totawew mêna sakihitowin ochi chapanak ochi wêya. yis oma, nêyanan kê opikeyahk usichi ni chapanak tapiskoch kechi ispa'yiwina mêna okanaweyi'mawasowak âyis ni mamanan, âyis ochi tipahikun apachitachik usichi ohkoma, kiskiyehtamahk ânima kêchîyi'wun ochi la famille ânima âwâsis pimatisiwin. Nêyanan tâ kê musinahikunis'iyahk ânima n'ohkomnan wêya Bobbi mâka âyis nêyanan kê weyô'tisiwin keyapich t'ayayahk Delia, nêyanan kichi o'chapan'âwâsisâk wêya êkwana kehtayi n'ohkom mêna Bobbi wêya êkwana oskiyi n'ohkom.

For as long as we can remember, our Aunt Betty and our mom would take us to the graveyard to see our Great-Kookum. As little girls, we would go for sleepovers at Betty's apartment. Betty always taught us about ghosts and death. When we would go to Holy Cross cemetery, she would show us Kookum and Mosom's graves, and tell us stories about growing up. That's where we remember learning so much about Old Kookum.

Iskô kâ kiskisiwew'iyahk, nêyanan aunt Betty mêna ni mamanaw kê tohtahikoyahk antê wateh'kan uskekanis tâ ni to wapamayahk nêyanan chapan. Kâ âwasisoyahk iskwesisak, nêyanan kê tohteyak tâ kapesiyahk antê Betty's pis'kichi'wêki'nânisa. Betty mânakakike kiskinohumakaweyahk âniki chêpiya mêna pooni pimâchisowin. Tânispê kâ tohteyahk Holy Cross Cemetary, wêya kê wahpatahikoyahk n'ohkom mêna moshom's wateh'kana, mêna kê wehtakoyahk âchimona âya ochi tâ ohpikewin. Êkota'ânima nêyanan kâ kiskiseyahk kê kiskinohumakawiyak êkoh n'ohkomnan.

Old Kookum loved to sit in her rocking chair and hold Sullivan as a baby. From the stories, it sounds like she could do it for hours. That chair now sits in Josie's house, and we all still rock in it from time to time. According to our mother, Old Kookum couldn't get enough of rocking the great-grand daughters as we were all born. Our Mother tells a story of how Old Kookum still rocked Cynthia when she was in her 30s. She loved to hold her family close.

N'ohkomnan kê sahkitum t'apit pechiyi son la chaise mêna tâ tahkonat Sullivan ka'awasisoyit. Ochi ânihi âchimona, k'iteht'kwun tâskoch wêya kê kasketat ikosi t'itohtak iskô tipahikuna. Êkwa'nima la chaise êkwa chepatastew ânta Josie's waskihikun, mêna kâhkiyâw nêyanan keyapich apachitayak kâhke'twâm kêsikâw. Êkosê isi ni mamanan, kehtaya nohkomaw nâmoya kasketat êkwehiko ochi tâ wewepisot o'châpân tânisa kâkê pimatsochik. Ni mamanân pekiskwâtum âna âchimona ochi tânisi kehtâyâhk n'ohkomnan keyâpich kê wewepisot Cynthia tânispê wêya k'ayat in her 30s. Wêya kê mitoni mêyotahk tâ michi'minat âmê sa famille.

Doreen Bergum: Sharing the words of my mother Mary Vaness Dumont — Always remember "You are good enough and don't let anyone tell you that they are better than you!"

Kâ puhkwênumawêyan pêkiskwêwina ochi ni mama Mary Vaness Dumont - "Kêya oma mêyo ê-koyikohk mêna kâya pukitina pukwâ'wiyak tâ wêhtamowis wêyawâw nâwach ê mêyo pimâtisit iskô kêya!"

It has been an honour serving as Elder/Knowledge Keeper for the Métis Nation of Alberta, Region 3 since 2011. [She has

Left: Doreen Bergum with Métis puppets. Right: In Métis vest and skirt
Photo: Doreen Bergum

also received an Esquao award in 2019 for her work within the Métis community.]

Kêchi yimitowin âtoskataman oma Elder/Knowledge Keeper kichi li Métis Nation of Alberta, Region 3 iskô 2011. [Westa mêna ohtitikow ânima Esquao Award in 2019 kichi âtoskêwin ânta li Métis mâmâw'e'âyâhk.]

I became a champion jigger, winning competitions at Edmonton, Calgary, Batoche, John Arcand Fiddle Fest, and Lewistown, Montana. I now teach jigging at Cypress Hills and in Olds. I have the Olds Métis Youth Dancers and we perform in the Olds area.

Ni kê pê otahowân nêosimowin, êti otahoyân mawine'hito'wina ântê Edmonton, Calgary, Batoche, John Arcand Fiddle Fest, mêna Lewistown, Montana. Nêyâ êkwa ê-kisisnohamakeyan nesosimowin ântê Cypress Hills mêna ântê Olds. Ni tayan ânki Olds Métis Youth Dancers mêna nêyanân meta weh'kasoyâk ânte Olds uskês.

Walking in the footsteps of our ancestors: it is with great pride and gratitude sharing and educating people on our Métis culture and spirit!

Êti pimohtêyân tâhkoskêwina ochi nêyanân wâhkoma'kunâk: êkwa ânima mitoni kêchi kiste'yimow mêna nanaskomowin, pahkwênumâwêwin mêna kiskino'humâkêyân âyisêniwâk oma kêyanâw Métis nistim'pimâchihowin mêna âchâk.

Keep safe, stay healthy and God bless!

Kunawemso, to mêyo'yayin mêna Manito âsâwe'hihta!

Doreen Poitras: Doreen is retired from working in the telecommunications industry. She is a past board member of the City of Edmonton's Rejuvenation of Parks project and served for six years on the board of Urban and Capital Housing. She is also a past board member of the Edmonton Indigenous Seniors Center.

Doreen received an Esquao Award in 2019 for her volunteer work within the Métis community. In her spare time, she enjoys painting commissioned feathers and antlers, and golfing with her friends.

Bertha Clark-Jones (as told by Gail Gallupe): She (Bertha Clark-Jones) had only gone to grade nine because after that she was able to get into the air force. It didn't stop her though. She was a good reader.

Wêya êke tohteht iskô kâ ati kiskino'humaht keka'mitahtaht âyis mwestas êkwa ânima wêya ê'kasketaht tâ machêtat ânima Air Force. Nâmoya kê nakiniko wêya mâka. Wêya ê mêyo âyimichiket.

It's true when they say learning is lifelong achievement, which I believe she proved herself over the years. So being adept at reading and writing, she became the President of the first Alberta Native Woman's Society which is still going today. From there,

Left: Doreen Poitras with her son. Right: At the 2019 Esquao Awards
Photo left: Poitras family. Photo right: Colette Poitras

they branched out and did another society called the Aboriginal Woman's Society (AAW). She advocated for the welfare of any mother who needed it who was Indigenous.

Tâpwe tânispe kâ itwêchik kis'keyih'tamowin ânima misa'kamê pimâtisiwin kêsêtawewin, tâna ni tâpweten wêya kechi'nâhow pâschi pêyak uskêwina. Ikosi châstâpew ânima âyimichêkêwin mêna musinahikêwin, kê atoskatahk President ochi nistum Alberta Native Women's Society tâna kêyapich kê pimpayek ânoch. Êkota ochi, puskêmaw mêna osêtachik kotuhk mâmâwêhitowin êsihkatêk Aboriginal Women's Society (AAW). Wêya natot'westamâkêt âschi nêsoh'kuma'kêwin kichi niko'twâw mikâwe kâ nitawehtak êkwa ânima wêya Indigenous.

They would help them out — they would advocate if they had trouble with the courts then they went to court with them. They got translators for the Cree and Dene speaking women and men. So, this kept her very busy and very happy.

Wêyâwâw ê wêchihâchik - wêyawâw natot'westamâkechik kêspin âyimpaywin usichi oyusi'wewi'kamik êkospê wêyawâw kê itohtechik oyusi'wewi'kamik âschi wêstawâw. Ê kachitinâchik pêkiskwestum'âwêwahk kichi Cree mêna Dene kê pêkiskwêchik iskwewahk mêna nâpewahk. ikosi, ooma kê kanawêmkot mitoni otamatoskew mêna mitoni mêyowe'yihtamok.

She did get an award for the Golden Jubilee medal in 2002. Then she received the Lifetime Achievement award and a National Aboriginal Achievement award for the foundation. It's now named Indspire.

Wêya âchitinum kêchi musinahikun ôchi Golden Jubilee Medal in 2002. Êkospê wêya otihtikot ânima Lifetime Achievement Award mêna ânima National Aboriginal Achievement Award âya kichi wêyus'chêkêwin. Êkwa ânima ê sêkatêk Indspire.

Mom's name is now registered in the hall of registries for Aboriginal veterans. She also went and fought for their rights — for Aboriginal veteran's rights. A lot of reserves lost good men, because of the discrimination against them. When they came back, they had no property. They couldn't go back to their reserves.

Ni mama ôwêhowin musina hikêwinaka kunawê'yihtumihk ânta musina hikêwinaka kunawê'yihta kichi Aboriginal Veterans. Wêya mêna ni to notinkêt wêyawâw kichi rights -kichi Aboriginal Veterans rights. Mistâhi reserves kê wanihâchik noti'nikêwahk âyis ochi ânima pêwe'yimitowin mayi'wêche'wêwahk wêstawâw. Kâ pêkêwichik nâmoya tâ kê kêwêchik ântê wêyawaw reserves.

These are things my mom found out about, and my mom fought for. There is a well-established Aboriginal veterans' group and they are well looked after. This brings me to the time my mom had to go to France.

Oki kêkwîya ni mama êti kiskêyihtum, mêna ni mama kê notinkêt kichi. Êkota âstew mâchitawêwin Aboriginal Veterans mâmâwêpiwin mêna wêyawâw kweyes ê-kânâwêmkâwchik. Ota êkwa ispê ni mama pohko tâ yihtohtêt France.

She phones me up and she says, "Gail, would you like to come on a little trip?" And I said, "Well, where?" She said, "Well, we're going to France." I said, "France, why?" And she said, "Because we've been asked to go as members of veterans in Alberta and across Canada to commemorate and bring home the spirits of their fallen soldiers that never made it across the seas back home to Canada after the Second World War."

Weya pê sêwepitamawit mêna itwew, "Gail, ki nohtê wêchiwin oma âpsis sepwetiwin. Mêna nitwan, "well tânte?" Wêya itwew, "Well ê-wihtoteyahk ântê France." N'itwan, "France, tanehki?" Mêna itwew, "Ayis, ê pê wêchimkawiyahk tayitohtêyahk owechihêwak ochi veterans ânta Alberta mêna kuskêwêt Canada kêchyimitowin mêna pêkêwêtahewahk âchahka âniki fallen oonotinkêwahk êka kâ kuskêwêt kêchi'kume tâ pêkêwêchik ote Canada uskoch Second World War."

So, of course I was delighted to be able to have this experience with my mom and we went off, we went and the stories were good because there were a lot of other people she met there that had been in the war. We visited a lot of countryside, as well as the Juno Beach site.

Ikosi, tâpwê ânima ni mêyehtên tâ âyâyân oma kiskeyih'tumowin usichi ni mama mêna ni sipwêtêhnan, nêyanân mêna âniki âchimona kê mêyosik âyis êkotê mistâhi kotuk âyisêniwak kê nakiskawat kâkê âyâchik ânta notinkêwin. Mistâhi ni wapahtênan êkwa ânima uskê. Nêyanân kêwêkiyahk timew uskêhkan âschi ânima June uskêhkân.

We visited a lot of memorials. We went to Belgium and Holland. And when we got off of the bus one day the people there were lined up and they were crying and coming up to the veterans and hugging them. It was a very, very moving moment for my mom. My mom always carried little stuff around with her to give to people. She always had a whole bunch of Canada pins which she had gotten from our town mayor and she'd give those out. She gave them to the children; they all loved that, but she also had a little tiny little flag. She took this little flag, and it was a windy day, and you could just imagine ships coming up to Juno beach and trying to lie down there on those bad days. But it was very windy. The waters were choppy. She got her little rain hood on and she took her little flag, and she went and planted it into the soil. She said, "Here, I'm here. I'm from Canada." And then she got back on the bus. And actually, it was a picture in the paper there. So those are the things my mom wasn't ever afraid to do. And she liked to — she was proud of, and loyal to Canada. And so she took her messages quite a few places.

Nêyanân kêwêkiyahk mistâhi kakiskisototaht. Nêyanân kê tohteyahk ântê Belgium mêna Holland. Mêna kâ nêtuchiweyah poosiwin pêyak kêsikâw âyisêniwahk kiposkâtochik mêna wêyawâw kê matochik mêna pêtohtêwahk âniki veterans mêna âkwus'kitinêwachik wêstawâw. Êwuko mitoni mêyo têhiwin kichi ni mama. Mêna, nêyanân kâ wapahtamahk, ikosi ni mama kâkike tahkonum âpisâsiki kêkwîya tâ meyât âyiseniwahk. Wêya kâkike k'âyat mistâhi Canada saponi'kunisa tâna wêya kê kachitina ochi nêyanân nêkân'apiw otenâhk mêna wêya ê-mekit ikonanhi. Wêya ê-meyat ikonanhi âwasisâk; weyawâw kâhkiyâw ê-mêyotahkik ekwa'nima, mâka wêya mêna âyât âpisasik ukotason. Wêya otinam oma ukotason, mêna yotin kêsikâw, mêna keyawâw kâkê mâmitonitâmek nâpehkwâna kâ petakopayiki ânta Juno Beach mêna kê kakwe pimi'sini'kichik êkota ispê ânhi mayi kesikâwa. Make mitoni kê yotehk. Ânima nipe mahkaskun. Wêya potiskam ânima kimiwun kesow'ustotin mêna kê otinahk ânima apisasik ukotason, mêna kê tohtet mêna kistikew êkw'ânima ânta uskê. Wêya êtwew, "Ota, Ni tayan ota. Nêyâ ochi Canada." Mêna êkospe wêya kawi êti posit poosiwin. Mêna tâpwe, êwuko ânima musini'payiwin êstek ânta âchimo'usinahikun êkote. Itam, êkonanhi kêkwîy ni mama êka kê

Bertha Clark in uniform and receiving the Jubilee medal
Photos: Gail Gallupe

sekisit wêhkâch tatohtâhk. Mêna wêya kê mêyotam tatohtâhk. Êkwa ânima mumichisewin mêna âsota makew tape'win âschi Canada. Mêna itam, wêya ê-tohtatat âchimona, mitoni mistâhi places.

Now back in the day my mom would always recruit me, she would bring me to the meetings. And I'm glad now, because if it weren't for my mom, I myself would not have the pride, integrity, ethics, or the knowledge of the culture of the Métis People. It was because of her. She revived it in our family.

Êkwa kâyas oma ni mama êkwechimit tâ wechihak, wêya kê pê tohtahit ântê mamawapeya. Mêna, ni mêyoten êkwa, âyis kespin êka wêya ochi ni mama, Nêyâ nâmoya ni tayan mumichisewin, kwayusk'watisiwin, âniskes kuma'kewin, âhpo kiske yihtamo'win nistum pimâchihowin ochi Métis âyiseniwak. Wêya ânima ochi. Wêya pimâchihewiyahk nêyân li famille.

Juanita: I shared my story about sitting at the table and having my grandmother say that we shouldn't identify. When I reflect on that, it's like, that was a piece of me that was taken away. But as a parent, now we constantly try to make the best choices for our kids. We try to decide what is going to help our children succeed in life.

Ni pêkiskwaten n'achimon nântâw k'apiyahk ântê la table mêna n'ohkom kê itwet ânima êka t'istaweyih tâkosiwin. Kâ mamitonitaman êkwa ânima, êkw'ânima tâskoch, êkwa ânima pâhki nêyâ kê muskamkawiyan. Mâka êkwa nekehikowiyan, nêyanan êkwa tapi'tawi payiw tâ osehtayahk ânihi mamwayes ê mêyosiki nawasona'mawin kichi ni chiwasimsinanahk. Nêyanân kese'yihtamahk kêkwîy tâ wêchihayakohk ni otawasimsinanak tâ kuskihowichik oma pimatsowin.

So, I can't be angry about it because they were honestly making what they thought would be the best choice in life, and I may not be the person I am now had they not made those choices. But for me now, I bring my kids to work and they get to be at Métis Crossing. They get to spend time with our Elder, with our Knowledge Holders, with our crafters.

Ikosi, nêyâ nâmoya kâkê kisowasin êkwa ânima âyis weyawâw kwuyusk'watisichik kâ tohtakik kêkwîy kâ tetakihk ânhi mamwayes ê mêyosiki nawasona'mawin kichi pimatsowin, mêna âhpwetikwe nâmoya âyisêniw nêyâ oma êkwa kespin êka osehtachik êkonanhi nawasona'mawina. Mâka nêyâ oma êkwa, ni pesowawahk ni chiwasimsak ânta âtoskewin mêna weyawâw kâ nahi'payik ta'âyâchik ântê Métis Crossing. Weyawâw kaskitawak tâ kiskino'humawekichik ochi nêyanan Kehte'yiseniw, usichi nêyanan Knowledge Holders, usichi nêyanan âtoska'tomowina.

I was at home with my son and he was flipping through a social studies textbook and it came to a section on the Métis Nation of Alberta, and he's like, "Mom, this is President Poitras and that's about Métis Crossing. This is us." I'm like, "Wow, I know that's us," but the generational change where he was so proud, he's so proud to know that we are here. That we're a part of this, that we're creating something really amazing for, not only the Métis People, but it's respected in the Province of Alberta and it's going to become pretty important to the whole tourism industry in Canada. So, he now is very proud to say "I'm Métis and my mom works at Métis Crossing, and this is who I am."

Nêyâ oma neki âyâyân âschi ni kisos mêna wêya kê kweski'pitahkk sapo ânima Social Studies masinahikun mêna penokwun ânima pâhki ochi Métis Nation of Alberta, mêna wêya tâskoch, "Mom, âwa oma President Poitras mêna êkwa ânima Métis Crossing. Keyanaw oma." Nêyâ oma tâskoch, "Watstkach, ni kisketen ânima keyanaw" mâka ânima âniskotapan kâ meskochipayik êkohk kê mumichisew, wêya êkohk mitoni kê mumichisew tâ kiskeyitahk ota âyayahk. Ânima keyanaw pâhki ochi oma, ânima keyanaw ê-osetayahk kêkwîy mitoni mamaskatumowin kichi, nâmoya puko li Métis âyiseniwahk, mâka êkwa ânima mêyo totumakewin ânta the Province of Alberta mêna êkwa ânima tâ peyispayiw mitoni kechiyiwun ochi kaykew kâ sekatek tourism industry in Canada. Ikosi, wêya êkwa mitoni mumichisew tâ êtwet "Nêyâ Métis mêna ni mama âtosket ântê Métis Crossing, mêna âwa oma âwêna nêyâ."

Whereas just two generations ago, it was like, "No, you don't talk about that." And I bring that into my role here in a very meaningful way because I'm not alone. After 1885, there were lots of families that chose not to identify, but it's a piece that's been missing. So, all of those people who now after the Truth and Reconciliation Commission are saying, "Hey, I know this is a piece of me, but I don't know how to find out about it."

Mâka mwechi nêso âniskotapana uspin. Êkwa ânima tâskoch, "Nâmoya, keya kiya pekiskwata êkwa'nima." Mêna nêyâ ê-pehtatayan ânima totamowin ota kâ mitoni itwemukahk âyis nâmoya ê-pêyakoyan. Mwestes 1885, mêchet ânki li famille êka tâ istaweyih'tâkosichik, mâka êkwa ânima pâhki kâkê nâmoya âyayan. Ikosi, kâhkiyâw ânki âyiseiwak âwêna êkwa mwestes ânima Truth and Reconciliation Commission kâ k'itwechik,

"Hey, ni kiskiten oma pâhki ochi nêyâ, mâka nâmoya ni kisketen tânisi tâ miskaman êkw'anima."

They can now come to Métis Crossing and ask questions, difficult questions, in a very safe place. And I can relate to that. It's very meaningful when I talk to any of our partners, whether it's a corporate partner or a government partner, because the story that I'm sharing comes from my heart. And it's a common story that other people, other Métis People share.

Wêyawâw tâ kê petohtewak ântê Métis Crossing mêna tâ kwehchikemowak kakwe'cheke'mowina, âyiman kakwe'cheke'mowina, ânta puspew nêta. Mêna nêyâ kâkê wehtam êkw'anima. Êkw'ânima mitoni itwemakahk tânispê kâ pekiskwatakik nikotwaw âtoske'wechi'wakunak, mutwanche âtoske'wechi'wakunak âhpo kechi okimakanahk âtoske'wechi'wakunak, âyis ânima âchimowin kâ pahkwenuman kê pe ispayek ochi mite. Mêna êkwa ânima pakwehtamik âchimowin ânima kohtuk âyiseniwak, kohtuk Métis âyiseniwak kâ pakwehtamkichik.

And for those people who, who grew up in a very Métis community, in a very Métis family, they have such wonderful stories to share that I can learn from. It's just such an opportunity to be here and to participate in listening to those.

Mêna âniki âyiseniwak âwena, âwêna kâ opikichik ânta mitoni Métis mamawi ê âyahk, ânta mitoni Métis famille... weyawâw âyâchik mamuska'teyih'takwun âchimona tâ pahkwenumawichik ânima tâ kiskino'huma'kaweyan ochi. Êkw'ânima kâ nahipayik ota t'ayayahk mêna tâ weche'hiwaniwiyahk tâ natohtamahk êko'nanhi.

It's really cool. We work a lot at Métis Crossing to share the Métis story and it's not my story as a Métis person. It's not President Poitras' story as a Métis person. It's the story of the Nation. We have such a diverse Nation with diverse experiences of all the Métis People within.

Êkw'ânima makwa hike'win. Nêyanan âtoskêyâhk mistâhi ântê Métis Crossing tâ pahkwenumahk ânhi Métis âchimona mâka nâmoya nêyâ âchimowin tapis'koch Métis âyiseniw. Nâmoya President Poitras' âchimowin tapis'koch Métis âyiseniw. Êkwa ânima âchimowin ochi ânima Nation. Keyanaw âyayahk iskô mechi petos Nation usichi petos kiskeyih'tumowina ochi kâhkiyâw li Métis âyiseniwak pechiyi.

When we started this process, we asked our community members: what do we want people to know about the Métis? What do we want them to feel about the Métis People when they leave here and how do we want their worldview to have changed? To me, that's very fundamental because it's changing the worldview that allows me to be who I am now, who allows me to proudly share this with my children. Whereas 30 or 40 years ago, it was something that our parents actively chose not to share.

Tânispê kâ machetayahk oma êsi toh'tamik, nêyanan kê kwechima'yakik keyanaw mamawi'e'ayahk owichihewak: kêkwîy ê ni tawehtamok âyiseniwak tâ kisketakik ochi ânki Métis? Kêkwîy ê ni tawehtamok âyiseniwak tâ moosetakik âya ochi ânki li Métis âyiseniwak ikospe kâ sepwetechik ota ochi mêna tânisi ni tawehtamok weyawâw misiwe'uske kâ kunawa'pahtumihk tâ meskopayek? Nêyâ oma, êkwa ânima nistum kiskeyih'tumowin âyis ânima tâ meskopayek ânima kunawa'pahtumihk ânima kâ pukitinam'kawiyan tâ âyâyân âwêna nêya êkwa, kâ pukitinam'kawiyan tâ mumichisewyan tâ pahkwenuman usichi ni'chiwasimsak. Mâka mwechi nistotamtinaw âhpo nêyotamtinaw uskekana uspin, êkwa ânima kêkwîy ni nékéhikowak kê nawasochik nâmoya tâ pahkwenuman.

And for me, I want people to know that Louis Riel was not a traitor. I want people to know that Louis Riel brought the Province of Manitoba into the Dominion of Canada. If it wasn't for that Provisional Métis Government, Canada may not be what we know today. So, the foundational piece that the Métis Nation played in the building of this country is not something we learned in school.

Mêna nêyâ kichi, ni tawemawahk âyiseniwak tâ kisketakik ânima Louis Riel nâmoya wêya misimi'wiskiw. Ni tawemawahk âyiseniwak tâ kisketakik ânima Louis Riel kê petaht the Province of Manitoba ânta the Dominion of Canada. Kespin êka ânima Provisional Métis Government, Canada âhpwetikwe nâmoya kêkwîy kâ ti'kiskitamahk ânoch. Ikosi, ânima weyus'chikewin ânima Métis Nation kâ tipahahk oma kâ osêtachik oma ki'taskenaw nâmoya kê kiskeyi'tamakawiyak ânta kiskisno'huma'kumik.

And I need people to know that the Métis People shouldn't have been road allowance people. They shouldn't have been forgotten people. They shouldn't have been hidden in plain sight because we were an active part in building this country. And it's something that we should be very proud of.

Mêna nêyâ nitaweyiten âyiseniwak tâ kisketakik ânima li Métis âyiseniwak nâmoya tâ kê wêkichik ânta road allowance. Weyawâw nâmoya tâ kê wankiskihiyakik âyiseniwak. Weyawâw nâmoya tâ kê kasochik ânta kâ wapi'michik âyis nêyanan âtoskatamahk oma osetayahk oma ki'taskenaw. Mêna êkwa ânima kêkwîy mitoni tâ kê mumi'chisiw'yahk.

I am so fortunate to be in a position to sit at these tables and to listen to our Elders and to our business owners and to our entrepreneurs and to our artists about how they want to share our culture.

Nêyâ oma ni pupe'wewin tâ âyâyân apiwin tâ âyapiyan ântê li tables mêna tâ natohtaman ânki keyanaw Kehte'yiseniwak mêna keyanaw âtoske'wechi'wakunak, mêna keyanaw âtoske'otipemsowak mêna keyanaw âtoska'tomowinak âya ochi tânisi ê-nohtê pahkwenumâchik keyanaw nistum'pimâchihowin.

Métis families, whether they now live in Fort Vermilion or Edmonton or Calgary passed through here (Métis Crossing). So, their histories or families could be connected to this place. And now that Métis Crossing is here and we have this gathering center here, and people say to me, "The feeling we get when we walk onto this land is a feeling of connection, of belonging." Which is neat because maybe people haven't always felt connected, and like they belonged in many places. So, to have that here is really special.

Li Métis familles, mutwanche âhpo weyawâw êkwa kê wêkichik ântê Fort Vermillion âhpo Edmonton âhpo Calgary kê meyaskamik oti (Métis Crossing). Ikosi, weyawâw kâyas âchimona âhpo li familles âniskoh'taw oma nêta. Mêna êkwa ânima Métis Crossing ota k'astek mêna nêyanan âyayahk oma mamawu'pihk'kamik ota, mêna âyiseniwak nêyâ kê itwechik, "Ânima kâ moositayahk ânima kâ pimohteyahk oma uskê êkwa ânima moosetawin ochi âniskoh'pichikun, ochi tipe'yehtak'osiwin." Tanma mitoni mêyosin âyis âhpwetikwe âyiseniwak nâmoya moositachik âniskoh'pichikun, mêna tâskoch weyawâw tipe'yehtak'osiwichik mêchet uskeya. Ikosi, tâ âyayahk oma ota mitoni kechi.

Lisa Wolfe: I got involved in cadets when I was about 13. I went through the cadet system. I'm very pro training the youth and working with the youth and teaching them how to work as part of a team leadership and mentorship and just learning in general. After cadets, I went and joined the Canadian Air Force. When I was 18, I swapped over and went into the Air Force. I was promoted from Officer Cadet to Second Lieutenant. And then from Second Lieutenant to Full Lieutenant.

Âtoskâtamân ânki oskiyi simakunsewak nânto nistosap ê si piponyân. Ni âtoskâten ânima oskiyi simâkunsewak puminihkewin. Nêyâ oma mitoni sâsâpokiskeyitum ê kiskinohumâkeyan oskiyik mêna âtoskeyân âschi oskiyi mêna ê kiskinohumakik tânisi te si âtoskechik pâhki mamawi kiskinotahiwin mêna kiskeyitumowin mêna mâchi kiskeyihtamowin. Mwestus oskiyi simakunsewak, ntohten tâ mâchitayân

Canadian Air Force. Tânispe âyinanew'osap kâ si piponyân, ni meskotastân mêna ni tohtân ânta Air Force. Nêyâ kê yâhko'tahewiyân ochi Officer Cadet iskô Second Lieutenant. Mêna ochi Second Lieutenant iskô full Lieutenant.

It was probably about 1991/92, and I just had my daughter Victoria. And right around that time the wars in Afghanistan were just starting to pick up a little bit and Saudi Arabia. And they were talking about deployments and stuff and being a single mom at that point I didn't really want to leave town, and I don't really want to leave my daughter here. So, I ended up getting involved with the Edmonton Police Service at that time.

Âhpwetikwe nânto 1991/92, mêna nêyâ mwechi nehtâwikiyan ni tânis Victoria. Mêna êkospê notinitowina ântê Afganistan mekwach ê mâchi payeki âpsis ântê Saudia Ariabia. Mêna weyawâw ê pekiskâtâhkik nanto oonotinekewa tâhtotechik mêna kahkeyâw kekway mêna ê pêyakoyân okâwemâwin, ikospe moya ênohtê sepweteyan otenaw ochi, mêna nâmoya nânto ênohtê nakatak ni tânis ota. Ikosi, ni mâchi âtoskâtâmân ânki Edmonton Police Service ikospe.

For me, it was giving back to the community and working with kids. I initially started in a job development program for Indigenous persons. Back then it was called the Aboriginal Job Development Program that the Edmonton Police Service had put on to incorporate more Indigenous People to the service.

Nêyâ kichi, kâwi mekiyân êkotê yisi mâmâwe k'âyâhk mêna âtoskeyân âschi âwâsisâk. Nêyâ nekânisi ê mâchitayân ânma âtoskewin osetayân mêyo watumo'hewin kichi Indigenous âyiseniwâk. Ikospe kê sekâtek Aboriginal Job Development Program âniki Edmonton Police Service kâkê âstachik tâ êwuko âstachik Indigenous âyiseniwâk ânima âtoskewin.

There were six of us in our group (in the program) and everybody knew who we were. Everybody knew our names. In some ways, you end up with the spotlight on you. And I think that it's great in some respects, because they're promoting like... we see that we need to move into this direction. We need to be more diversified and bringing those recruitment people into the service, because you lose the understanding when you don't have any culture or any identity within the service. The people that you're serving come from certain select communities, you need to have people that speak languages, understand the background, understand the history behind that so that you can deal with them.

Êkotê nikotwâsik nêyanân mechitowâhk (ânta mêyo wâtumo-hewin) mêna kâhkeyâw'aweyak ê kiskitakik âwena weyawâw. Kahkeyâwyak ê kisketâkik ni wehowinân. Tâskoch, ê-musinâstek ânma kâhkeyâwyak. Mêna ni tehten êkwa ânma mitoni mêyo-sin, âyis weyawâw yâkotahewichik tâskoch.... ni wahpatenân ânma nêyanân nitawe'yihtam êkosi tâ wuskâweyak. Nêyanân nitawe'yihtam nâwach t'otinamihk âyiseniwak mêna kê petâchik kâke masinâhikechik âyiseniwak ânta âtoskewin âyis ki wânehten nisitohtamowin tânispe moya ki tayân nistum pimâchihowin âhpo nikotwâw isteyweyih'tâkosiwin pechiyi ânta âtoskewin. âyiseniwak k'âtoskemakuchik pespayiwak ochi nawasunum mâmâwi ê âyâhka, keya nitawe'yihtaman t'âyayin âyiseniwâk kâ pekiskwechik petos pekiskwewina, nistohtam ânma background, nistohtam ânma kayâs âchimowin pechiyi êkwânma itâm keyawâw t'atoskatamâhchik weyawâw.

There was an opportunity when I had a chance to be Coordinator for the Job Development Program. It has since morphed into the Diversity Job Development Program, Indigenous Job Development Program. And when we were in the diversity side of it, we used to work a lot with not just pulling in Indigenous People, but also pulling in people from the Chinese community, from the Vietnamese community, the Russian community, Ukrainian, but specifically people, because Edmonton is a huge, diverse community.

Êkota kâ nâhipayek tânispe âyayân koche tâ âtoskeyan ânma Coordinator kichi Job Development Program. Ispê pê mesko-payin iskô Diversity Job Development Program, Indigenous Job

Development Program. Mêna tânispe kâ âtoskatamâhk t'otinamihk âyiseniwak, nêyanân ê kê âtoskeyahk mistâhi âyiseniwak moya pohko Indigenous âyiseniwak, âya mêna âyiseniwak ochi ânma Chinese mâmâ'e'âyâhk, ochi Vietnamese mâmâ ê âyâhk, ânma Russian mâmâ'e'âyâhk, Ukrainian, mâka tântowa âyiseniwak, âyis ôchi Edmonton êkohk ê misâk, t'otinamihk mâmâ ê âyâhk.

And in some ways, because I had four kids, it was really busy. And now kind of looking back on it, it's like, wow... It was really busy, but it was a good, busy. There was a lot of giving back to the community.

Âteht ôte yisi, âyis ôchi âyawakihk neyo âwasisak, mitoni ôtumiyowiyân. Mêna êkwa kâ wapahtamân, tâskoch, wow... Mitoni ê otumiyowiyâhk, mâka mêyosin, ôtumiyowiyâhk. Êkotê mistâhi êmekiyâhk kâwi yisi mâmâ ê âyâhk.

I've got two girls that are graduated, one that's going on for a Bachelor of Arts right now, the other one's pursuing acting and modeling, and the boys are just finishing up school and one's doing football and the other one's working towards doing blacksmithing.

Ni tayân nêso iskwesisak kah kesi kiskinohumakachik, pêyak kâ tohtet ânma Bachelor of Arts mekwach, kotuk totamâkewin mêna tâpis'ehtâwin, mêna ânki napesisâk mwechi kesetawâk kiskinohumâkewin mêna pêyak êtohtâhk takiskâchikun mêna kotuk âtoskatâhk t'ayitohtak ôyehisowin.

But they all have their culture and heritage. So how do we give back? We give by back by actually going out to the events we give back by networking and getting out in the community. We give back by just being the volunteer that wants to do something because sometimes people don't know how to do something or what to do.

Mâka kahkeyaâw âyawawâk weyawâw nistum pimâchihowin mêna ânisko'kumakewin. Itam, tânisi tâ mekiyâhk kâwi?

Nêyanân ê mekiyâhk kâwi âya ôchi ântê kekway kâ ispayek, ê mekiyâhk kâwi kâ mâmâwapêyak mêna êtohteyâhk mâmâ kê âyâhk. Nêyanân ê mekiyâhk kâwi âya ochi kâ nisokumakeyâhk kekway kâ nohtê'totamâhk âyis âskaw âyiseniwahk nâmoya kisketamohk tânisi kekway tâ totâhkwaw âhpo kekway tâ totâchik.

So, for me I gave back a lot with my knowledge as a police officer and working on different things like the End Poverty Commission. I sat on that commission because I grew up poor. I understand what it's like to grow up poor. I know what it's like not to go buy clothes or have clothes and do hand me downs but it doesn't mean everybody needs to live that way. No, we work really hard to get out of that so that we can have a better way of life for our kids. For me, I really enjoy working with young adults and seeing them, aspire and attain their dreams of what they always wanted to do.

Ikosi, nêyâ kichi, mistâhi kawi ni kê mekin kêkwîy kâ kisketaman âya ochi oma semâkunis mêna âtoskatamân petos kêkwîya tâskoch End Poverty Commission. Êkota âyapiyan âyis ê kê ohpikeyân ê-kitimakisiyân. Ni nisitohtamowin kêkwîy ânima tâ nitimakisiyân. Ni kiskihten tâniki oma êka kê âtâwiyan âyiwansa âhpo tâ yâyân âyiwinsa mêna tâ mekâwiyan âyiwansa mâka moya kâhkeyawyâhk ikosi puhko tâ wekit. Nâmoya, nêyanân âtoskeyân mitoni mistâhi to otinamasoyâhk ikota ochi itam nêyanân tâ âyâyâhk nâwach ê mêyosik pimatsowin ôchi nêyanân âwasisâhk. Nêyâ, mitoni ni mêyoten âtoskeyan ôskiyak âschi mêna tâ wapimakwâw, mostawi'nikewin mêna kuskeh'tamâsochik kêkwîy kâkê nitawetakihk.

Pearl Calahasen: There are some people in life, in our lives who come to us, and I think they're given to us by the Creator to make sure that we can survive whatever is laid out before us. With that, I was the first graduate of my family.

Âyawahk ateht âyiseniwak kâ pimatisochik, oma keyanaw kâ pimatisoyahk kâ pehtotechik, mêna ni tiheyiten weyawâw ê pê mekawiyahk ochi Manito tâ kechinahoyahk tâ pimâtisiwiyahk puko kêkwîy kâ pê âstek nêkân keyanaw. Usichi êkwa ânima, nêyâ oma nêkân tâ kesi kiskino'humakaweyan ochi ma famille.

There was great hopes attached to that. The biggest dream of my life was to be an airline stewardess, imagine that. Because how does a poor girl who comes from a poor family without any connections, get to see the world? I wanted to see the world. I wanted to know what happens out there. Whatever I learned I could bring back to my family. And as it turned out when I went to Ottawa I was accepted as the stewardess.

Êkwa'nima âyakik kechi puko'seyi'mowina ânis'kohpita êkota. The biggest dream oma ni pimatisowin ânima Airline Stewardess, iteyih'tam êkwa'nima. âyis kêkwîy oma kâ kitimaksit iskwesis ochi kâ kitimaksichik famille mâke'kwiy'ayat âniskoh'pichikun, tâ notina tâ wapahtak misiwe uskê? Nêyâ kê nohtê wapataman misiwe uskê. Nêyâ kê nohtê kisketaman tansi êspayik êkote. Kêkwîy kâ kiskino'humakawiyan ni kâkê pehtan kawi ochi ma famille. Mêna tâskoch kâ ispayek tânispê kâ tohteyan Ottawa n'otinamihkwak tapis'koch stewardess.

There was a series of tests I had to go through. And those series of tests, they're really restrictive tests and they found out I had a heart problem. So, they said that they couldn't accept me.

Êwuko êtohtakika wawapahtamik nêyâ puko tâ tohtaman. Mêna ikonanhi wawapahtamika... ikonanhi mitoni meyaw'ateht'puko wawapahtamika mêna weyawâw miskomok ânima nêyâ âyâyân mite ahkosiwin. Ikosi, weyawâw êtwewak ânima êka kaskitachik tâ ôtinamihkchik.

I cried and cried and cried and called my grandma and said, "What's happening, Grandma? I thought the world was supposed to be really good. The world was supposed to give us ways for us to be able to deal with things?" and I cried for days and days on end. And my grandma said "It's not meant to be.

You're not meant to be there. So, therefore come home." So, I came back home and didn't know what I wanted to do.

Ni mâton mêna mâton mêna mâton mêna ni tepwewaw n'ohkom mêna n'ititwon, "Kêkwîy ispayek, N'ohkom? N'itehiyitamân miswe uskê ite'yihtamân mintoni tâ mêyosik. Miswe uskê ite'yihtaman tâ mâkoyak nântâwsi tâke totamihk ochi keyanâw t'astoskatâmak kêkwîy?" mêna ni mâton iskô tahto kêsikâw. Ikosi ni pekiwan mena namoya ikisketaman kekwiy ke nohte totaman.

I started teaching adults who didn't know how to read or write because many of our own people don't know how to read or write. And so, as a result I thought oh, this is my calling.

Ni mâchi kiskinohumawak âyiseniwak âwêna êka kasketachik tâ âyimechikechik âhpo musinahikechik âyis mêchet oki keyanaw âyiseniwak nâmoya kasketawak tâ âyimechikechik âhpo musinahikechik. Mêna ikosi, ispayiw ni tehiyiten, 'oh, ôma nêyâ kiskeyih'tumowin.

And so, as a result, I was doing really well in my Education Degree, and I was going for my master's degree. I got my master's degree, and this was the push from the women in my community. From there I was going to get my PhD.

Ikosi, ôma ôchi ispayek, mitoni ni mêyo âstokan nêyâ ôma Education Degree, mêna nêyâ ê nohtê âtoskatam my master's degree. Ni kachitinen my master's degree, mêna natotamok iskwewak ânima ânta mamawi'e'ayahk. Ochi êkotê nêyâ tâ kachitiniman my PhD.

And then, I was called. I was called by the people of the community of Lesser Slave Lake, the Indigenous women and men who called and said, "We need you to run. We want you to run." And I thought, what am I running from? I don't need to run anymore.

Mêna êkospe, ni pê tepwâtikawin. Ê tepwâtikiyan ôchi

âyiseniwak âniki mamâwi'e'ayahk ôchi Lesser Slave Lake, âniki Indigenous iskwewak mêna nâpewak âwena kâ tepwâtikâwchik mêna êtwechik, "Nêyânân ê nita'weyihtam'ahk tâ pimpâhitâyin. Nita'weyihtamahk tâ pimpâhitâyin. Mêna ni tehiyiten, kêkwîy ê pimpâhtâyan ochi? Nêyâ nâmoya kâtâch tâ pimpâhtâyân keyâ'pich.

And they said, "We'd like you to run for (MLA) in Lesser Slave Lake." And I didn't know that was coming open. So, the eight Elders called and kept calling and they were Métis men and Métis women, and First Nations men, and First Nations women who got together, all of them. They didn't recognize each other as Métis or First Nations. They recognized themselves as Indigenous People who have struggled and needed someone to speak on their behalf. And so, they came to me. And so, I thought, Oh my God, how are we going to do this? First of all, we don't have any money. Secondly, we don't have any organization, and thirdly, I don't know if I could even do this.

Mêna ikosi, "nita'weyihtamahk tâ pimpahitayin ochi (MLA) in Lesser Slave Lake." Mêna nâmoya kê kisketaman êkwa'nima êti ohtenipayek. Ikosi, âniki âyina'neyo Kehtayak tepwatichik mêna tâ tepwatichik mêna weyawâw li Métis nâpewak mêna li Métis iskwewak, mêna First Nations nâpewak, mêna First Nations iskwewak kâ mamawapichik, kâhkiyâw âniki. Weyawâw nâmoya kê wapamsochik tâskoch Métis âhpo First Nations. Ê-wapamsochik tâskoch Indigenous âyiséniwak âwéna kê timakisichik mêna nitawe'yihtumok âwiyak tâ pekiskwatamochik weyawâw kichi. Mêna ikosi, weyawâw ê-penatichik. Mêna ikosi, ni tehiyihten, "Oh ni Manitom, tânisi tâ itotaṃahk oma? Nêkân pêyak, nâmoya makikwiy sooniyaw. Kehtwam, nâmoya âyayak mamawi'towin, mêna nistwaw, nêyâ nâmoya ni tehiyiten kespin ni kâkê tohten oma.

And so, they said, "Yes, you can, you can walk in two worlds, you speak the languages, you speak English and you speak Cree. We know you have not lost your cultural ways. We understand that you're strong. We understand that you have taken on many

Pearl Calahasen campaign ad
Photos: Métis Nation of Alberta

things that probably people haven't taken on. We believe that you can do this."

Mêna ikosi, weyawâw êtwewahk, "Tâpwe, keya kâ kuskêtan, kâkê pimohten ânta nêso miswe uskea, ki pekiskwan ânhi pekiskwewina, ki pekiskwan English mêna ki pekiskwan Cree. Nêyanan ni kisketenan kêya nâmoya kê wanitan ki nistum pimatisiwin take'tota'mihk. Nêyanân nisi'tohtamnan ânima keya ê muskawseyin. Nêyanan nisi'tohtamnan ânima kêya kê otinaman mêchet kêkwîy ânihi âhpo êtikwe âyisêniwak nâmoya kê otinakik. Nêyanan kê tâpwehtamahk ânima kêya kâkê itohtên ôma.

So as a result, I said, okay. And when I said, okay, it was like somebody grabbed me by my neck and just sort of led me to different places, and the Métis Nation at that time came forward and helped me. They were very strong and made sure that they were there to support me, to help me with my printing, to help me with my communications, to help me with whatever I needed.

Pearl Calahasen being sworn in to the Alberta Legislature
Photos: Métis Nation of Alberta

Pearl Calahasen
Photos: Métis Nation of Alberta

Ikosi oma ochi ispayek, n'itwan, okay. Mêna tânispê k'itweyan, okay, êkwa ânima tâskoch âwiyak otehtinit ochi mikwa'yaw mêna mwechi nêkânêwehit ântê petos uskê tipahas'kanisa, mêna li Métis Nation ikospe ânima pê nêkânechik mêna wêchi-hichik nêyâ. Wêyawâw mitoni kê sookisêwahk mêna kechi'na-howichik tâ wêchihichik, tâ pumihewichik, tâ wêchihichik âschi ânm kâ musinahikeyan, te wêchihichik âschi ânima wehta'ma-towin, tâ wêchihichik âschi kêkwîy ânima kâ nitawe'yihtaman.

It took everybody, it didn't take one group. It took everyone to be able to come together to be able to ensure that there was going to be an individual that could be there for them.

Êwuko âpachihachik kahkewaw âyahk, nâmoya puko pêyak mêchetin. Êwuko âpachihachik kahkewaw âyahk tâ mamaw'asta tâ kechinahowchik ânima âwiyahk tâ âyâht weyawâw kichi.

They wanted to make sure that there will be an individual there to be able to stand up for them, and they wanted to make sure that their issues would come to the table. That's exactly what I did.

Weyawâw êti kechinahowchik ânima âwiyahk t'âyâht tâ natot-wes'tamâ'ket weyawâw kichi, mêna weyawâw êti kechinahow-chik ânihi pekwe'yihtomina tâ pê ispayikik ote la table. Êkwa ânima sooskwach kâ itohtaman.

There was no time for personal stuff. When you become elected your personal life is open to everybody. So, if you tried to lie or something, somebody is going to find out anyway, so what the hell is the point? You know — just tell them the truth right from the beginning.

Nâmoya time kichi tipiyawe' tipeyih'tamowin kêkwîy. Tânispê kâ nâwusonayek ki pimatisiwin pê yohtenam kichi kâhkîyâw iyahk. Ikosi, kespin kê kochitayin tâ keyaskiyin âhpo kêkwîy, âwiyahk tâ miskatum misawach, ikosi tanehki mâchimanito-nahk êkwa'nima? Kiskehiten - sooskwach tâ wehtamwachik tâpwêwin iskô kâ mâchipayek.

When I first got elected, it was like the world changed. It just flipped. It was like right immediately every day they get something like about two hundred calls, and I would try to answer every single one of them.

Tânispê nêyâ nêkân kâ nâwusonayihk, êkwa'nima tâskoch misiwe uskê kê meskotâstek. Sooskwâch kê meskochpayin. Tâpiskoch seemak kâhkeyâw kesikâw weyâwâw k'ayachik nânto nêso mitâtâht omtânawâw sewepitama'tona, mêna nêyâ nikochetan tâ pekiskwatamn tahto kahkiyaw êko'nanhi

Those two hundred calls in that day was somebody [who] was in dire need, right? And so, how do you then prioritize that call? I used to go from the time that they called, I just go through the calls throughout and there were times when I would call them at two o'clock in the morning or six o'clock in the morning just because that was the only time that I had. You start [in the legislature] at seven in the morning for breakfast meetings and then you're there until two in the morning. I didn't realize that it took so much out of you.

Êko'nanhi néso mitâtâht omtânawâw séwépitama'tona ké âwiyak [awina] mitoni nitawé'yihtak, tapwé? Ména ikosi, tânisi tâ nékanét'nistumochi ékwa'nima séwépitama'ton. Nêyâ kê itoteyan ochi kâ séwépitama'tona, nêyâ sookwach go through ânhi séwépitama'tona mêna there were times tânispê kâ séwépitamok nanto nêso tipahikun kâ kekisepa âhpo kotosik tipahikun kâ kekisepa mwechi âyis ikonanma puko only time that I had. Keya ki mâchitan [in the legislature] tepakohp tipahikun kâ kekisepa ochi kekisepa mechisowin mamawapo'wina mêna êkospe keya êkota ki tayan iskô nêso tipahikun kâ kekisepa. Nêyâ nâmoya kiskeyihitaman ânima êkohk it took êkohk out of you.

I asked the Elders because [it was] eight Elders [who] came and asked me to run... Every time I'd do an election, I'd say, "Am I done now?" They say, "No, you're not." And I said, "What? But I should be done, shouldn't I?"

Pearl Calahasen with her husband Ivan
Photos: Métis Nation of Alberta

Ni kwechimawahk ânki Kehtayak âyis [it was] âyinanew Kehtayak [who] petohtechik mêna kwechimchik tâ pimpahtayan... kâ nâwusonayek, nêyâ ketwan, "Ni poyon'che êkwa?" Weyawâw tâ itwewahk, "Nâmoya, keya." Mêna nêyâ nitwan, "Kêkwîy? Mâka tâ kê pôyôyan?

"No, you're not. The tip of the iceberg hasn't even been touched."

"Nâmoya, keya. Keya moya âhpo the tip of the iceberg âhpo pê tasekan."

So I said, "Wow, I'll never get done."

Ikos ni êtway, "Wow, nêyâ nâmoya wekach kâ ni pôyôn."

They said, "Well, we'll let you know when you're done."

Weyaw êtwewak, "Itam, nêyanân kâ wehtamkôyek ispê kâ pôyôyin."

And then this last round, like that was seven elections. Right.

And that's painful. They said, "You'll know, you'll know."

Mêna êkospe ôma êskôyanik, tâskoch êkwa ânima tepakohp kâ nâwusônayek. Tâpwe. Mêna êkwa ânima ahkwun. Weyawâw êtwewak, "Keya kâ kiskihiten, kâ kiskihiten."

And I said, "Can I leave? Can I quit?"

Mêna ni itwan, 'Kâkê sepwetan? Kâkê pôyôyan?"

And they said, "No, you can't quit. But you'll know when you're ready."

Mêna weyawâw êtwewak, "Nâmoya, keya kâ ê pôyôyin. Mâka kâ kisketen ispê keya kesayaw."

And I said, "What the heck does that mean?"

Mêna nêyâ nitwan, "Kêkwîy ânima êkwa'nima êtweyin?"

So, anyway, I knew the last election. I knew that was going to be my last one.

Ikos, pukowesiyi, ni kiskiyitên iskoyanihk nâwusonawin. Ni kiskiyitên êkwa'nima iskoyanihk.

But you do [it] because you have to. You have to do the best because people are relying upon you. Their lives are hinging upon your decisions.

Mâka ki tohten âyis kêya puko tâ tohtamin. Kêya puko tâ tohtamin kêchiyihk âyis âyisêniwak ê ni tawemiskwaw. Wêyawâw opimatisowin mumisê'totam ânhi keseyih'tumowina.

Muriel Stanley Venne: Muriel established the Institute for the Advancement of Aboriginal Women (IAAW) in 1994. She hoped to create an organization that would highlight the accomplishments of Indigenous women, all while building community and providing supports to those in need.

Muriel muskawastaw ânima Institute for the Advancement of Aboriginal Women (IAAW) ânta 1994. Wêya pukosêyimot tâ osêhtaht mamawihitowin'âtoskêwin ânma kâ pisisika'pahtumihk ânhi kuski'tâmâsowina o'chi Indigenous iskwewak, mêkwach osêhtâchik mamawe ê âyâhk mêna mêyêwâhk ôtinamawew o'chi âniki kitimâkisichik.

Muriel was also instrumental in producing *The Rights Path Alberta,* a comprehensive publication that informs Indigenous People about their human rights. Through her work with IAAW, Muriel has advocated for systematic change within Canadian law and the criminal justice system and how they respond to systemic violence against Indigenous women, arguing that the issue is "symptomatic of the mistreatment of Indigenous women by the criminal justice system."

Muriel mêna osêhtaht The Rights Path-Alberta, ânima nistotâmowin musinahikun kâ âchimostatâht Indigenous âyisêniwak nântâw wêyawâw kwayus'tatisiwina. Misehwêhte wêya âtoskêwin usichi IAAW, Muriel ê-pêkiskwatamowat kichi puminikêwin mêskotâpowin ânta Canadian oyusiwêwin mêna ânima nipatakew kwayus itotama'kêwin mêna tânisi wêyawâw nuskomowichik ânima puminikêwin muchi'tohtumowin uschiye Indigenous iskwewak, kê wêhkatâhk ânima muchi'tohtumowin ânima "kâ pisis'kâpâh'tâmihk o'chi kitimahêwin kichi Indigenous iskwewak o'chi ânima nipatâkew kwayus itotâmâ'kêwin."

The IAAW, under Muriel's leadership is an advocate for Indigenous women. They also celebrate the strength and beauty of Indigenous women each year at the Esquao awards.

Ânima IAAW, sêpa Muriel ôchi nêkânêwin ânima kê pêkiskwâtamowât kichi Indigenous iskwewak. Wêyâwâw mêna mochikê'tamochik sokisiwin mêna kuta'wusisiwin o'chi indigenous iskwewak pâhpêyak uskê ânta Esquao Awards.

Muriel has received a variety of honours for her work. These include but are not limited to: The Alberta Human Rights Award (1998), the Order of Canada for her human rights advocacy and for bringing national attention to the crisis of murdered and missing Indigenous women and girls (2005), the Governor General's Commemorative Award for the Persons Case (2005), the Queen Elizabeth II's Golden and Diamond Jubilee Medals, and the Alberta Centennial Medal, as well as a Distinguished Citizen Honourary Bachelor of Arts Degree from MacEwan University (2010).

Muriel otihtikot mêchêt kêkwîya pêtos o'chi kêchi'yimitowina kichi wêya âtoskêwin. Êwuko mêna māka nâmoya êkonanhi puko: The Alberta Human Rights Award (1998), the Order of Canada âya kichi wêya kwayus'tatisiwina natotwes'tamâkêwin mêna kichi ê pêtohtat mamawi'tipe yihta'kosiwin natoh'tamowin o'chi âstumi'payiw ânma Murdered and Missing Indigenous Women and Girls (2005), the Governor General's Commemorative Award for the Persons Case (2005), the Queen Elizabeth II Golden and Diamond Jubilee Medals, and the Alberta Centennial Medal, âya mêna ânima Distinguished Citizens Honourary Bachelor of Arts Degree from MacEwan University (2010).

Muriel is a strong advocate of ensuring that Indigenous history, particularly Métis history is included in textbooks so that youth have the opportunity to learn about the rich history and culture of the Métis People. Muriel's legacy will continue on, as her daughter, Rachelle has taken on the role of CEO of IAAW and has joined Muriel on the path for equality and respect for Indigenous women.

Muriel wêya sôhkisew kâ pêkiskwâtâmowat ta kechi'nahôyêt ânima Indigenous âtâyokân, wawayês êkwa âtâyokân tâ âstêki musinahikuna ikosi oskiyi tâ âyâchik kâ nahi'payêk ta kiskêyitamahk nantâw ânma kâ wêyootsik âtâyokân mêna nistum pimâchihowin o'chi Métis âyisêniwak. Muriel ânima onukutuma'kêwin tâ âhkume'yihta âya ochi otânisa, Rachelle otinum âtoskêwin CEO ochi IAAW mêna êti ânisko'kunan ânma mêskanâw pêyakwun âyâwak ispeteyih'takwun mêna tâ mêyo tohtâwewachik Indigenous iskwewak.

Mary SkyBlue Morin: I spent most of my life working myself out of poverty from living on the other side of railroad tracks where there were no town services, living in shacks made of plyboard with cracks in the wood to the outside, keeping the fire stoked all night to keep warm. We lived in tents for the summer gathering food and saving on rent. As a single parent I have been homeless with children, once in Edmonton (1998) due to a delayed contract payment and once in Calgary (2002) due to being laid off without much notice. Each time I had to live with a cousin, an auntie and a sister-in-law for two or three months while I worked to save money for a security deposit and first month's rent for another apartment. I have moved to places of employment and my children have had to start school at these new places. I persisted through these times making my standard of life better than my mother's, telling my daughter and my son to make their lives better than mine. They are the witnesses to my life experience.

In 1985, I had the opportunity to coordinate the 100th anniversary of the Batoche Resistance coordinating a number of event committees to present a week of celebration to the Métis Nation.

In 2010, I met Marlene Lanz of the Métis Nation of Alberta Region 3. She asked me to do an all-day Michif workshop for the Métis community in Calgary which led to workshops for the Métis locals in MNA Region 3. Michif Cree language sessions also started with the MNA Region 3 youth. In 2016-2017, I conducted weekend workshops for the Métis locals in MNA Region 3 area. A handbook was developed to prompt discussion on the Michif l anguage and culture. The handbook was published for reference. In 2018 and 2019, we added Michif Cree cultural camps to practice our Michif language. This translation work eventually led to the development of the Michif Cree Language Phrases APP. Translation was also provided for a Michif Cree Monopoly game and other games for MNA Region 3.

In returning to Edmonton, Michif Cree language workshops were conducted with the MNA office staff and various Michif

Cree video recording sessions with the MNA Métis youth. Michif Cree translations were provided to the Rupertsland Institute of Métis Excellence for education material development. In partnership with Rupertsland Institute of Métis Excellence, the Edmonton Public Library has video recordings of the Michif Cree language as I developed for historical reference.

All My Relations... Kahkeyo ni wahkohmakunak....

Dianne Ludwig: I went back to school and I got my Social Work degree, and I went to work for Social Services in Lac La Biche. I lasted eight months and I just about had a nervous breakdown. I have never in my life seen kids so beaten up, so neglected as I did when I worked for social services... I couldn't take it so I had to take a leave. After I left social services I went to work as a parole officer, and I liked that part of it. Then I worked for Métis Child and Family Services, Native Counselling.

Just about every one of my jobs had to do with working with people because I love working with them, all of them. Then of course I came to Portage College. It was Native Cultural Arts, and I thought, boy that's the one for me. So, I went back to school again and I took that course. Because I knew how to do all the stuff they were presenting in the courses that they had, but you know how it is, you always need that white piece of paper saying "You can do this." So that's why I went back to school. I became an instructor in the Native Cultural Arts program and that's how I got into the school.

N'itohtên kawi tâ kiskino'humakawiyan tâ kachitinaman ânima Social Work Degree, mêna n'itohtên tâ âtoskiyân âsichi Social Services antê Lac la Biche. Ni kuskêtan iskô nanto âyinanew pêsimohk mêna kêkach n'itayân k'âhkosihk mâmitone'yichikunihk. Nâmoya wêkach ni pimâtisiwin ni wâpimawak âwâsisâk kê pukuma'whâwichik, ikohk wunkiskisi'totawew iskô kê itotâman k'atoskêyan ochi social services... Nâmoya ni kuskêtan t'atoskataman ikosi nêya puko tâ sipwêhtêyan âchiyaw. Mwestus kâ sipwêhtêyan social services n'itowe âtoskân tâskoch ânima parole officer, mêna ni mêyohtên êkwa'nima. Êkospê ni âtoskân ochi Métis Child and Family Services, Native Counselling. Kêkach kahkiyaw n'atoskêwina k'atoskâtâmân usichi âyisêniwak âyis ni sakihitên k'atoskâtâmân wêyawâw usichi, kahkiyaw uniki. Êkospê tâpwe ni pêtohtân oti Portage College. Êkwa ânima Native Cultural Arts, mêna ni teyihitên, boy êkwa'nima nêya kichi. Ikosi n'itohtan kawi ânta kiskino'humakêwin âsumêna mêna n'otinên êkwanima mâmâwi'kiskino'humatowin. Âyis kê kiskeyihtamân tânisi t'itotâmân kâhkiyaw kêkwîy wêyawâw kâ wapahti'hikêchik mamaw'kiskino'humatowina k'âyachik, mâka kiskiyihitên tânisi êkwa'nima, kêya kakikê ânima kâ wapiskahk li papier êtastêk "Kêya kâ kaskêtan oma." Ikosi ânima tânihkê âsumêna kâ itohtêyan kiskino'humakêwin. Ni mâchi âtoskâtên kiskino'humakêwinew ânta Native Cultural Arts Program mêna ikosa ânima kâ pukitin'kâwiyân ânta kiskino'humakêwin'kumik.

I got into the school teaching Cree, and then teaching the arts. So, I could do both things and that was a plus for me from what I learned as a young person, and I've put that to good use. I taught girls how to make moss bags and with that there is a lesson right? With everything that I taught these kids, I taught them the lesson behind what I was delivering. That made it a lot better.

Ni pukitin'kâwiyân ânta kiskino'humâkew'kumik kê kiskino'humâkew'iyan Nêhiyâwêwin, mêna êkospê kê kiskino'humâkew'iyan ânihi osêchikêwina. Ikosi, nâmoya ni kuskêtan nêswayi kêkwîy tâ itohtâmân mêna êkwa'nima ke mitoni mêyopayin nêyâ kichi ochi kêkwîy kâkê kiskino'humâkew'iyan usichi oskîyi âyiseniw, mêna ni mêyo âtoskâtên êkwa'nima. Ni kiskino'humâwak iskwesisak tânisi t'osêtachik uskeya waspisona mêna êkwa'nima usichi kiskino'humâkewin, tâpwe? Usichi kâhkeyâw kêkwîy kâ kiskino'humâkew'akik oki âwasisak, ni kiskino'humâkew'akik weyâwâw ânima kiskino'humâkewin ochi kâ whetâm'wâkwaw. Êkwa'nima mitoni mêyo payo.

Now, I can walk down the street and these kids never forget you. You treat them good and you respect them and they never forget you, never ever.

Êkwa, ni kuskêtan tâ pimohtiyan pimohtêskunaw mêna oki âwâsisâk nâmoya wêhkâch kêya kê wânkiskichik. Tâ mêyo totum'wachik mêna tâ mêyo totêm'wachik mêna nâmoya wêhkâch tâ wânkiskichik kêya, nâmoya wêhkâch.

I truly believe everybody that comes into this world has a gift, and my gift is to work with the youth, and I try to pass that knowledge on to them. I try to pass that knowledge on to them and I tell them how important it is for them to learn that and never forget who they are and be proud of who they are. Don't ever be ashamed of who you are. Walk it proud, walk it proud of who you are and don't ever be ashamed that you're Métis, or First Nations or whatever because there's so much to learn out there. There's so much to learn about your culture.

Ni tâpwêtên kâhkiyâw'âwêyahk kâ pê pimatisit oma misiwe'uskê ê âyât kuskihowin, mêna nêya ni kuskihowin ânima t'âtoskêyan âsichi oskîyi, mêna ni kochêtan tâ mêyâwak êkwa'nima kiskino'humâkêwin yisi wêyâwâw. Ni kochêtan tâ mêyakik êkwa'nima kiskino'humâkêwin mêna ni wêhtâm'wâwak êkohk ê kêchiyiwun wêyâwâw tâ kiskino'humâkechik êkwa'nima mêna nâmoya wêhkâch tâ wânkiskichik âwêna wêyâwâw mêna tâ kiste'yimow'ichik âwêna wêyâwâw. Kâyâ wêhkâch tâ nêpewisiyik âwêna kêyâwâw. Tâ pimohtêyêk ewuko kiste'yimowin, tâ pimohtêyêk ewuko kiste'yimowin âwêna kêyâwâw mêna kâyâ wêhkâch tâ nêpewisiyik kêyâwâw Métis, âhpo First Nations âhpo kêkwîy âyis êkota êkohk kiste'yimowin kohk tâ kiskino'humâkâwiyêk misewe'uskê. Êkota kêyâpich mistâhi tâ kiskino'humâkâwiyêk nântâw ki nistum'pimâchihowin.

It's been a good life. I can't ever say that it wasn't. I have a lot of things that I've taught my children and I'm not sorry that I was given six children to raise. It's beautiful, beautiful, beautiful. And I'd do it all over again.

Kê mêyo pimâtisiwin. Namoya wêhkâch ni kâkê itwân êka ânima ikosi. N'itâyân mêchet kêkwîy kâkê kiskino'humâkik nitâwâsimsak mêna nâmoya ni mêhtâtên ê kê mêkâwiyân ikotosik âwâsisâk tâ opikinâwâsoyân. Mitoni mêyo nâkwân... mêyo nâkwân, mêyo nâkwân. Mêna ni t'itotên kâhkiyâw âsumêna.

Afterword

Marilyn Lizee

Even as a little girl, I knew who I was. I knew I was not an Indian, and I knew that I was not white. I belonged somewhere in between, and I was alright with that. Growing up I always wanted to help people. Whether I was playing imaginary games where I went on great adventures and saved lives, or just helped my neighbours with their groceries, I felt a sense of purpose. Later, when I attended junior high school outside of my home community — I think the teachers saw this in me as well. Sometimes it was a good thing, other times not so much. I was a leader, and a protector of the other children. So, when one of them got in trouble, I was called to the office, but I was okay with that.

Today, as I look at my son and grandson, I see that same quality in them. It is one of the greatest gifts that was given to me by my parents, grandparents, and my ancestors, and I am grateful that it has been passed down to my children as well. It is a piece of myself and my family that will live on in the generations to come.

That is the passion behind this book. I truly believe that we all have a story to tell, and that these stories can help people in ways that we do not always see. The Métis Matriarchs in this book have all touched my life in one way or another. Their knowledge, compassion, hardships, and triumphs need to be shared. Our children need to read about strong, resilient Métis women. They are the cornerstones of our society, and we need to ensure that their Métis culture, heritage, and traditions are passed on so that we can bring those who have been lost and wandering, home.

This book has been a dream of mine, and my sisters at New Dawn Métis Women's Society for many years. I am truly grateful for the willingness of these beautiful Métis women who agreed to come forward and share their stories with us. Métis women are the leaders of our communities; they are our vision makers, the storytellers, and the keepers of our families. Their wisdom, guidance, and strength have created foundations made of stone that allow us to continue forward with confidence and pride. It is a foundation that we continue to build our Nation on, and for that, I humbly say, "Thank You." I know this is not enough; there are no words to describe the kind of gratitude that I feel for every one of you. Your strength as Métis women is admirable, and I acknowledge your courage for being willing to come forward and tell your story.

To Dr. Lorene Shyba, Publisher of Durvile Publications, I want to acknowledge and thank you for believing in me, Bailey Oster and Colette Poitras, by making this long time dream a reality! Mere words cannot express how much your trust in our work means, again thank you.

To President Audrey Poitras, Métis Nation of Alberta, I want to acknowledge all the hard work you have done over the years supporting our women's group by any means possible, you are also a vital part of this book becoming a reality!

To Bailey Oster, you made this a reality, all your hard work, editing, transcribing and dedication is the reason this book is being published.

To Colette Poitras your dedication to your Nation, and all the partnerships that you created and were willing to share with us, is the reason this book is being published, and for that I am forever grateful.

We are hoping that this book will be the first of many, and that more Métis women will come forward and tell their stories, because we all have a story to tell.

I have a lot of tales, my Kookum told me, that I still live by today, one day I will tell my story. But not yet.

—Marilyn Lizee, Editor

Acknowledgements

Bailey Oster

FIRST, I would like to thank all the amazing women who gave their time, energy, and stories to us; without you, this book would have been impossible. Each of these women are truly the keepers of our families, and of our Métis culture.

I would also like to thank my mother, Colette Poitras, who has dedicated her life to promoting the stories of Indigenous Peoples. She gave a presentation at the New Dawn Annual General Meeting in 2018 which was the catalyst behind the idea for this book. Without her connections, hard work, and passion, this project would never have been possible.

To Krista Leddy who did the amazing cover art, and Mary "SkyBlue" Morin who did the Michif translation, thank you for all your hard work. Their additions to this text are invaluable and the book would not be what it is without them.

I cannot go without mentioning President of the Métis Nation of Alberta, Audrey Poitras. She is an inspiration to Métis women across the Homeland and we are proud to call her our President. I would also like to thank Melanie Omeniho and all Les Femmes Michif Otipemisiwak (Women of the Métis Nation) for their hard work and dedication to promoting Métis women across our Homeland.

Thank you to Matt LeMay for being a supporter of this project and developing our accompanying documentary and to Jason Madden for his amazing endorsement of this book. I also cannot forget to thank Dr. Paul Gareau, Kimberly Fraser-Airhart, and Dr. Yvonne Poitras Pratt for taking time out of their busy schedules to help guide me through writing some of the essays within the book.

I would also like to thank all the staff at the Métis Nation of Alberta including Madison Tipler, Madison Quintal, Amy Dillon, Leanne Miller, Patrick Bako, Margaret Hawrysh, and Kaylee Townend. Each of these individuals had a hand in making this dream a reality through their unyielding support and patience.

Thank you for financial support provided by Aboriginal Affairs and Northern Development Canada; this support allowed us the opportunity to make this book into a documentary, and to hire a translator who could make our dream of having this book in both English and Michif a reality.

This book was made possible by Lorene Shyba and Raymond Yakeleya of Durvile & UpRoute Books. Without their belief in this project, and desire to promote the stories of Métis women, this book would have never been published. Thanks also to Jennifer Theroux for her proofreading.

Lastly, I want to thank every Métis woman who has come before us and paved a path we are now able to walk confidently. You were the inspiration for this book, and I hope we made you proud.

Bibliography

Adese, J., & Andersen, C. (2021). *A People and a Nation: New Directions in Contemporary Métis Studies.* University of British Columbia Press.

Bakker, P. (1997). *A Language of Our Own: The Genesis of Michif, the Mixed Cree-French language of the Canadian Métis.* Oxford University Press.

Brady, J. P. (n.d.). *The St. Paul Half-Breed Reserve.* Retrieved from the Gabriel Dumont Institute. Retrieved April 8, 2021 from *http://www.Métismuseum.ca/resource.php/03835*

Brown, J. (1980). *Strangers in Blood: Fur Trade Company Families in Indian Country.* University of British Columbia Press.

Brown, J. (1983). "Women as Centre and Symbol in the Emergence of Métis Communities." *Canadian Journal of Native Studies* 3(1) 39-46.

Callihoo, V. (1960). "Our Buffalo Hunts. *Alberta Historical Review,* 8(1).

"Canada's Residential Schools: The Métis Experience." (2015). United Kingdom: *Truth and Reconciliation Commission of Canada.*

Devine, H. (2004). *The People Who Own Themselves: Aboriginal Ethnogenesis in a Canadian Family,* 1660-1900. University of Calgary Press.

Dobbin, M. (1981). *The One-and-a-Half Men: The Story of Jim Brady and Malcolm Norris, Métis Patriots of the Twentieth Century.* New Star.

Ens, G. (1996). *Homeland to Hinterland: The Changing Worlds of the Red River Métis in the Nineteenth Century.* University of Toronto Press.

Gareau, P. L., (2021). "Mary and the Métis: Religion as a Site for New Insight in Métis Studies." In J. Adese & C. Andersen (Eds.). *A People and a Nation: New Directions in Contemporary Métis Studies.* (pp. 188-212). UBC Press.

Hrycun, L., Tough, F., Kermoal, N., Rossiter, J., Madden, J., & Davis, Z. (2018). *Métis Scrip in Alberta* [Pamphlet]. Rupertsland Centre for Métis Research.

"Les Femmes Michif Otipemisiwak - Women of the Métis Nation." (2021). "Our Story." Retrieved April 10, 2021. *https://en2.metiswomen.org/our-story/*

Logan, T. (2008). "A Métis Perspective on Truth and Reconciliation." *Truth to Reconciliation: Transforming the Legacy of Residential Schools.* (80). Aboriginal Healing Foundation.

McDougall, B., & St. Onge, N. (2013, Winter). "Manitoba History: Rooted in Mobility: Metis buffalo hunting brigades [1]." Manitoba Historical Society. Retrieved April 10, 2021. *http://www.mhs.mb.ca/docs/mb_history/71/metis-brigades.shtml*

Muzyka, K. (2020, February 13). "Forced to Live on Roadsides: The Dark History of Métis Road Allowances." CBC Radio. Retrieved April 8, 2021. *https://www.cbc.ca/radio/unreserved/from-scrip-to-road-allowances-canada-s-complicated-history-with-the-m%C3%A9tis-1.5100375/forced-to-live-on-roadsides-the-dark-history-of-m%C3%A9tis-road-allowances-1.5100660*

Paquin, T., Préfontaine, D. R., & Young, P. (2003). *Traditional Métis Socialization and Entertainment.* Gabriel Dumont Institute.

Payment, D. P. (2009). *The Free people = Li gens libres: A History of the Métis Community of Batoche, Saskatchewan.* University of Calgary Press.

Poitras Pratt, Y. (2019). *Digital Storytelling in Indigenous Education: A Decolonizing Journey for a Métis Community.* United Kingdom: Taylor & Francis.

Poitras, C. (2021). "The Métis experience." In Yakeleya, R., Yakeleya, E. (Authors), & Stewart, S. (Ed.), *We Remember the Coming of the White Man* (Special edition) (pp.38-43). Durvile & UpRoute Books.

Racette, C. (1985). *Contrasting Worlds 1: Métis Development and the Canadian West.* (pp.10). Gabriel Dumont Institute.

Sawchuk, J. (1998). *The dynamics of native politics: The Alberta Métis experience.* Purich.

Sawchuk, J., Sawchuk, P., & Ferguson, T. (1981). *Métis Land Rights in Alberta: A Political History.* The Métis Association of Alberta.

Seraphim, J. (n.d.). *Wild West Show: Métis women's roles in the resistances.* National Arts Centre. Retrieved April 03, 2021, from https://nac-cna.ca/en/wildwestshow/historique/les-roles-des-femmes-Métisses-dans-les-resistances

Teillet, J. (2019). *The North-West is our Mother: The story of Louis Riel's People, the Métis Nation.* Harper Collins Canada.

Wall, D. (2008). *The Alberta Métis Letters: 1930-1940 policy review and annotations.* DWRG Press.

Women of the Métis Nation (2019). Métis perspectives of missing and murdered women, girls, and LGBTQ2S+ People. Les Femmes Michif Otipemisiwak.

SPIRIT OF NATURE SERIES

SERIES EDITORS: RAYMOND YAKELEYA & LORENE SHYBA

DURVILE & UpRoute Books

PUBLISHING AUTHORS WHO HAVE THE FORESIGHT TO BRING NEW KNOWLEDGE TO THE WORLD

THE TREE BY THE WOODPILE
By Raymond Yakeleya
ISBN: 9781988824031

LIVING IN THE TALL GRASS
By Chief R. Stacey Laforme
ISBN: 9781988824055

LILLIAN & KOKOMIS THE SPIRIT OF DANCE
By Lynda Partridge
ISBN: 9781988824277

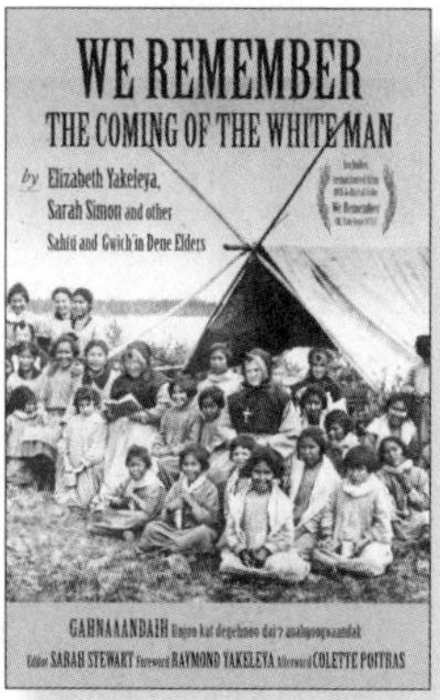

WE REMEMBER THE COMING OF THE WHITE MAN
Eds. Stewart & Yakeleya
ISBN: 9781988824246

WE REMEMBER SPECIAL EDITION
Eds. Stewart & Yakeleya
ISBN: 9781988824635

STORIES OF METIS WOMEN
Eds. Oster & Lizee
ISBN: 9781988824215

FOLLOW US ON FACEBOOK
"DURVILEANDUPROUTE"

DURVILE IS A PROUD CANADIAN INDIE PUBLISHER.
DISTRIBUTED BY UNIVERSITY OF TORONTO PRESS (UTP) IN CANADA
AND NATIONAL BOOK NETWORK (NBN) IN THE US.

DURVILE & UpRoute Books

SPIRIT OF NATURE SERIES

VISIT DURVILE.COM
OR CLICK THE QR CODE FOR
MORE INFO ON THESE TITLES

SIKSIKAITSITAPI: STORIES OF THE BLACKFOOT PEOPLE
By Payne Many Guns *et al*
ISBN: 9781988824833

WHY ARE YOU STILL HERE?: A LILLIAN MYSTERY
By Lynda Partridge
ISBN: 9781988824826

NAHGANNE TALES OF THE NORTHERN SASQUATCH
By Red Grossinger
ISBN 9781988824598

CHILD OF MORNING STAR EMBERS OF AN ANCIENT DAWN
By Antoine Mountain
ISBN: 9781990735103

MIDNIGHT STORM MOONLESS SKY
By Alex Soop
ISBN: 9781990735127

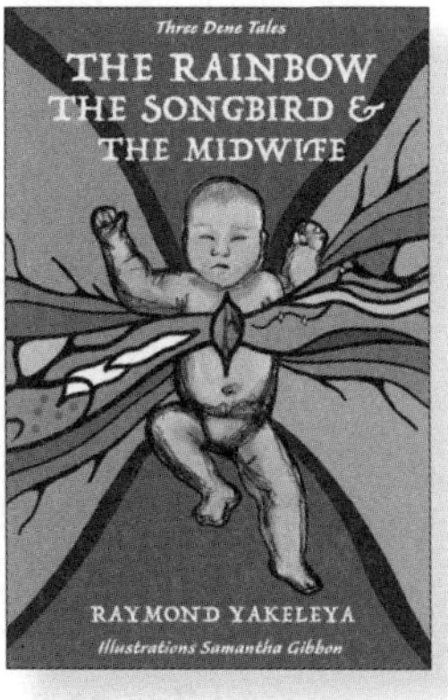

THE RAINBOW, THE SONGBIRD & THE MIDWIFE
By Raymond Yakeleya
ISBN: 9781988824574

A percentage of publisher's proceeds and author royalties have been donated or committed to The Elizabeth Yakeleya Fund; "Home In Our Hearts" for Ukrainian Evacuees; The Canada Ukraine Foundation; Doctors Without Borders; Calgary Communities Against Sexual Abuse; The Canadian Women's Foundation; The Salvation Army; (MMIWG) Missing and Murdered Indigenous Women and Girls; Days for Girls International; Red Door Family Shelter, Toronto; Indigenous Family Shelter, Winnipeg; The Schizophrenia Society of Canada; and The Elizabeth Fry Society.

Contributors

Bailey Oster, *Author and Editor*

Bailey Oster is a Métis woman with roots in the Red River Settlement and St. Paul des Métis. Bailey received her Bachelor of Arts in Sociology with a research focus in restorative justice. She currently works as a manager within the Youth Programs and Services Department at the Métis Nation of Alberta. She was elected as the youngest ever Vice President of New Dawn, the Métis Women's Organization within Alberta at nineteen years old and still currently holds the position.

Marilyn Lizee, *Afterword and Editor*

As President of New Dawn Metis Women's Society, Marilyn Lizee has had a long career in Métis politics that goes back prior to 1996. She continues to take many responsibilities within her Métis community, including her role as Senior Cultural Chair of the Métis Nation of Alberta's Cultural Committee. She also works with, and for, President Audrey Poitras. It is her passion for her culture and her identity as a strong Métis woman that gives her pride and motivation to continue her journey forward.

SkyBlue Morin, *Michif Translation*

Mary SkyBlue Morin is a Michif cultural knowledge keeper and a speaker of the Michif Cree and Ile-a-la-Crosse Michif language. She learned the language as a child and has continued to speak it to this day. She has been working as a Michif Cree writer, translator, and teacher since 2010.

Contributors

Audrey Poitras, *Foreword*

Métis Nation of Alberta (MNA) President, Audrey Poitras, is one of the highest profile Métis women in Canada. Audrey's career in Métis politics began in 1996 when she was elected to lead the Métis Nation of Alberta as its first female President. From Métis identity to Métis rights and recognition, Audrey remains a key figure among Canada's political leaders. From being named the 2016 Indigenous leader of the year, to being one of the most influential people in 2005 and among Canada's 100 in the same year, in 2011, Audrey received a National Aboriginal Achievement Award for Politics, and today, elected for her 8th term as President of the Metis Nation of Alberta, Audrey is the longest serving President in the history of the Metis Nation.

Krista Leddy, *cover beadwork art*

Krista Leddy is a proud Métis woman whose family comes from the historical Métis communities of St. Albert and Lac Ste. Anne. She is an artist, storyteller, and a holder of traditional knowledge and skills. She is also an advocate for Métis reconnecting with the community, using art and stories as ways to weave them back into the beautiful sash of Métis identity.